INDIVIDUALISM IN MODERN THOUGHT

The usage of 'collective' concepts such as Society, State, Church and Class is essential to both the social sciences and to everyday discourse. But what in reality corresponds to such concepts? Proponents of methodological individualism argue that it is individual human action, with its unintentional and unpredictable consequences, which shapes any collective concept.

Individualism in Modern Thought is a comprehensive survey of methodological individualism in social, political and economic thought from the Enlightenment to the 20th century. Exploring the works of such figures as de Mandeville, Smith, Marx, Spencer, Durkheim, Menger, Simmel, Weber, Mises, Hayek, Popper and Parsons, this study underlines the contrasts between methodological collectivism and methodological individualism. The detailed analysis offered here also reveals the theoretical presuppositions behind the collectivist and individualist traditions and the practical consequences of their applications. Infantino concludes in favour of individualism.

This work touches upon issues in social and political theory, intellectual history, political philosophy, political economy and sociological theory. The relationship between the individual and the constitution of society is of key interest to Infantino, who draws upon the ideas of Hayek to develop his own unique approach to the issues examined.

Lorenzo Infantino is Professor of Sociology at Libera Università Internazionale degli Studi Sociali, Rome.

ROUTLEDGE STUDIES IN SOCIAL AND POLITICAL THOUGHT

INDIVIDUALISM IN MODERN THOUGHT

From Adam Smith to Hayek

Lorenzo Infantino

London and New York

First published 1998
by Routledge
11 New Fetter Lane, London EC4P 4EE

Simultaneously published in the USA and Canada
by Routledge
29 West 35th Street, New York, NY 10001

© 1998 Lorenzo Infantino

Typeset in Garamond by Routledge
Printed and bound in Great Britain by Biddles Ltd, Guildford and King's Lynn

British Library Cataloguing in Publication Data
A catalogue record for this book is available from the British Library

Library of Congress Cataloguing in Publication Data
Infantino, Lorenzo, 1948–
[Ordine senza piano. English]
Individualism in modern thought: from Adam Smith to Hayek / Lorenzo
Infantino.
(Routledge studies in social and political thought: 14)
Includes bibliographical references and index.
1. Individualism–History. I. Title. II. Series.
HM136.I46513   1998
302.5'4'09–dc21   97-52179
CIP

ISBN 0–415–18524–6

TO MY PARENTS

CONTENTS

PREFACE

One of the errors most frequently committed within the social sciences is the reification of collective concepts. We can clarify this question by means of some points made by Gaetano Salvemini. After presenting a particular 'collection' of facts as an illustration, he wrote:

> We give them a single name: 'The French Revolution'; which enables us to bring to mind the complex picture of events without having to repeat the details in order every time. But the use of personal, concrete names has made us so used to seeing a real entity behind each name that we very often end up by personifying collective and abstract names also. In the same way that we think of illness as a concrete entity existing outside and above the sick person, so we treat the Revolution as something existing outside and above the people who lived in the Revolutionary period.[1]

Salvemini added:

> There is nothing to stop us from saying that the Revolution destroyed feudal rights, as long as we remember that these words mean that, after the fall of the Bastille, the peasants no longer wanted to pay feudal dues, the Deputies of the Constituent Assembly did not succeed in making people observe them, the members of the Legislative Assembly almost entirely abolished them by law, those of the Convention completed the work of taking away their force by law.[2]

Salvemini explained that the danger begins when we make the Revolution operate 'like a person of flesh and blood, like a historical occurrence distinct from events and creator of those same events'.

Hence, the problem lies not in *whether* but in *how* to use collective concepts. We need them, because they are the shorthand that enables us to communicate with great immediacy and economy of time, but they are not entities endowed with a separate life, either autonomous or, as Salvemini said, 'distinct from events and creator of those same events'.[3]

However, the reification of collective concepts is a widespread practice. Society, the State, the Church, class, race, party, and many other *Kollectivebegriffe* are used by the cultural tradition that goes by the name of *methodological collectivism*, as if they had a reality independent of individuals and individual actions, to which we intend to refer concisely. This is an obstacle to the understanding of social events, and in particular of the birth and development of norms and institutions. In fact, as soon as autonomous reality is bestowed on collective concepts, they become a force, itself also autonomous, which leads to the consideration of the actions of individuals in terms of effects and never of causes.

It is not understood that society, as Georg Simmel maintained, is an 'inner bond' of the relationship of interaction that individuals bring into being;[4] it is not comprehended, as Karl Popper emphasised, that 'what really exists is people', but that 'what does not exist' is society understood as an entity 'distinct' from individuals.[5]

Therefore, only people exist. They act on the basis of ideas, norms, beliefs; and they bring about intentional and unintentional results. If human actions generated only the desired consequences, there would be no need for social sciences: the intentions of the actors would already make everything clear. But we act outside ourselves, always measuring ourselves against the other, and this comparison produces a 'cascade' of unforeseeable events.

In other words, the origins and development of social norms are not the consequence of the intervention of mysterious forces. They are the result of human actions. But it is often a matter of unintentional or unintended results of actions directed towards other goals; and even if one is in the presence of results which were consciously pursued, this does not exclude the possibility that they may in their turn produce unprogrammed social consequences. This shows, among other things, how necessary it is to free oneself from every claim to omniscience, from that presumptuousness which often leads to belief in the myth of the great Legislator or Planner who, sure of his ability to bend the situation to his own designs, aims at moulding and remoulding norms and institutions intentionally. This is the myth of the collectivistic tradition which, as Friedrich A. von Hayek emphasised, was unfortunately shared by the utilitarian tradition, from Bentham to the theory of general economic equilibrium and beyond.

It follows from this that the method of the social sciences cannot be other than what Carl Menger has called 'compositive'; this is a method which attributes the birth and development of norms to the 'composition' of individual actions. Furthermore, it follows that the task of these same social sciences is to study the unintentional or unintended results of intentional human actions.

These are the main themes of this book. I have tried to construct a 'common ground' around them, making use in particular of the works of Bernard de Mandeville, Adam Smith, Herbert Spencer, Carl Menger, Georg Simmel, Max Weber, Ludwig von Mises, Friedrich von Hayek and Karl Popper.

That is all. It only remains to acknowledge my debts. In particular, I have benefited from the seminars and frequent meetings on the problems addressed in this volume, which have taken place since its establishment at the Centre for the Methodology of the Social Sciences, of LUISS (Libera Università degli Studi Sociali – Rome), where Dario Antiseri has been very generous with his suggestions and has untiringly encouraged me to complete my work. I asked Antiseri himself and Sergio Ricossa to read the whole typescript with critical attention. I hope I have not abused their friendship. The text has been read also by Massimo Baldini, who has never failed to encourage and stimulate me during the writing of the book. I submitted the chapter on *The early Parsons: between sociology and economics* and the one on *Durkheim and the application of collectivistic method* to Paolo de Nardis and Enzo Vittorio Trapanese respectively; both read it with great care.

I have benefited from the remarks of all of these first readers of my book and I offer them my sincere gratitude. The responsibility for the views expressed, however, is exclusively mine.

1

INTRODUCTION

The 'abuse of reason'

Friedrich von Hayek, the scholar who in this century gave most attention to the problem of the unintended consequences of intentional human actions, wrote:

> Life of man in society, or even of the social animals in groups, is made possible by individuals acting according to certain rules. With the growth of intelligence, these rules tend to develop from unconscious habits into explicit and articulated statements and at the same time to become more abstract and general. Our familiarity with the institutions of law prevents us from seeing how subtle and complex a device the delimitation of individual spheres by abstract norms is. *If it had been deliberately designed, it would deserve to rank among the greatest human inventions. But it has, of course, been as little invented by any one mind as language or money or most of the practices and conventions on which life rests.*[1]

In other words: many social institutions arise unintentionally, without being planned by anyone. And yet the advance of modernity has often been accompanied by a claim to omnipotence. A culture has been established which is determined to see in social institutions the intentional result of human action. We have moved from the idea of an *intentional order* attributable to the will of God to that of an intentional order attributable to the designs of man. The task of planning has been ascribed to reason, that of realisation to politics, leading to the claim that it is possible to 'reconstruct the universe through pure ideas, axioms and principles'.[2] This is the origin of the extremism of Reason, which lost 'the awareness of its own limits' to the point of 'annulling other influences: will, feeling, the physical body'.[3] Individual and collective life have suffered in this way from the pathological attitude that Hayek called the 'abuse of reason',[4] a 'philosophical vice' which propels the person affected by it towards social 'constructivism'.[5]

1

We have been led into this attitude by 'the rationalism of René Descartes and his followers',[6] whose ideal Voltaire, his 'greatest representative',[7] expressed in the following terms: 'If you want good laws, burn those you have and make yourselves new ones'. This is the triumph of utopianism, the claim that it is possible to model social reality freely, by means of a 'unitary direction' entrusted to a class of 'chosen ones'. It demonstrates that the 'constructivist' mentality fails to understand the difficulty of putting together a complex society by means of a centralised organisation, the sure result of which, as will be explained in more detail, is the loss of individual autonomy and of the capacity to develop.

Political economy and the discovery of unintentional order

However, there is a different tradition of thought, which has challenged the 'abuse of reason' and has suggested a very different answer to the problem of social order. The first to try to systematise an answer were Bernard de Mandeville and David Hume, followed by the Scottish social philosophers of the eighteenth century.[8] In particular, Adam Smith, the founder of modern political economy, climbed on the shoulders of Mandeville and Hume. These authors all maintained that a 'great society', or, to use an expression more familiar to us, an 'open' or 'extended society' is such if it embodies an *unintentional order*. That is, they 'discovered' the possibility of rejecting the 'unitary direction' of collective life; they believed that order should not be 'given' by a superior being to subjects who operate in society, but that order can be the *unintentional* result of the action of individuals. From this derives a theoretical scheme which we can name briefly the 'Mandeville–Smith model'. Let us begin with an illustration.

Beside the aims which each man pursues individually and knowingly, his actions also obtain, unintentionally, another objective: they serve the conditions (I use the term 'conditions' not in a juridical sense, but with the meaning that can be deduced from the theory of evolution as 'conditions', to which the action of Ego must adapt itself in order to fulfil its course) dictated by the Other and thus give rise to the norms which regulate social relations. In this way, order is brought into being by the very individuals who act, without their being aware of it, and without the intervention of a 'social brain' to coordinate their movements.

This is shown by a now classic extract from Smith:

It is not from the benevolence of the butcher, the brewer, or the baker, that we expect our dinner, but from their regard for their own interest. We address ourselves not to their humanity but to their self-love, and never talk to them of our own necessities but of their advantages. Nobody but a beggar chooses to depend chiefly upon the benevolence of his fellow citizens.[9]

Expressed in Mandeville's words, this is equivalent to saying that 'all of us, turning the vices and weaknesses of others to our own advantage, seek to obtain a living in the easiest and most direct way that our talent and capacity allow'.[10]

Hence, there is in our life an ineradicable 'double entry account',[11] activated by the interest of each person to pursue his own ends. Such ends are not pursued in a social vacuum. Each person needs the intervention of the Other, and for that reason has to 'serve' him. Consequently, it happens that, if he wants to be able to enter what he wishes to accomplish on the credit side of his existential 'account', the actor has to submit himself to the conditions imposed by the Other.

The Other can, in his turn, obtain a service from the former, as a result. Thus, *unintentionally*, a network of conditions or norms which generalise and regulate social 'commerce' is born.

The first objection raised against this kind of explanation of social order is that it 'strips' man, exalts his less 'noble' aspect, and believes in the possibility of bringing about unintentional order. There is a paradox here: to formulate such a charge is to propose, as we shall see in more detail, to place the individual under the 'guardianship' of an intentional order, which means that his judgement of man is no less pessimistic. But that is not the point here. It is not a fault to base a model of social order on personal 'interest'; on the contrary, it is an advantage, because it predisposes us to receive from man not the best, or perhaps the impossible, but rather what that same man can most easily give. This does not exclude the possibility of there being minorities able to do more and better; but it protects us from thinking that this 'more' and 'better' can be generalised. Mandeville wrote: 'The most knowing, the most virtuous, and the least self-interested Ministers are the best; but in the mean time there must be Ministers'.[12] Consequently, there have to be systems of control, as a counter balance to 'interests', because in such a case even 'common prudence is sufficient to hinder a man of very indifferent principles from stealing'; indeed, he knows that he is in a 'great danger of being detected, and has no manner of security that he shall not be punished for it'.[13]

It is thus clear that the Mandeville–Smith model gives autonomy to individuals and recognises their 'personal interest', which becomes the motive of action. There is no intention of suppressing this interest, a suppression which is, in any case, incompatible with the life of a 'great society'. The mediation of interests is not performed consciously by an entity put in authority over individuals, but it happens unintentionally, by means of the very action of the individuals who act. One can say that a model of this kind points towards 'isolating' the *minimum presuppositions* of social life. That is, it impels us to activate mechanisms which drive the actor in relation to the minimum conditions required for collective living. The individual is not asked to renounce his own interests and to soar to exemplary heights of nobility; instead he is asked to submit himself to 'conditions' which make possible the pursuit of his own interests and the interests of others.

The birth of sociology and intentional order

What the 'abuse of reason' was not able to do with political economy in its early days it did with sociology, in particular with French positivist sociology with all its emphasis on the claim that no human society can exist 'without an intelligence which directs it'.[14] Saint-Simon called for 'the coming of a unitary direction of society'.[15] Comte said that 'the exercise of a general and combined activity is the essence of *society*'.[16] Durkheim maintained that individualism does not turn 'all wills' towards the same 'social' end[17] and that one can accuse the theorists of individualism of 'ensuring dissolution of society'.[18]

Therefore, sociology was born with the idea that society ought to be an intentional order, organised and directed by a specific 'intelligence'. Like every other form of 'constructivism', that of sociology demonstrates a double conceit here. It maintains that it would not be possible to give up the idea of society understood as an aware organisation of collective life, and it is the victim of the illusion that it is possible to organise consciously a complex society. On the contrary, the existence of such a society is linked to the possibility of an unintentional order, of a social dynamic which does not have to depend on 'unitary direction'.

When considering the possibility of organising society in a conscious way, Saint-Simon did not hesitate to judge the concept of individual liberty as 'vague and metaphysical' and to regard it as an 'obstacle to civilization'.[19] Comte labelled individualism and liberty of conscience as 'revolting monstrosities'.[20] Durkheim equated individual autonomy with egoism, to which he attributes the sole capacity to create anomie.[21]

The sociology of Saint-Simon and Comte was taken to extremes by Marx, who saw in the rights of man 'the rights of the member of civil society, i.e. of egoistic man, of man separated from other men and the community',[22] and proposed the conscious organisation of society by way of a single plan brought to fruition after the 'strictest centralization' of power in the hands of the State.[23]

However, all of these authors, with whose names the birth and early development of sociology are closely linked, displayed hostility when making comparisons with political economy, a discipline from which, as has already been stated, comes the proposition of an unintentional order, of a 'great society' which renounces the idea of a 'unitary' social direction. Saint-Simon maintained that the 'science of production' is not economics but politics, because only the latter knows how to pursue that common end towards which all men ought to direct their steps.[24] Comte accused the economists of having dissociated economic phenomena 'from the analysis of the intellectual, moral and political state of society'; indeed, of having created the 'sterile aphorism' of liberty, and of not seeing the need for a 'special institution' which would fulfil the function of unitary coordination.[25]

Marx declared that 'the goal of the economic system is the *unhappiness* of this system', adding that 'the only wheels which political economy sets in motion are *greed* and war *amongst the greedy competition*'.[26] Durkheim continually made economists his target, and he puts himself in opposition to Herbert Spencer and Georg Simmel, from whose writings the possibility of unintentional order emerges.

In the seminal nucleus of sociology, therefore, there is a firm rejection of the model on which political economy is based; there is a 'revolt against individualism'.[27] That has often led to a situation of mutual diffidence between economists and sociologists. From this side of the sociological frontiers, economic theory has seemed like the realm of 'anomie'; from beyond the economic frontiers, sociology for its part has been represented as incapable of deciphering the order of a market society. As Joseph Schumpeter has emphasised, this has not made relations between the two disciplines very fruitful in the past, and it is possible that it may not do so in the future.[28]

The 'revolt against individualism'

The rejection on the part of a certain sort of sociology of the model on which political economy is based is the consequence of what we have called the 'double claim' of constructivism. This consists in considering that unintentional order is impossible and that, on the contrary, the conscious organisation of a complex society is possible. We must be very careful about this because, in the contrary case, the 'revolt against individualism' becomes incomprehensible and even paradoxical. This is exactly what happens in the writings of Robert Nisbet, who maintains, in defence of Durkheim, that 'we should have to look far to find a mind more "modern" in social and political affiliation' than that of the French sociologist,[29] and adds that even in the 'body of his social theory' Durkheim's spirit is rationalist–positivist, derived in large part from Descartes.[30]

Later in the book, we shall see again the influence that German culture exercised on Durkheim, but in the following paragraphs we see how, in the struggle against the 'open society', positivism finds an ally in idealism. Here, it must at once be said that Nisbet, defensively associating Durkheim with rationalism, overlooks the fact that Descartes himself in his *Discours de la méthode* sang the praises of intentional order: 'To take a purely human instance, I believe that Sparta flourished so well not because of the excellence of its laws taken one by one . . . but because, being all the invention of one man, they all tended towards the same end.'[31] Thus, when Durkheim is constructivistic, he is not so in spite of Descartes, but rather because he is affected by the 'abuse of reason' which arises precisely from Cartesian philosophy.[32]

What is the point? The question was made clear by Friedrich von Hayek, who wrote that those who are opposed to constructivism dwell on:

> the fact that . . . to make reason as effective as possible requires an insight into the limitation of the powers of conscious reason and into the assistance we obtain from processes of which we are not aware, an insight which constructivist rationalism lacks. Thus, if the desire to make reason as effective as possible is what is meant by rationalism, I myself am a rationalist. If, however, the term means that conscious reason ought to determine every single action, I am not a rationalist, and such rationalism seems to me to be very unreasonable.[33]

Using Popper's language, it could be said that 'constructivism' is an 'uncritical' or naive rationalism, and that those who are opposed to it and denounce its claims are 'critical rationalists'.[34] The 'revolt against individualism' which gave birth to sociology has its place within foundationist rationalism, with which modernity is strongly imbued.

In this way, a profound gap has opened up between the life of the market society and a large part of culture. On the one hand, a way of life based on the autonomy of the actors and their consequent competitive co-operation has been affirmed. This has placed in the limelight the uncertainty of the human condition; in fact, one can symbolise the market as a permanent 'discovery procedure',[35] a place in which the attempt to falsify productive solutions and models of life knows no respite – all is fallible or, if one likes, the only certain thing is uncertainty. On the other hand, a contrary culture has developed, made presumptuous by its very naivety, which has aimed at resolving the problem of order by means of a 'unitary direction' of society. This means denying the equality of the subjects and entrusting to some of them the task of regulating individual and collective life. It has not been realised that this claim coincides precisely with the ambition to assert a 'privileged point of view on the world', to hand over the monopoly of truth to a class of 'chosen ones'. Here we can see the illusion that one is better able to defend the human condition from uncertainty by the centralised 'taming' of individual energies. But the uncertainty remains because it cannot be eliminated; and the result is simply the paying of a double price, expressed by the suppression of individual autonomy and by the consequent reduction of the means through which one can confront the 'perils' of life.

The alliance against the open society

Hayek observed that errors sometimes turn into 'dogmas' because they are shared by cultural currents in conflict with each other on other questions.[36]

One of the errors of constructivism consists – as has already been said – in thinking that unintentional order is impossible. We are concerned here with a point that is not the exclusive domain of Comte's positivism; it is present also in Hegel's idealism. Hegel maintained that the individual is an 'abstract person' incapable of controlling the 'spiritual powers which, in their unfettered freedom become elemental beings raging madly against one another in a frenzy of destructive activity'.[37] He believed that civil society is 'division' and appearance, a splitting, the realm of selfish individual interests, of the breaking of ethical community bonds.[38] He considered it necessary to 'suppress' the 'spirit of individualism'.[39] He saw in the market system the manifestation of 'the abstracting process which effects the subdivision of needs and means'.[40]

In 1824, Gustave d'Eichthal, a pupil of Comte's, wrote as follows to his master, after attending Hegel's lectures: 'There is a marvellous agreement between your results, even though the principles are different, at least in appearance . . . the identity of results exists even in the practical principles, as *Hegel is a defender of the governments, that is, an enemy of liberals*.'[41] Moreover, d'Eichthal sent a copy of the *Système de politique positive* to Hegel, who praised the first part of it.[42] In his turn, Comte declared outright that Hegel seemed to him 'the man most capable to push the positive philosophy in Germany'.[43]

The fact is that Comte's positivism and Hegel's idealism are united on common ground. After taking into consideration the dates of publication of some of their works, Hayek commented: 'Although Comte was twenty-eight years younger than Hegel, we should regard them as being in effect contemporaries, so that it is legitimate to think of influence by Comte on Hegel as much as of Hegel on Comte'.[44] The link might appear paradoxical; Hayek himself pointed this out. He said that 'the curious fact' is that this 'proximity' has always been remarked upon 'with the air of surprise and discovery'.[45] However, the points of agreement, far from being occasional, are systematic, and their influence on the social sciences has been much more important than, perhaps forgetting the debt owed by Marx to both of them, 'has yet been realised'.[46]

It is clear then that the common ground which unites Comte and Hegel is undoubtedly their rejection of unintentional order. Both were hostile to the individual and wished to 'oppress' him within the 'community'. Hence their alliance against the 'open society'. The positivist imperative of the 'unitary direction' of society (in which politics has to affirm its own primacy over economics), the Hegelian concept of the State as 'the actuality of the ethical idea'[47] and the prediction, which, too, is Hegelian, of war as 'Spirit' and 'form' in which 'the essential moment of the ethical substance . . . is present in its actual and authentic existence',[48] are the elements which, in various combinations, have led to the different manifestations of totalitarianism. This appears even more evident if one considers that, politically, the concept of 'community' does not have only one solution.[49] That is, it can be referred to political situations marked by a different principle of legitimation (race, nation, class, etc.), but united by the idea of intentional order.

Therefore, the accounts balance perfectly. Even if it is justified differently, the objective which is always aspired to is, according to Ludwig von Mises' expression, the 'omnipotent government', that is the total dominion of the politico-administrative apparati over the life of the individual.[50]

From the methodological point of view, this happens through the systematic violation of Hume's law, which distinguishes facts from values and which therefore inhibits the derivation of prescriptions from descriptions.[51] This means that scientific explanations and ethical valuations exist, but they must be kept separate – ethics cannot be extracted from science (nor can ethics suggest conclusions to science). In other words, reason cannot found an ethical system – the exact opposite of what supporters of intentional order do. This is why Max Weber wrote:

> As Hellenic man at times sacrificed to Aphrodite and at other times to Apollo, and, above all, as everybody sacrificed to the gods of his city, so do we still nowadays, only the bearing of man has been disenchanted and denuded of its mystical but inwardly genuine plasticity. Fate, and certainly not 'science', holds sway over these gods and their struggles.[52]

That is to say, the separation between science and ethics is the basis of the 'politeism' of values, of the 'open society'. Their unification, on the other side, produces a 'closed system', where reason is called in to 'justify', as used to happen before the assertion of the process of secularisation, a social Absolute of which a privileged group claims to be the depositary.

2

BERNARD DE MANDEVILLE AND ADAM SMITH

The theory of the 'great society'

Man, a social animal

Bernard de Mandeville categorically excluded the possibility of society's having originated from a 'contract' – a pact endorsed by individuals who have no previous bond. Men are not any more able to arrange a pact of this kind than are 'horses'.[1] 'Societies never were made that way'.[2] A person who possesses feelings which are not already regulated by norms cannot 'have a regular way of thinking, or pursue any project of social co-operation'.[3] In the most peremptory way, Mandeville insisted that the social condition cannot be programmed by individuals who are strangers to this same condition. In fact, no one can 'reason but *a posteriori*, from something that he knows, or supposes to be true',[4] no creature can 'Know the Want of what it can have no Idea of'.[5] The 'difference between right and wrong' cannot be spoken of except between men who already 'live in society'.[6] When the individual considers the problem of collective living, he already benefits from the social condition.

Hence, contractualism falls into a very serious contradiction: it separates the individual from society, placing him in a 'state of nature' in which he leads his own life in isolation, and yet ascribes to him the gifts of language and reason which impel him to 'create' society through the terms of an appropriate pact. But language and reason are a social product: if the individual possesses them he is already living in society, and there is no need to have recourse to any 'contract' in order to establish it; if he does not possess them, he cannot be directed by them towards endorsing the social pact. Mandeville emphasised this strongly:

> If we examine every Faculty and Qualification, from and for which we judge and pronounce Man to be a sociable Creature beyond other Animals, we shall find, that a very considerable, if not the greatest Part of the Attribute is acquired, and comes upon Multitudes, from their conversing with one another. *Fabricando fabri fimus*. Men become sociable, by living together in society.[7] . . . It is hard to guess, what Man would be, entirely untaught.[8]

9

Man's sociability, therefore, is a product of living together. Again, Mandeville wrote:

> Let us examine a man's whole life, from his infancy to his Grave, and see, which of the two seems to be most natural to him; a Desire of Superiority, and grasping every thing to himself; or a Tendency to act according to the reasonable Notions of Right and wrong; and we shall find that in his early Youth the first is very conspicuous; that nothing appears of the second before he has received some Instructions, and that this latter will always have less Influence on his actions, the more uncivilised he remains.[9]

One can consquently say that the 'Brain of a Child, newly born, is *Carte Blanche*'.[10] This is why 'the best thing we can do to Infants after the first Month, besides feeding and keeping them from Harm, is to make them take in Ideas . . . and dispose them . . . to imitate us.'[11] 'The brain at first serves as Slate to Cypher.'[12] And 'the more we are persuaded that the greatest Excellencies the best Men have to boast of, are acquired, the greater Stress it will teach us to lay upon Education.'[13]

Smith's ideas are not very different from those of Mandeville. Smith, too, maintained that man can 'subsist only in society' and that the state of nature has never existed.[14] In fact:

> Were it possible that a human creature could grow up to manhood in some solitary place, without any communication with his own species, he could no more think of his own character, of the propriety or demerit of his own sentiments or conduct, of the beauty or deformity of his own mind, than of the beauty or deformity of his own face. All these are objects which he cannot easily see, which naturally he does not look at, and with regard to which he is provided with no mirror which can present them to his view. Bring him into society and he is immediately provided with the mirror which he wanted before.[15]

It is here that '[the mirror] is placed in the countenance and behaviour of those he lives with, which always mark when they enter into, and when they disapprove of his sentiments; and it is here that he first views the propriety and impropriety of his own passions, the beauty and deformity of his own mind'.[16]

Thus, our ideas of beauty and ugliness, of intelligence and dullness, of suitability and unsuitability, have their origins in the society in which they are generated, i.e. by interaction, by the 'meeting' of men who participate in collective life.[17] Only children are excluded from this process because they receive their 'first ideas' about their surroundings passively from other people.[18] However, if a man were from his birth:

> a stranger to society, the objects of his passions, the external bodies which either pleased or hurt him, would occupy his whole attention. The passions themselves, the desires or aversions, the joys or sorrows, which those objects excited, though of all things most immediately present to him, could scarce ever be the objects of his thoughts.[19]

So Mandeville and Smith are wholly in agreement on the inseparability of the binomial man – society. Interaction is the source of all the norms which regulate collective life and of the capacity to 'fix' within oneself the meanings of action, that is the capacity to think about them, to make them the object of reflection.

Needs and the division of labour

Mandeville analysed carefully the reasons which bind us to each other, and excluded very clearly the possibility that society could be generated and kept together by 'benevolence'.

Anyone who believes that falls into the utmost absurdity, 'wrongs his own Understanding' and is the victim of 'ignorance' and 'folly'.[20] 'If we examine into the Nature of all Bodies Politick, we shall find, that no Dependence is ever had, or Stress laid on any such Affection, either for the raising or Maintaining of them'.[21] Mandeville added:

> I am willing to allow, that among the Motives, that prompt Man to enter into Society, there is a Desire which he has naturally after Company but he has it for his own Sake, in hopes of being the better for it; and he would never wish for either Company or any thing else, but for some Advantage or other he proposes to himself from it. What I deny is, that Man naturally has such a Desire, out of a Fondness to his Species, superior to what other animals have for theirs. It is a compliment which we commonly pay to ourselves.[22]

Mandeville was even more explicit. He declared that need *'is the cement of civil society'*.[23] Society is

> entirely built upon the Variety of our Wants, so the whole Superstructure is made up of the reciprocal Services, which Men do to each other.[24] . . . How to get these Services perform'd by others, when we have Occasion for them, is the grand and almost constant Sollicitude in Life of every individual Person. To expect, that others should serve us for nothing, is unreasonable; therefore all Commerce,

that Men can have together, must be a continual bartering of one thing for another. The Seller, who transfers the Property of a Thing, has his own Interest as much at Heart as the Buyer, who purchases that Property; and if you want or like a thing, the Owner of it, whatever Stock or Provision he may have of the same, or how greatly soever you may stand in need of it, will never part with it, but for a Consideration, which he likes better, than he does the thing you want.[25]

Mandeville could not have put it more clearly: *'The reciprocal services which men render to each other are the foundation of society'*.[26] This means that a developed society is one in which 'No number of Men, when once they enjoy Quiet, and no Man needs to fear his Neighbour, will be long without learning to divide and subdivide their labour'.[27]

Smith's position on the division of labour is not unlike that of Mandeville. He argued as follows:

[man] stands at all time in need of the co-operation and assistance of great multitudes, while his whole life is scarce sufficient to gain the friendship of a few persons. In almost every other race of animals each individual, when it is grown up to maturity, is entirely independent, and in its natural state has occasion for the assistance of no other living creature. But man has almost constant occasion for the help of his brethren, and it is in vain for him to expect it from their benevolence only. He will be more likely to prevail if he can interest their self-love in his favour, and shew them that it is for their own advantage to do for him what he requires of them. Whoever offers to another a bargain of any kind, proposes to do this. *Give me that which I want and you shall have this which you want,* is the meaning of every offer.[28]

This is the scheme on which society is based and which the division of labour takes to its logical conclusion. In fact, when it is established

it is but a small part of a man's wants which the produce of his own labour can supply. He supplies the far greater part of them by exchanging that surplus part of the produce of his own labour, which is over and above his own consumption, for such part of other men's labour as he has occasion for. Every man thus lives by exchanging, or becomes in some measure a merchant, and the society itself grows to be what is properly a commercial society.[29]

Thus, it happens that 'the most dissimilar geniuses are of use to one another'.[30]

Hence, Mandeville and Smith replied to the question of *how* society is possible by describing 'naked' man impelled to action by the sole aim of satisfying his own needs. More noble aims, considered on the level of 'Apologies, Excuses and Common Pleas' are put in parentheses.[31]

Mandeville did not hesitate to write:

> Ashamed of the many frailities they feel within, all Men endeavour to hide themselves, their ugly Nakedness, from each other, and wrapping up the true Motives of their Hearts in the Specious Cloke of Sociableness and their concern for the Publick Good, they are in hopes of concealing their filthy Appetites and the Deformity of their Desires.[32]

At this point, a question arises spontaneously: if men really were as they are described in this extract, would society be possible?

Can a 'commercial society' survive?

Mandeville and Smith replied in the affirmative:

> though among the different members of the society there should be no mutual love and affection, the society, though less happy and agreeable, will not necessarily be dissolved. Society may subsist among different men, as among different merchants, from a sense of its utility, without any mutual love and affection; and though no man in it should owe any obligation or be bound in gratitude to any other, it may still be upheld by a mercenary exchange of good offices according to an agreed valuation.[33]

What then is the minimum condition for the existence of society? The expression 'agreed valuation' means that the *exchange* should provide reciprocal advantages that it should produce a positive-sum game. Thus the comparison between the points of departure and those reached by means of the exchange should be favourable to the latter: Ego should find in the Other's service the means by which he can improve his own position; and the Other in his turn should be able to obtain advantages from Ego's services. This is what makes society useful and ensures its survival.

However, there is a risk: it is that each may seek to transform the social 'transaction' into a zero-sum game, that Ego may wish to 'make use of' the Other's services without giving any in return. In this case, the benefits are not reciprocal. The Other does not have any interest in continuing the exchange with Ego: the survival of society itself is threatened. In other words, Ego has maintained a process which goes against himself: preventing the Other from pursuing the advantages of exchange is equivalent, in fact, to rendering void his own availability to continue the relationship. The result which every 'exchanger' ought to pursue is therefore a 'profit' which does not destroy the possibility of more profit. This is why Smith emphasised that 'honesty is the best policy'.[34]

Nevertheless, it can happen that social actors are blinded by appetites and passions. How is it possible to defend oneself from this? Mandeville wrote:

> If Virtue, Religion, and future Happiness were sought after by the Generality of Mankind, with the same Sollicitude, as sensual Pleasure, Politeness, and worldly Glory are, it would certainly be best, that none but Men of good Lives, and known Ability, should have any Place in the Government whatever . . . The most knowing, the most virtuous and the least self-interested Ministers are the best; but in the meantime there must be Ministers. Swearing and Drunkenness are crying Sins among Seafaring Men, and I should think it a very desirable Blessing to the Nation, if it was possible to reform them: But all this while we must have Sailors.[35]

What is to be done? It should be understood, Mandeville added, that 'there is no Man that has any Pride, but he has some Value for his Reputation' and that even 'a Man of very indifferent Principles' will refrain from stealing if he 'would be in great Danger of being detected, and has no manner of Security that he shall not be punish'd for it'.[36]

Even if we have to turn to people who are not those we would wish to turn to, society can still survive. 'To secure and perpetuate to Nations their Establishment, and whatever they value' it is sufficient to have 'wise laws, to guard and entrench their Constitution, and contrive such Forms of Administration, that the Common-Weal can receive no great Detriment from the Want of Knowledge or Probity of Ministers'.[37]

So we do not have to entrust ourselves to men, but to laws, to control, and to the sanctions facing the person who is found out. In other words, we have to realise that what we wish to 'ascribe to the Virtue and Honesty of Ministers, is wholly due to their strict Regulations . . . a Nation ought never to trust to any Honesty, but what is built upon Necessity; for *unhappy is the people, and their Constitution will be very precarious, whose welfare must depend upon the Virtues and Consciences of Ministers and Politicians* and not upon respect for the laws'.[38] To use an expression closer to us, we can call all of this *the certainty of the law*.

Smith fully agreed. He went as far as to say outright:

> If there is any society among robbers and murderers, they must at least, according to the trite observation, abstain from robbing and murdering one another. Beneficence, therefore, is less essential to the existence of society than justice. Society may subsist, though not in the most comfortable state, without beneficence; but the prevalence

of injustice must utterly destroy it. . . . [Beneficence] is the ornament
which embellishes, not the foundation which supports the
building. . . . Justice, on the contrary, is the main pillar that upholds
the whole edifice.[39]

Hence, Mandeville and Smith maintained that even if society were
composed of men 'lacking firm principles' it would still be possible. Their
'naked' man is moved only by base passions. But society survives because the
law and its sanctioning mechanisms make it evident to this man that adhering
to social norms leads to fewer inconveniences than violating them; that is to
say, the free expression of his own 'appetites' is a more costly act than
respecting the rules which direct collective life.

The law, the instruments of control and sanctions, can thus oblige an individual to raise the level of his own behaviour up to the *minimum* level necessary
for the survival of society. This is a conviction expressed again and again by
Smith. The following extract is typical:

The rules of justice may be compared to the rules of grammar; the
rules of the other virtues, to the rules which critics lay down for the
attainment of what is sublime and elegant in composition. The one,
are precise, accurate and indispensable. The other, are loose, vague,
and indeterminate . . . A man may learn to write grammatically by
rule, with the most absolute infallibility . . . But there are no rules
whose observance will infallibly lead us to the attainment of elegance
or sublimity in writing.[40]

There are no rules, therefore, which can guarantee the excellence of human
behaviour. However, there are norms by which correctness can be imposed on
each individual; this is sufficient to make 'social commerce' possible.

The advantage of Ego and the advantage of the Other: the 'invisible hand'

In the 'commercial society' outlined by Mandeville and Smith, the services
rendered by the Other appear in the guise of a means by which we can satisfy
our needs. The reciprocal services which the actors render must conform to the
'agreed valuation'. This is the same as saying that the actors themselves ought
to be free to determine the 'conditions' under which the *exchange* must take
place. The word 'condition' indicates the service or the 'price' to which each
must submit himself in order to have the Other's service in exchange. But how
can I 'persuade a Man to serve me, when the Service, I can repay him in, is such
as he does not want or care for?'[41] 'Money obviates and takes away all those
Difficulties, by being an acceptable Reward for all the Services Men can do to
one another.'[42] This is why 'to procure all the Comforts of Life and what is

15

called temporal Happiness' without money is like trying to communicate without language.[43]

Money, just like language, is the common denominator of the exchanges. It frees us from the necessity of correlating one specific service with another specific service, and it creates the suppositions for the intensification and development of 'social commerce'.

Payment in money is the most complete form of *generic obligation* which frees the relationship from a specific object or a specific person and which makes the 'condition' or means that services assume in relation to the Other absolutely clear. This is the idea on which Mandeville and Smith's theory is based, an idea well expressed by jurists when they maintain that the personal *motives of exchange* are not normally relevant. It follows from this that the social actors set up a continual 'double entry': they write in the credit account what they obtain from others and in the debit account what they owe to others in order to have their goods and their services.

A common aim transcending the ends pursued by individuals is not being considered here. There is only the valuation of the personal result. The expectation of each man is to reach his own goal, yet this achievement is possible only by submitting oneself to the 'condition' demanded by the person from whom we ask some goods or services. That is, when we deliberately pursue our objectives, we pay a 'price' which is entered in the debit column of our account and in the credit column of the Other's account. Thus we set in motion a mechanism of social cooperation regulated by the very 'conditions' or norms which that same exchange produces. It is a mechanism which knows no respite, because human needs cannot be suppressed, and which continually modifies the 'prices' by which 'social commerce' takes place. It is possible to isolate some 'frames' from this process:

1 Each of us needs the Other in order to realise our own projects.
2 It is not possible to know in advance what part of our plan will be accepted by the Other, who is not only one of our potential providers of 'means': he is first of all a *limitation* or a *fetter* because he asks us 'not to do' or to abandon a part of our plan (our plan must therefore be multiplied by a coefficient k, produced by the measure – from one to zero – of the Other's availability).
3 It is necessary to add a 'deal' to the advantage of someone else, to submit oneself to 'conditions' not pursued intentionally but dictated by the one from whom we ask collaboration.
4 The exchange takes place if both of the actors involved judge it to be convenient, namely if it produces a positive-sum game.
5 From the 'limitations' which the Other imposes on our plan and which we impose on his, as well as from the reciprocally accepted 'conditions', are born the norms, to which it was not previously possible to give shape, that

regulate the *exchange* (from now onwards, if not otherwise specified, when we use the term 'conditions' we shall mean also 'limitations').

6   Cooperation refers to the moment at which the plans of Ego and the Other intersect, so that, in respect to the final objectives, which stand beyond the relationship itself and which can therefore be unknown to the Other, the actors render to each other an unintentional 'collaboration'.

7   The consequences, which do not enter into the plans of Ego and/or the Other and which are likewise generated by their actions, are also unintentional.

What is the point? It is just as Mandeville wrote:

> The vast Esteem we have of our selves, and the small Value we have for others, make us all very unfair Judges in our own Cases. Few Men can be persuaded that they get too much by those they sell to, how Extraordinary soever their Gains are, when at the same time there is hardly a Profit so inconsiderable, but they'll grudge it to those they buy from.[44]

But this continual comparison between ourselves and others allows us to measure ourselves one against the other, beyond each one's intentions. We can therefore understand that the norms which arise from our mutual relationships form 'standards of judgment',[45] within which, at least in part, are our preferences. Hence, we all share the condition of *price makers*, but we are also *price takers*. When the norms are considered together, they in fact represent a map of coordinates. It is true that this map is subject to continual variations. However, these follow different rhythms and times so that relative stability of the *map* enables it to function also as a 'network' of reference, to fulfil a 'parametric function'. In other words, we reciprocally submit ourselves to limitations and 'prices'; these limitations and 'prices' become the tables by which we seek to make forecasts, by means of which we calculate the possible yield of our enterprises and of our resources in a given socio-historical context.

As Smith points out, in this way the individual decides autonomously to channel his own efforts, and he can in the meantime, and unintentionally, contribute to the purposes of others by submitting himself to the 'price' which they ask for their services. On the contrary, a norm which is imposed by authority and which does not arise from the free interaction of social actors is not the measure of the relationships which actually exist in society. It is something superimposed and misleading; it is equally so if exchange is impeded by force or in some other way. It must be free. In fact, if the 'parametric function' of prices already fixed can drive individuals to channel their resources towards objectives which are no longer profitable, the 'fall of profit in them and the rise of it in all others immediately dispose them to alter this faulty distribution'.[46] 'Without any intervention of law, therefore, the private interests and passions of men naturally lead them' to seek better yields. By transferring our resources into the sector in which we expect to gain a better result, we unintentionally divide and distribute the capital of every society 'as nearly as possible in the proportion which is most agreeable to the interests of the whole society'.[47]

It seems, Smith added, that the individual 'is in this, as in many other cases, led by an *invisible hand* to promote an end which was no part of his intention. Nor is it always the worse for the society that it was no part of it. By pursuing his own interest he frequently promotes that of the society more effectively than when he really intends to promote it. . . . It is evident', Smith emphasised, that 'every individual can, in his local situation, judge much better than any statesman or lawgiver' what 'species of domestick industry' he should invest in.[48]

Thus the significance to be attributed to the expression 'invisible hand' becomes clear. It is not a mysterious force: it is a system of indices. In other words, each individual seeks to make use of the resources and information available to him for his own advantage. Within this information is the system of prices produced by previous transactions. This makes it possible to calculate the yield of new enterprises and to correct earlier errors of 'destination', even if this does not exclude the possibility that the new decisions, coming into operation together with the decisions of others and thereby modifying the system of prices, may turn out to be wholly or partly unsound.

In his *History of Astronomy*, Smith dwelt at length on the ancient belief that ascribed events which could not otherwise be explained to the benevolence or displeasure of intelligent, although invisible, beings; he recalled the belief in the 'invisible hand of Jove'. In the *Theory of Moral Sentiments* and in the *Wealth of Nations*, the 'invisible hand' is a central point of the result produced unintentionally by the intentional action of the individual. This means that, what in a non-secularised society is attributed to the divine will as supreme ruler of human destiny, is now seen as the *emergent* outcome, not planned by individual action. Here individuals, without their realising it, are *price makers*. When the actions of individuals are put together, they produce, without a previous plan, the 'conditions' which make 'social commerce' possible. But these 'conditions' also form the map which gives direction to subsequent actions, and which provides to each person the standards by which he can programme the use of his own resources. The consequence is that the individual is in this case a *price taker*.[49]

Does this mean that individual preferences are dictated by monetary calculation? No. 'Pecuniary wages and profit, indeed, are everywhere in Europe extremely different, according to the different employments of labour and stock. But this difference arises partly from certain circumstances in the employments themselves, which, either really, or at least in the imagination of men, make up for a small pecuniary gain in some, and counter-balance a great one in others.'[50] In other words, it is possible to choose a profession considered to be more 'honourable', even if it yields a smaller income, and so on. However, the 'limitations' and 'prices' make certain preferences exorbitant or impossible, and they are therefore eliminated.

Ateleological development

Furthermore, it now appears clear that in Mandeville and Smith's theory we are very far from 'constructivism'. As we have seen, society does not arise from an original contract with terms agreed by individuals who previously lived in isolation. It is the 'natural' condition of man; when the individual begins to think about collective life, he already benefits from the social condition.

That is not all. For Mandeville and Smith, society is not even 'kept together' by a 'unitary direction' harmonising the actions of individuals. Cooperation derives, without any planning, from the attempt to achieve individual aims. Norms are none other than the unintentional product of the exchanges which succeed one another. They change according to the changes in the preferences of the various social actors. Thus, Mandeville and Smith were evolutionists. They were 'Darwinians before Darwin';[51] that is, they thought in terms of the superiority of those institutions and norms which could most effectively and appropriately respond to the demands of communal life. They thought of the division of labour as an unintentional product; it 'is not originally the effect of any human wisdom, which foresees and intends that general opulence to which it gives occasion'[52]; it is not born from a particular mind, nor is it planned by anyone. When men grasped its existence and significance it was already well developed. This is why, in referring to it, one can say what Mandeville himself wrote on the subject of language: 'It is impossible, that any Creature should know the Want of what it can have no Idea of.'[53]

Norms and the division of labour, therefore, belong to the universe of the unintentional products of intentional action. If they survive, it is because they answer to the needs of the social actors. They are not the rigid 'diving bell' which a superior 'mind' lets down from above, nor stages of a journey towards a prefixed goal. Smith expounded the concept very lucidly:

> The man of system . . . is apt to be very wise in his own conceit; and is often so enamoured with the supposed beauty of his own ideal plan of government that he cannot suffer the smallest deviation from any part of it. He goes on to establish it completely and in all its parts, without any regard either to the great interests, or to the strong prejudices which may oppose it. He seems to imagine that he can arrange the different members of a great society with as much ease as the hand arranges the different pieces upon a chess-board. He does not consider that the pieces upon the chess-board have no other principle of motion besides that which the hand impresses upon them; but that,

in the great chess-board of human society, every single piece has a principle of motion of its own, altogether different from that which the legislature might choose to impress upon it. If those two principles coincide and act in the same direction, the game of human society will go on easily and harmoniously, and is very likely to be happy and successful. If they are opposite or different, the game will go on miserably, and the society must be at all times in the highest degree of disorder.[54]

A conclusion must be drawn from all of this. In Mandeville and Smith's theory, politics (or the state) is never the variable which gives a solution to the problem of social order. This problem arises from the human condition, a situation in which the individual is not self-sufficient: he needs the Other. He experiences want also as insufficient availability of his neighbour to provide goods and services for the realisation of his own projects. This means that in every action the economic variable intervenes, and that *there is not* a natural identity of interests. From this comes the question of the compatibility of individual actions, namely the problem of social order. For Mandeville and Smith, each individual seeks to fulfil his own needs by means of intentional actions which, hence, do not benefit from an order already fixed; instead they produce this order laboriously and unintentionally, because each person, while pursuing his own ends, contributes towards the fulfilment of the ends of others. The services of each are a means, and each is the beneficiary of the activity of others.

Therefore, the order which is produced does not derive from the planning or from the mind of anyone, whether man or divinity, nor does it point towards a predetermined end. Thus, socio-economic elements are not subordinated to politics, because each piece on the chess board conserves its 'own principle of movement'. In other words, politics is not required to fulfil the task of building the social order intentionally or to lead individuals towards a common Destiny. Smith wrote:

> The factions formed sometime ago under the names of Whig and Tory were influenced by these principles: the former submitted to government on account of its utility and the advantages which they derived from it, while the latter pretended that it was of divine institution, and to offend against it was equally criminal as for a child to rebel against its parent.[55]

Unintentional order is represented by the first position, which Smith makes his own and which diminishes politics from the place of purposes to that of a means at the service of civil society. It is a position which presupposes the establishment of the process of secularisation; that is, it presupposes the emergence of a profane area left free by the channelling of religion into a separate course. Politics, economics and science set themselves up as reciprocally dependent functions; politics no longer controls the life of individuals in the name of religion.

This is why Giovanni Sartori writes:

> the separation of social from political passes across the division between political and economic. This is the main path . . . it was the economists – Smith . . . and the free trade theorists in general – who showed how life in association prospers and develops when the State does not intervene; who showed that life in association finds in the division of labour its own principle of organisation; and then showed to what extent life in association is extraneous to the State. Society is not only a distinct *social system* . . . in relation to the political system. It is more: it is the social system that gives rise to the political system.[56]

Sartori also adds in a note that 'the history of the discovery of the idea of society is still to be written' and emphasises that Werner Sombart's essay, *Die Anfänge der Soziologie*, which places Mandeville and Smith earlier than French positivist sociology, 'still deserves' to be read.

Mandeville: the service rendered by others is always a means

The analysis by Mandeville and Smith shows that, even if individuals have precisely personal aims, society is possible because each man permanently needs the Other. This constitutes a platform which Mandeville and Smith never abandoned and on to which they climbed to explore a more complete and complex social framework. The theory of man which they used does not start from 'quantifiable' interests. For Mandeville, the human being is desire:

> Man never exerts himself but when he is rous'd by his Desires: While they lie dormant and there is nothing to raise them, his Excellence and Abilities will be for ever undiscover'd and the lumpish Machine, without the Influence of his Passions, may be justly compar'd to a huge Wind-mill without a breath of Air.[57]

Hence, passions are the propelling force of our life. They push us into action and satisfying them is what we call 'happiness'.[58] 'We are ever pushing our Reason which way soever we feel Passion draw it, and self-love pleads to all human Creatures for their different views, still furnishing every individual with Arguments to justify their Inclinations'.[59] Therefore, reason is only an instrument at the service of passions. The magnetic needle of life points towards happiness. It is impossible that man 'should act with any other View but to please himself . . . and the greatest Extravagancy either of Love or Despair can have no other Centre'.[60] 'There is no Merit in saving an innocent Babe ready to drop into the Fire . . . we only obliged ourselves; for to have seen it fall and not strove to hinder it, would have caused a Pain which Self-preservation compell'd us to prevent'.[61] And when we share 'with another in his Misfortunes, Self-love makes us believe that the Sufferings we feel must alleviate and lessen those of our Friend, and while this fond Reflexion is soothing our Pain, a secret Pleasure arises from grieving for the Person we love'.[62]

In other words, the pursuit of happiness on the part of one person does not necessarily impose costs on others. His passion can impel him to fulfil the good of others, but this cannot cancel the fact than in such a case there is nothing altruistic: the only objective is to give an outlet to one's own passion or to fulfil one's own desire. Hence, the social relationship can serve us to realise an aim which lies outside the relationship itself, or can serve us for the pursuit of a purpose which lies within that same relationship, as happens when the Other is the object of our passion or our desire. And yet, in both cases, the availability of the Other (not forgetting the 'costs' which are added to the planned action of the actor) is a means by which Ego seeks to achieve his own interests. In the second of the two cases, men usually speak of 'altruism'. But altruism is a sort of 'optical illusion', something of which we do not understand, or perhaps do not wish to understand – the mechanism. Thus, citing Montaigne, Mandeville went as far as to declare that some men deceive others, but that 'much the great number impose upon themselves'[63] and referring to Bayle, wrote that, when he has to choose between reason and desires, man always decides in favour of the latter.[64]

There is also a 'service' provided by the Other through which we construct our image of ourselves. It is his judgement.

> It is common among cunning Men, that understand the Power which Flattery has upon Pride, when they are afraid they shall be impos'd upon, to enlarge, though much against their Conscience, upon the Honour, fair Dealing and Integrity of the Family, Country, or sometimes the Profession of him they suspect; because they know that Men often will change their Resolution and act against their Inclination, that they may have the pleasure of continuing to appear in the opinion of Some, what they are conscious not to be in reality.[65]

It is for this reason that 'sagacious Moralists draw men like Angels, in hopes that the Pride of at least Some will put 'em upon copying after the beautiful Originals which they are represented to be'.[66] That is to say, our behaviour is conditioned by the expectations and judgement of others and by the image of ourselves which they send back to us. Mandeville said:

It is incredible how necessary an Ingredient Shame is to make us sociable: it is a Frailty in our Nature; all the World, whenever it affects them, submit to it with regret, and would prevent it if they could; yet the Happiness of Conversation depends upon it, and no Society could be polish'd if the Generality of Mankind were not subject to it. . . . from [our] infancy throughout [our] Education, we endeavour to increase instead of lessening this Sense of Shame; and the only Remedy prescrib'd is a strict Observance of certain Rules to avoid those Things that might bring this troublesome Sense of Shame upon [us].[67]

Thus, virtues are a social product. So is courage, which 'is artificial, and consists in a Superlative Horror against Shame, by Flattery infused into Men of exalted Pride'.[68] So is every other 'virtue'.

If you ask me where to look for those beautiful shining Qualities of Prime Ministers, and the great Favourites of Princes that are so finely painted in Dedications, Addresses, Epitaphs, Funeral Sermons and Inscriptions, I would answer *There*, and no where else . . . This has often made me compare the Virtues of great Men to your large China jars: they make a fine Shew, and are ornamental even to a Chimney; one would by the Bulk they appear in, and the Value that is set upon 'em, think they might be very useful, but look into a thousand of them, and you'll find nothing in them but Dust and Cobwebs.[69]

This means that the qualities which we attribute to human actions are generated by the social mechanism of sanctions, that is, by the negative consequence suffered by the person who removes himself from socially defined standards. Hence, collective life draws benefits from men's desire to be 'thought well of' and from their 'Love of Praise and even of Glory'.[70] From this it follows that 'all shameless people that are below Infancy and matter not what is said or thought of them, these, we see, no body can Trust. . . . Such are justly called Men of no Principles, because they having nothing of any Strength within, that can either spur them on to brave and virtuous Actions, or restrain them from Villainy and Baseness'.[71]

Hence, the importance of what today we call primary socialisation. Mandeville wrote: 'The multitudes will hardly believe the excessive Force of Education, and in the difference of Modesty between Men and Women ascribe that to Nature, which is altogether owing to early Instruction'.[72] It is this that makes us sensitive to 'shame', that spreads 'the seeds of all Politeness', and that generates that 'established Pride' which is the source of the effort made by those who already possess titles 'not to seem unworthy' and by those ambitious people who do not have them 'to deserve them'.[73]

Smith: the service rendered by others is always a means
(on the principle of 'sympathy')

On these subjects also, Smith's position is no different from that of Mandeville. For Smith, too, man is the desire to be happy. And yet happiness does not consist only in 'being loved'; it consists also in knowing 'that we deserve to be beloved'.[74] This means that the image which others have of us and which they send back to us, or could send back to us, is an essential component of our life and forms part of that intersubjective mechanism to which Smith gave the name of 'sympathy'. Let us go through it step by step.

Man 'naturally desires, not only to be loved, but to be . . . the proper object of love'.[75] He desires not only praise, but praiseworthiness; or to be that thing which, though it should be praised by nobody is however the . . . object of praise'.[76]

> The love and admiration which we naturally conceive for those whose character and conduct we approve of, necessarily dispose us to desire to become ourselves the objects of the like agreeable sentiments, and to be as amiable and as admirable as those whom we love and admire the most. Emulation, the anxious desire that we ourselves should excel, is originally founded in our admiration of the excellence of others. Neither can we be satisfied with being merely admired for what other people are admired. We must at least believe ourselves to be admirable for what they are admirable. But in order to attain this satisfaction, we must become the impartial spectators of our own character and conduct. We must endeavour to view them with the eyes of other people, or as other people are likely to view them. When seen in this light, if they appear to us as we wish, we are happy and contented. But it greatly confirms this happiness and contentment when we find that other people, viewing them with those very eyes with which we, in imagination only, were endeavouring to view them, see them precisely in the same light in which we ourselves had seen them. Their approbation necessarily confirms our own self-approbation.[77]

If this is the situation, it is not difficult to understand that the highest social norms arise unintentionally from the desire to be the 'object of praise'. Smith wrote:

> He who admires the same poem, or the same picture, and admires them exactly as I do, must surely allow the justness of my admiration. He who laughs at the same joke, and laughs along with me, cannot well deny the propriety of my laughter. On the contrary, the person who, upon these different occasions, either feels no such emotion as

24

that which I feel, or feels none that bears any proportion to mine, cannot avoid disapproving my sentiments on account of their dissonance with his own . . . To approve or disapprove, therefore, of the opinions of others, is acknowledged, by every body, to mean no more than to observe their agreement or disagreement with our own.[78]

In other words, 'Every faculty of one man is the measure by which he judges of the like faculty in another. I judge of your sight by my sight, of your ear by my ear, of your reason by my reason, of your resentment by my resentment, of your love by my love. I neither have, nor can have, any other way of judging about them.'[79]

Smith adds: 'It is seldom [our judgements] are quite candid . . . It is so disagreeable to think ill of ourselves, that we often turn away our view from those circumstances which might render that judgment unfavourable.'[80] 'This self-deceit, this fatal weakness of mankind, is the source of half the disorders of human life.'[81] This weakness is not 'altogether without a remedy'.

Our continual observations upon the conduct of others, insensibly lead us to form to ourselves certain general rules concerning what is fit and proper either to be done or to be avoided. Some of their actions shock all our natural sentiments . . . We hear every body about us express the like detestation against them . . . We thus naturally lay down to ourselves a *general rule*, that all such actions are to be avoided, as rendering us odious, contemptible or punishable, the objects of all those sentiments for which we have the greatest dread and aversion. Other actions, on the contrary, call forth our approbation, and we hear every body around us express the same favourable opinion concerning them. Every body is eager to honour and reward them. . . . It is thus that the *general rules of morality* are formed.[82]

Hence, the highest social norms arise without being planned by anyone; they are an unintentional result produced by the desire to 'be observed, to be considered, to be noticed with sympathy, complacency and approbation'.[83] It is vanity that interests us, not ease nor pleasure.

But vanity is always founded on the conviction that one is the 'object of attention and approval'.[84]

In this process, the ability to put oneself in the Other's place is essential. It is precisely this that Smith calls 'sympathy'. It 'does not arise so much from the view of the passion [of another] as from that of the situation which excites it.'[85] It puts us, as has already been said, in the conditions of seeing ourselves as others see us or as they would see us if they knew everything about us.[86] This is why Albert Salomon rightly said that:

Smith's theory of society is necessarily a theory of sympathy. But in this context sympathy cannot be defined as compassion, empathy or any imitation of feelings. Thus Smith suggested the concept of sympathy as a measuring rod for perfect conduct in societal relationships.[87]

It is in fact by this that we can 'measure' our conduct through the expectations and judgement of others and consequently seek to adapt ourselves to whatever is demanded of us so that we are accepted, in the social interchange, as an 'other party'. However, since we judge others, and others judge us, the law which eventually arises is a two-headed Janus, a sort of 'third person' which incorporates in itself the *perspective* of Ego and that of the Other.[88]

All of this refers to the origin of norms. But what attitude does the individual take towards norms in force in a given socio-historical context? To quote Adam Smith:

> The regard to those general rules of conduct is what is properly called a sense of duty, a principle of the greatest consequence in human life and the only principle by which the bulk of mankind are capable of directing their actions. Many men behave very decently and through the whole of their lives avoid any considerable degree of blame, yet they never felt the sentiment upon the propriety of which we found our approbation of their conduct, but acted merely from a regard to what they saw were the established rules of behaviour.[89]

There is a coincidence with the norm. Let us try to make this question clearer.

For Smith, social norms constitute a sort of 'impartial spectator' with whom every man has to keep account in every moment of his life. The relationship of participation which each man maintains with the 'impartial spectator' can be directed by the effort to act 'as oneself'; that is: what the 'third person' dictates to us is in this case made to seem authentically 'ours'. But it is not; it is an acceptance imposed solely by the desire not to depart from the established rules and by fear of suffering the consequences of violating them. However, it can also happen that the individual transforms the 'impartial spectator' into a 'man within the breast', into a 'great inmate'.[90] In such a situation, not only 'outward conduct' but also 'inward sentiments and feelings' are affected.[91] In both cases, however, the Other's services are the means by which Ego pursues his own objectives. They are clearly so at the moment when his 'service rendered' enables us to go further, towards a target beyond the exchange, and they are so when the actor's good lies in the same relationship, which in this case constitutes the mirror from which to take one's own image. Apparently, in this circumstance what happens is that we give up our own interests for the interests of others. But 'it is not the love of our neighbour, it is not the love of mankind which . . . prompts us'.[92] It is the 'selfish interest' which coincides with the social 'profile' that we have designed for ourselves; a profile, however, that we realise through the medium of the availability of the Other.[93]

Whether what moves us is the aim of reaching a certain place beyond the relationship or whether it is something located within the relationship itself, the point is, according to Smith, that human society could not exist 'if mankind were not generally impressed with a reverence' for the social norms.[94] Hence, the importance of the process of primary socialisation.

Therefore, his conclusions agree with those of Mandeville. But there is more. The 'isolated' motivations of Mandeville and Smith coincide with Max Weber's 'instrumentally rational' action and 'value-rational' action. He saw precisely in the first type of choice a solution which uses the 'service rendered' of others as a 'condition' for aims which lie beyond the relationship, and he reserved the second definition for the project which realises its purposes within the relationship itself.[95]

The 'Adam Smith problem'

The close agreements between the sociological theory of Mandeville and that of Smith make it possible to re-assess the criticisms which Smith directed at Mandeville and to throw some light on the so-called 'Adam Smith problem'.

In the *Moral Sentiments* we read that there is:

> another system, which seems to take away altogether the distinction between vice and virtue, and of which the tendency is upon that account, wholly pernicious: I mean the system of Dr Mandeville. Though the notions of this author are in almost every respect erroneous there are, however, some appearances in human nature which, when viewed in a certain manner, seem at first sight to favour them. These, described and exaggerated by the lively and humorous, though coarse and rustic eloquence of Dr Mandeville have thrown upon his doctrines an air of truth and probability which is very apt to impose upon the unskilful.[96]

And yet directly afterwards Smith added:

> Whether the most generous and public-spirited actions may not, in some sense, be regarded as proceeding from self-love, I shall not at present examine. The decision of this question is not, I apprehend, of any importance towards establishing the reality of virtue, since self-love may frequently be a virtuous motive of action. I shall only endeavour to show that the desire of doing what is honourable and

noble, of rendering ourselves the proper objects of esteem and approbation, cannot with any propriety be called vanity.[97]

But was it not Smith who wondered: 'From whence, then, arises that
emulation which runs through all the different ranks of men, and what are the
advantages which we propose by that great purpose of human life which we
call bettering our position?'[98] And his answer was: 'To be observed, to be
attended to, to be taken notice of with sympathy, complacency and approbation, are all the advantages which we can propose to derive from it. It is the
vanity, not the ease, or the pleasure, which interests us.'[99]

Hence, there is not the distance between the two authors that Smith
claimed. However, the questions can be clarified further. Werner Sombart
wrote that there are 'two thinkers who are the source of two currents of social
thought, whose manifold waters can be followed through the centuries, the
fathers of the social optimism and pessimism of the modern era';[100] according
to Sombart himself, these thinkers are Shaftesbury and Mandeville. Should we
then place Smith in the wake of Shaftesbury? Not so. In order to understand,
however, it is not necessary to resort to social optimism and pessimism. The
fact that he denies that man has an innate moral sense means that Smith is
already in territory quite different from that of Shaftesbury and Hutcheson;
and it is in this territory that Smith finds himself together with Mandeville
and Hume. Mandeville's attitude of 'representing every passion as wholly
vicious'[101] could not have pleased the author of the *Moral Sentiments*. Yet, as
Elie Halévy maintained, Smith's teaching 'is the doctrine of Mandeville, set
out in a form which is no longer paradoxical and literary, but rational and
scientific'.[102]

The same thesis has been upheld by Edwin Cannan and by Jacob Viner.
Cannan wrote:

> We can scarcely fail to suspect that it was Mandeville who first made
> him realise that 'it is not from the benevolence of the butcher, the
> brewer, or the baker, that we expect our dinner, but from their regard
> for their own interest'. Treating the word 'vice' as a mistake for self-
> love, Adam Smith could have repeated with cordiality Mandeville's
> lines:
>
> > Thus vice nursed ingenuity
> > Which joined with time and industry
> > Had carry'd life's conveniences,
> > Its real pleasures, comforts, ease,
> > To such a height, the very poor
> > Lived better than the rich before.[103]

In his turn, Viner explained:

More important, in preparing the way for Adam Smith, was Mandeville's more elaborate reasoning in support of individualism and laissez-faire, resting on his famous argument that 'private vices' such as 'avarice' and luxury were 'public benefits' . . . Mandeville deliberately stated his conclusions in such manner as to make them offensive to moralists, but Smith accepted them in substance while finding a more palatable form for their expression.[104]

Hence, it is not possible to place Smith in territory opposed to that of Mandeville. Yet, the criticisms directed towards the latter by Smith have encouraged the idea that the corpus of Smith's thought might contain at least some contrasting elements. This is why Hayek wrote that 'It was somewhat misleading, and did his cause harm, when Adam Smith gave the impression as if the significant difference were that between the egoistic striving for gain and the altruistic endeavour to meet known needs.'[105] The fact remains that the so-called 'Adam Smith problem' has arisen in German literature. This theory considers it possible to divide Smith's works into two parts: the first, represented by the *Moral Sentiments*, is based on 'sympathy'; the second, developed in the *Wealth of Nations*, has selfish exchange as its central point. Thus the *Umschwungstheorie* has been developed, the hypothesis that the philosopher of 'moral sentiments' is different from the economist who sees in interest the only spur to action.

In 1848 Bruno Hildebrand accused the *Wealth of Nations* of 'materialism' in *Die Nationalökonomie der Gegenwart und Zukunft*. On the other hand, in 1853, in *Die politische Oekonomie von Standpunkt der geschichtlichen Methode*, Karl Knies was the first to insist on the incompatibility between Smith's moral philosophy and economics. However, the full exposition of this presumed contrast is to be found formulated in 1878 in *Adam Smith als Moralphilosoph und Schoepfer der Nationaloekönomie* by Witold von Skanzynski, basing it on the analogous theory expounded in 1861 by H. T. Buckle in his *History of Civilisation in England*.[106]

What is the point here? Anyone who accepts the thesis of the inconsistency between Smith the philosopher and Smith the economist shows, first, that he has not read what is said in the *Moral Sentiments* on the subject of the possible existence of a society of 'brigands and assassins' and, second, that he has not understood the significance given to the concept of 'sympathy'. For Smith, this concept is the instrument through which the expectations and the normative framework of society are formed, but it is not the motive of action. In other words, the means through which the framework of moral judgements and values is developed is one thing, the motivation of individual action is another. For Smith, as has been pointed out in the preceding pages, 'sympathy' is the ability to put oneself in the Other's place, to see what he 'expects' of us, to judge ourselves from his perspective. Consequently, sympathy is not a sentiment, but rather, from the 'sentimental' point of view, it is neutral because putting oneself in the Other's place does not mean sharing his 'sentiments'; it is simply equivalent to adopting his observation post.

The consistency of Smith's theory

The question can be made clearer, however. The type of argument used by Smith had already been used by Mandeville and, at much greater length, by Hume. If moral judgement is something which cannot be attained through pure reason and, if this judgement, contrary to what Shaftesbury and Hutcheson asserted, is not innate, where does it come from? Mandeville, Hume and Smith agree in declaring that normative standards are a product of social exchange. We have already quoted an extract from Mandeville in which he said that: 'Men often will change their Resolution, and act against their Inclination, that they may have the Pleasure of continuing to appear in the Opinion of some, what they are conscious not to be in reality.'[107]

Here Mandeville makes the conduct of the actor depend on the Other's judgement; the person who acts, that is, puts himself in the role of observer and fits his own action to the expectations and judgement of the Other. In Hume, this change of perspective is rendered possible by 'sympathy', which hence does not have a 'sentimental' connotation, but is simply the continuous 'displacement' that each man submits to in his relationship with the Other. Therefore, sympathy is a 'principle'[108] – it is the instrument which allows human minds to be 'mirrors to one another':

> not only because they reflect each other's emotions, but also because those rays of passions, sentiments and opinions may be often reverberated, and may decay away by insensible degrees. Thus the pleasure, which a rich man receives from his possessions, being thrown upon the beholder, causes a pleasure and esteem; which sentiments again, being perceiv'd and sympathiz'd with, encrease the pleasure of the possessor; and being once more reflected, become a new foundation for pleasure and esteem in the beholder.[109]

Hence, the idea of the substitution of perspective could already be found in Mandeville, while in Hume there is the idea of the Other as 'mirror' and 'spectator' and the emptying of the concept of 'sympathy' of all 'sentimental' connotation. Smith simply collected these concepts and used them to demonstrate the *fieri* of a system of social expectations and social norms. Therefore, the bond which unites the 'moral reflection' of Mandeville, Hume and Smith cannot be questioned. Nor can one assert, by endowing the concept of 'sympathy' with characteristics which it does not have, that there is a fundamental incompatibility between the *Moral Sentiments* and the *Wealth of Nations*.

There is more. The consistency between the two works lends itself to demonstration by another route. If there were a contradiction within Smith's theoretical works, the 'impartial spectator' would have to be incompatible with the 'invisible hand'. The inconsistency would not then concern the contents of Smith's two major works; it could already be found in the *Moral Sentiments* because in it Smith speaks not only of the 'impartial spectator', but also, even if only marginally, of the 'invisible hand'. Of this he says:

> The rich only select from the heap what is most precious and agreeable. They consume little more than the poor, and in spite of their natural selfishness and rapacity, though they mean only their own conveniency, though the sole end which they propose from the labour of all the thousands whom they employ, be the gratification of their own vain and insatiable desires, they divide with the poor the produce of all their improvements. They are led by an invisible hand to make nearly the same distribution of the necessities of life, which would have been made, had the earth been divided into equal portions among all its inhabitants.[110]

Consequently, what guides us in economics is the 'invisible hand', a system of prices which originates, as we have already seen, unintentionally from the personal plan to sell or buy. Prices are the 'conditions' which we contribute towards fixing, without our realising it, and to which we have to submit ourselves in order to fulfil our role on the market as consumer, contractor, and so on. However, we know that the 'impartial spectator' who is brought into existence unintentionally through our relationship with the Other is himself constituted by 'conditions' which must be respected if it is to be possible to fulfil any social role. So it is clear that the 'invisible hand' is only a 'section' of the whole network of 'conditions' produced by the intersubjective relationship. Therefore, there is no 'double thinking' in Smith. The proof of this is that the 'impartial spectator' and the 'invisible hand' signify one and the same thing: that, in a determined socio-historical context, we have to submit ourselves to 'conditions' in order to fulfil our personal objectives.[111]

Some conclusions

What we have discussed so far allows us to 'fix' the main questions arising from Mandeville and Smith's writings around certain points.

Preferences are not a product of reason

The problem that their thinking constantly revolves around is that of the compatibility of individual actions. Their fundamental question concerns order. They were drawn to the problem of the void left by the theological answer and sought to cover it with scientific deliberation. If the 'invisible

31

hand of Jove' is no longer what moves and accompanies the life of all men, what makes collective living possible? Mandeville and Smith moved within the territory of a cultural tradition which knew how to defend itself from the illusions and claims of naive rationalism. The theory which they developed presents man as a needy and fallible creature, incapable of replacing the divine Absolute with an Absolute created by the human mind, by Reason. Mandeville defined Descartes as a 'vain reasoner',[112] and similarly Smith spoke of Cartesian philosophy as 'illusive'.[113]

As we know, the theory that the *Wealth of Nations* was influenced by Physiocratic Rationalism was definitively swept away when Edwin Cannan recovered and published in 1896 the *Lectures on Justice, Police, Revenue and Arms* which Smith had given in 1763. Because of this, it became possible to verify that Smith had developed his own economic theories before his long stay in Paris in 1766.[114] Nevertheless, even without the evidence made available by this discovery, there is not a page in Smith's work that allows us to eliminate him from the ranks of 'critical rationalism'.

'Moral sentiments' do not originate from reason. This is a concept which Smith repeats at every opportunity and which is expressed in this way in one of the conclusive parts of the *Moral Sentiments*:

> Reason cannot render any particular object either agreeable or disagreeable to the mind for its own sake. Reason may show that this object is the means of obtaining some other . . . and in this manner may render it either agreeable or disagreeable for the sake of something else. But nothing can be agreeable or disagreeable for its own sake, which is not rendered such by immediate sense and feeling. If virtue therefore, in every particular instance, necessarily, pleases for its own sake and if vice as certainly displeases the mind, it cannot be reason, but immediate sense and feeling which in this manner, reconciles us to the one, and alienates us from the other. Pleasure and pain are the greatest objects of desire and aversion: but these are distinguished not by reason, but by immediate sense and feeling.[115]

This means that reason is only a 'function' of life, but it is not the source from which the theme of our existence comes. This is not surprising. In fact, for Mandeville and Smith the goal of each individual is the pursuit of happiness. Thus, one can say that what is found in the pages of these authors is, to use an expression of Max Scheler's, a 'non-formal ethics'[116] – that is, an ethic in which the subject of life is dictated by feelings, which measure the coincidence with ourselves, the happiness which each man is seeking. Therefore, reason is an instrument, a means of finding direction, but the existential contents pre-exist it.

Obviously, the search for happiness is individual. Mandeville wrote: 'It is impossible Man should wish better for another than he does for himself, unless where he supposes an Impossibility that himself should attain to those Wishes'.[117] This is echoed by Smith: 'Every man is certainly, in every respect, fitter and abler to take care of himself than of any other person.'[118] The boundary that separates Smith from 'constructivism' could not be clearer. It is not by chance that in the *Wealth of Nations* Smith challenged Quesnay's idea that the 'political body' could 'thrive and prosper only under a certain precise regimen, the exact regimen of perfect liberty and perfect justice'.[119] According to Smith, the situation is different: the effort

> which every man is continually making to better his own condition is a principle of preservation capable of preventing and correcting, in many respects, the bad effects of a political oeconomy, in some degree, both partial and oppressive. Such a political oeconomy, though it no doubt retards more or less, is not always capable of stopping altogether the natural progress of a nation towards wealth and prosperity, and still less of making it go backwards. If a nation could not prosper without the enjoyment of perfect liberty and perfect justice, there is not in the world a nation which could ever have prospered.[120]

The extract quoted above shows that Smith had thoroughly understood the 'constructivism' of the physiocrats; he had realised that Quesnay was a 'man of system', a definition Smith had coined in the *Moral Sentiments* to indicate – as we have already seen – someone who 'is apt to be very wise in his own conceit, and is often so enamoured with the supposed beauty of his own ideal plan of government, that he cannot suffer the smallest deviation from any part of it'.[121]

There is no doubt that Smith had hit the nail on the head. This can be seen also from this typical opinion expressed by Alexis de Tocqueville:

> According to the economists [the physiocrats] the State does not only have the task of governing the nation; it also has the task of moulding it in a particular planned way; it is responsible for forming the spirit of the citizens according to a pre-arranged model, equipping them with the principles and sentiments it considers necessary. In reality, its rights and powers have no limits; not only does it reform men, but it also transforms them; if it wished to, it could make them different from what they are! Baudeau says 'the State makes of men all that it wishes'. This remark sums up all their theories.[122]

This is why Overton Taylor declares that Smith's theory explains order through determined events, while the theory of the physiocrats is one of 'an ideal order to be achieved by a rational plan' of intervention.[123]

Thus, in the scheme to which Mandeville and Smith's deliberations give substance, there is a theory of man which stands in opposition to the rationalist theory. The individual is not moved by reason but by needs, passions and desires, which he seeks to satisfy. The ethic that derives from this cannot, therefore, be of a rationalistic type; instead, it is a 'non-formal ethics'.

The norm as relationship between services rendered

As this is so, social order is not a construction of reason, there is no planned beginning to society. Man has always lived in society; it is the place of his existence. In a broad sense, man is in every case a social being. In fact, his humanisation is a product of the inter-subjective relationship, which continually produces outcomes which are not due to human planning and 'wisdom'.[124] However, man is a social being also in a more restricted sense: that is in the sense that each of his actions contains 'limitations' and 'conditions' strictly speaking. Let us concentrate on this last point.

Mandeville and Smith's sociology is based on the idea of the social dispersion of knowledge; no one can be omniscient. As we already know, Smith wrote: 'What is the species of domestick industry which his capital can employ, and of which the produce is likely to be of the greatest value, every individual, it is evident, can, in his local situation, judge much better than any statesman or law-giver can do for him.' Immediately after this, he added:

> The statesman, who should attempt to direct private people in what manner they ought to employ their capitals, would not only load himself with a most unnecessary attention, but assume an authority which could safely be trusted, not only to no single person, but to no council or senate whatever, and which would nowhere be so dangerous as in the hands of a man who had folly and presumption enough to fancy himself fit to exercise it.[125]

If we use a favourite expression of Max Scheler and José Ortega y Gasset, we can say that in the Mandeville–Smith schema each man observes the world primarily from a personal 'perspective'.[126] This coincides with his own needs, his own passions, his own desires. Each sees the Other through the 'perspective' of his personal knowledge and projects. The objective of each is to fulfil his own plans. The services of the Other are a means towards this fulfilment; but the Other is also a series of 'limitations' and 'conditions' to which each must subordinate himself in order to have in exchange the availability of others without which his needs remain unsatisfied. When looked at from the perspective of the individual, the world is therefore a 'pragmatic field', a territory from which we seek to obtain advantages. Yet, the fact of seeking the services of the Other obliges Ego to satisfy Other's demands. Their respective perspectives intersect. Consequently, there emerges a 'double entry', a framework which defines the mutual positions of 'give' and 'have', of reciprocal advantages and of reciprocal limitations and conditions. This framework does

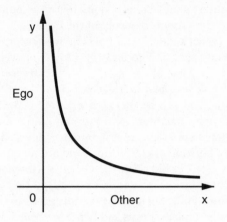

Figure 2.1 Curve of the 'social'

not arise from anyone's planning, but it is the unintentional result of the desire of each one to satisfy his own needs. All of this can be represented on a plan of Cartesian axes (see Figure 2.1).

If we give the positive value *a* to the interaction between the two subjects, since both derive advantage from the *exchange*, we have an equation where the value is the product of Ego's proposal *y* compared with the Other's response *x*. Hence, $a = xy$. On the graph, since the values of *x* and *y* are positive, and since these are the plans which Ego and the Other accomplish through their relationship, this produces a hyperbola.

This is a curve which lends itself well to depicting the social situation because obviously no concrete value of *y* exists for $x = o$, and vice versa. In other words, without the Other, Ego cannot fulfil his own plan; and, without Ego, the Other cannot ask anyone to satisfy his own needs – which is necessary for the pursuit of his own ends. Hence, the curve can never touch the axes, because then it would no longer define a social situation of interaction between two actors.

The place of Ego and the Other can be taken respectively by *autonomy* and by the *conditions* strictly speaking of an action. In this case, the curve signifies that in the social relationship the autonomy which is the origin of the action itself can never be suppressed (autonomy must therefore take a value higher than zero but cannot reach one, a whole number, because the limitations or bonds imposed by the Other would be lacking). It signifies that the 'conditions' are always present in every action; hence their value is greater than zero, but cannot reach one, a whole number, because Ego's autonomy would be lacking. That is to say, the 'conditions' are a 'to do' for the benefit of the Other; if Ego were obliged to act exclusively for Other's benefit, he would not have any personal 'motive' for action, there would be no 'double entry account', namely the voluntary decision to render services in favour of the Other.

The hyperbola is a two-headed Janus, an ideal 'third person' who incorporates the points at which the perspectives of Ego and the Other intersect. Therefore, it can be given the name of curve of the 'social'. *It is a curve which defines the identity of the actors, which is never complete without the intervention of the Other, without the 'limitations' and 'conditions' to which every action has to be subordinated.* It is a curve which does not have maximum or minimum points, but *places of possible living together.* This represents well the situation experienced by the social actors, who are never in a position of equilibrium and are therefore forced to pursue unceasingly their relationship with the Other, with whom they are obliged to seek continually points of mediation or co-adaptation, of acceptability of the social relationship. Thus, 'society' is the name given to the action of individuals who reciprocally render services and hence are beneficiaries of the activity of others. This is equivalent to saying that the agreement between the actors concerns the cost of the services which the Other performs for Ego and of those which Ego performs for the Other – services which serve both of them for their own ends. Consequently, the agreement affects the role of each as a provider of means, but not the ends which each person decides beforehand to pursue and towards the achievement of which, even if they are known, the 'Other party' cooperates unintentionally. In other words, each person 'controls' through his specific knowledge the means which he gives and those which he asks for, and he controls the immediate results of his actions.

Historical variability

The mechanism that produces the 'social' shows that the configuration of the 'third person' depends entirely on Ego's proposal and the Other's response; and therefore indicates that, when these variables change, the configuration of the 'social' also changes. Perceiving this, Leslie Stephen accused Smith of putting his trust in a mechanism in which 'the standard of morality seems to be too fluctuating to serve any intelligible purpose'.[127] But there is some superficiality in this accusation. Stephen did not realise the fact that what makes normative standards 'fluctuating' is not the mechanism as such; instead, it is the measure of the autonomy of the subjects. The greater the autonomy – that is, the actor's freedom of initiative – the greater the variability of the norms.[128] Not only that. Autonomy, which is thus the other face of the citizens' juridico-formal equality, certainly modifies normative standards. But this does not mean that this modification is a 'fluctuation' to be regarded with suspicion; to be more correct, it is the continual adaptation of norms and social values to the needs of the one who acts.[129]

The representation of the 'social' as the point of 'inter-section' of the action of Ego and the Other has the advantage of showing the relativism of norms and values; it demonstrates that the change of normative standards is a consequence, even if not always conscious, of the actions of social subjects, that in fact it makes plain that when Ego's proposal and/or the Other's response vary, the social norm, or the 'price' of one act in terms of another, also changes. In other words, men have nothing Absolute; norms which direct actions are always *relative*.[130] Even when the reduced autonomy makes them less 'fluctuating' they are still relative. Nor will they ever be able to become absolute: they are always the 'measure' produced by the relationship between Ego and the Other. This is why we find 'historical variability' in Mandeville and Smith; on the other hand, there is no determinism nor any indication of any ultimate necessary goal. In their pages, there is room only for evolution, that process which is chosen 'by a modest divinity, who does not know precisely what the being he wishes to create is like'.[131]

The State

If the social norm is the 'price' of one act in terms of another or the relationship in which one service rendered is exchanged with another, the significance that Smith attaches to the expression 'natural liberty' can be understood. This is not the liberty that man is supposed to have enjoyed in a state of nature that never existed: it is, on the contrary, the condition which a man enjoys when he is free to pursue what 'personal interest suggests to him'.[132] It is the situation in which individuals are placed on the same level before the law and 'every man, as long as he does not violate the law of justice, is left perfectly free to pursue his own interest as he thinks proper and to put his activity and capital in competition with those of every other man or class of man.'[133]

When this is looked at from the double *perspective* of the 'two-headed Janus', it means that at the moment when Ego 'intersects' with the Other, he has to agree with him (and the Other has to agree with Ego) to calculate autonomously the convenience of the exchange.

Each has interests which are affected by this, because the attempt to oblige the Other to render services that he does not consider convenient makes the relationship fail, and the one who has sought to 'force' the terms of the exchange loses completely the availability of others.[134] Thus, the mutual consent of the relationship makes possible the free calculation of advantage on the part of the 'exchangers' and the birth of a relationship that 'measures' the needs of each – that is, which stabilises the 'price' or the norm at the level of the importance of the reciprocal services. Another consequence is that the action (which is economic in every case, since it obtains goods and/or services in exchange for other goods and/or services) generates the normative conditions which make the action possible; hence it is also a juridical relationship.[135] This is why the State ought not to intervene in the enterprises of individuals. Its tasks should be:

(a) 'the duty of protecting the society from the violence and invasion of other independent societies';

(b) 'the duty of protecting, as far as possible, every member of the society from the injustice and oppression of every other member of it, or the duty of establishing an exact administration of justice';

(c) 'the duty of erecting and maintaining certain publick works and certain publick institutions, which it can never be for the interest of any individual, or small number of individuals, to erect and maintain, because the profit could never repay the expence.'[136]

Point (a) is so clear that it does not require comment. It is however appropriate to say a few words about the rest.

On the subject of the maintenance of justice – as we have already mentioned – for Smith, as for Mandeville, it is the principal condition of a society, the objective, which has to precede every other. In particular, one way to avoid injustice is to have clear rules of a general character. These originate from situations produced by interaction which become typical, namely, generalised models of conduct. They can obtain recognition (formal or *de facto*) from the State, but they are not an artificial creation of the State. The State is only an 'imperfect remedy' through which we seek to defend ourselves from human imperfections.[137] Thus, it is not necessary to call on the intervention of the legislator for everything: because he, being imperfect, is liable to multiply his own mistakes. His intervention can multiply injustices, upset the expectations of social actors and reduce their autonomy. In short, the certainty of justice becomes weak.

'External diseconomies'

As to point (c), the creation and maintenance of 'certain public works and certain public institutions', which could 'never be created and maintained by the interest of an individual', Smith showed that he had a clear understanding of the existence of what today we call 'public goods' – that is, goods the products of which, if private, could generate 'external economies', advantages which those who had produced them would benefit from without paying. In this case, therefore, steps are taken to finance this production compulsorily by means of taxes[138].

On a similar point, one could ask: Was Smith aware of 'external diseconomies', the negative consequences caused by private economic activity, or the costs not borne by the person who gives rise to them (one thinks of the smoke or the noise of a factory)? He did not address this subject. However, we have some points from which we can hypothesise his possible response.

For Smith, as already underlined, 'every individual . . . in his local situation, can judge better than any statesman or law-giver can do for him'. This declaration served as a basis for Hayek's assertion that the market is an 'information-gathering process', a process that is 'able to call up, and to put to use, widely dispersed information that no central planning agency . . . could know as a whole, possess or control'.[139] Therefore, if there are 'external diseconomies', this means that they are negative unintentional consequences of human intentional actions. And this happens despite the mobilisation of knowledge made possible by the market. If so, Smith would not have judged 'external diseconomies' as a 'failure of the market', but as a 'result' which would be impossible to detect without the collection of information made precisely by the market. Hence, the problem does not lie in the market; instead, it lies in our inability to put together a web of rights which allows the 'control' of such consequences. In other words, it would need an endowment of rights able to make possible the negotiation of means and to place in front of the manufacturer the following choice: to reduce pollution or not to reduce it, and in the latter case to pay pollution compensation to the citizens who suffer the negative consequences.[140]

Action is always economic

So we reach a crucial question: Is the individual of the Mandeville-Smith model the *homo oeconomicus* against whom the 'moralists'[141] often express their anger? There is no doubt that the man of whom Mandeville and Smith speak acts in an economic way. He operates in a 'pragmatic field', he seeks 'advantages' for the sake of which he puts up with 'costs'. Thus, his action cannot but be economic. However, his aims pre-exist his action. They tend eudaemonistically to bring about the coincidence of each man with himself, and they can therefore be concerned with sport, the affections, the arts, and so on.

On the concept of the *homo oeconomicus*, however, which we will return to later, a clarification should be made. Contrary to what is alleged, it is a symbol created not by the classical school of economics, but by the mercantilist school. To the latter, as Jacob Viner remarked, the image of a greedy and rapacious *homo oeconomicus* served to legitimise the intervention of the State, which it expected to fulfil the task of controlling and limiting mercantile 'selfishness'.[142] But belief in the usefulness of such intervention was a consequence of the fact that the mercantilists, unlike Mandeville and Smith, did not consider that the exchange could benefit both of the contracting parties. Hence, the need for a 'privileged point of view on the world', of the intervention of an organ reckoned to be endowed with a 'superior' understanding, 'not spoilt' by interests. That is, the State ought to determine the 'common good' – the social or collective best, understood as something external to and outside the individual operators, like a real 'third position'. But for Mandeville and Smith it is always the individual who acts; personal interests cannot be suppressed, the 'privileged point of view on the world' does not exist and it does not moderate selfishness, but gives a totally free path to those who think they represent, or are recognised as representing, the *social best*.

This is why Smith wrote that he had never 'known much good done by those who affected to trade for the publick good'.[143] And it is the reason why Hayek declared that 'justice has meaning only as a rule of human conduct', while 'no conceivable rules for conduct of individuals supplying each other with goods and services in a market economy would produce a distribution which could be meaningfully described as just or unjust'.[144] Hence, the conclusion that the 'common good' is not 'a particular state of things'; instead, it consists 'in an abstract order . . . which has to leave undetermined the degree to which the several particular needs will be met'.[145] In other words, 'the aim will have to be an order which will increase everybody's chances as possible – not at every moment, but only on the whole and in the long term'.[146]

3

WHICH METHOD?

A question about the philosophy of the social sciences

Unintentional order and the individualistic method

As we have seen in the preceding pages, the theory developed by Mandeville and Smith, unlike contractualism, does not envisage a *beginning* of society. Man is a social being *a nativitate*. What is human is a result of the relationship with the Other; it has its origin in society. Hence, the definition of 'social' belongs to the same human condition. Yet, in the works of the two authors, the term 'social' takes on, as well as a broad sense, a more specific and restricted sense. Let us see why.

The answer given by Mandeville and Smith to the problem of social order is based on the understanding that the *perspective* used by Ego does not exhaust the whole of reality. The Other puts himself in a different *perspective*, thus the same action has a *double* meaning. The butcher, the brewer, or the baker, whom Smith dwells on, are motivated by their own personal interest, which makes their activity an instrument serving this interest. But the same meat, beer and bread have a different personal interest for the one who acquires them. Each contracting party observes the same act of exchange from his own *perspective* and bestows on it a different meaning. Ego sees in the Other's services a means to attain his own ends, and the Other sees in those of Ego the means by which to achieve his own objectives. However, by submitting to the 'conditions' requested by the Other, Ego participates in the exchange and cooperates intentionally in the attainment of declared aims, and unintentionally in the pursuit of the ends, unknown to him or not necessarily known, of his 'other party' – which is what the Other also does when he accepts the 'conditions' dictated by Ego. Hence, to look at the *exchange* from only one *perspective* is equivalent to turning a blind eye to the contribution that each of the actors makes towards the pursuit of the Other's objectives. If, on the other hand, the two *perspectives* are put together, a relationship of reciprocal contribution to the attainment of the respective ends appears. Consequently, there is an element that specifically *unites* the 'exchangers'. This element is provided by the 'conditions' to which they mutually submit. These conditions, once they have been generalised, make possible a process of co-operation between unknown

41

people, or between people who do not need to know each other personally, and who also pursue ends which they do not have to declare to each other. These 'conditions' give content to the 'social' in *the strict sense*.

To clarify this further, we can usefully follow Rudolf von Jhering. He gave the name *subjective purpose* to what the actor pursues consciously, and *objective purpose* to the cooperation made possible by his acceptance of the 'social' properly called, that is, by his acceptance of the 'conditions' which each places on the action of the Other.[1] This means that the 'social' in the strict sense is a network of generalised 'conditions', or the 'price' to which each has to submit in order to pursue his own ends. In other words, the personal goal 'is an indispensable' presupposition 'for every action';[2] the conditions to which Ego submits safeguard the Other's objectives, while those accepted by the Other protect Ego's objectives. This is what makes the 'great society' possible, i.e. a cooperation based on the autonomy of the social actors in which the aims of Ego are not obstacles in the way of the aims of the Other. In fact, the 'conditions' are not a *prescription*; they do not impose an end, but leave Ego free to choose – that is, to decide his own objective and to consider whether it is worth the 'price' requested by the Other, and vice versa. As we have repeated several times, there is not a 'unitary hierarchy of ends' imposed by a social mind or a Legislator-Planner.[3] This is why Duncan Forbes has written that Scottish sociology emancipated itself from a 'superstition': it freed itself from the 'myth of the Legislator' or from intentional order; and that was the 'most original and daring *coup* of the social science of the Scottish Enlightenment'.[4]

The 'Scots' and, even earlier, Mandeville, were able to reach this conclusion because they avoided the trap of the 'creation of society', or the problem of its *beginning*. It follows from this that the subject under consideration is not man's social condition, nor the fact that society is his only place of existence; this is a sociality in a broad sense which no one disputes. Instead, what is being considered is the action, the *process* which this supports. Each man moves, acts, and completes his own actions for determined purposes. He is not the passive heir of the past nor the prisoner of an indisputable and unmodifiable 'whole'; he is an actor who, starting from a 'place of living together' which is never definitive, chooses his own ends and modifies the relationships of interaction with the Other. Therefore, he brings to life a social dynamic which confirms or generates the 'conditions' (the 'social' in a strict sense) which the relationship needs for working. It is here the origin of an order which is not attributable to the specific will of individuals engaged in pursuing their own personal objectives, and which establishes itself unintentionally, *alongside* individual purposes.

This is saying that Mandeville and Smith used an approach which observes simultaneously what is happening at a personal level and what results at the social level. However, this approach has been 'the subject of great resistance in sociology'.[5] In particular, it has been reproached for operating through an 'isolated' individual placed in a social and normative vacuum. But the target is not the method as such. The object of criticism is unintentional order, the 'great society', of which the individualistic method demonstrates the dynamic, i.e. the concatenation of acts of exchange which make it possible. It is asserted that the individualistic method is incapable of grasping the social element, the link that unites the life of each person with that of the Other, and that the model of living together which derives from it is impossible because of the absence of such a link. It is appropriate to spend some time on this question.

The 'individualistic' method makes clear the social link

If one reflects only on the fact that the individualistic method avoids posing the question of the *beginning* of society, by presenting man as a social being, *a nativitate*, the accusation against it loses any foundation. In the preceding pages, we have quoted two extracts, one from Mandeville, the other from Smith, which leave no doubts at all. We can recall them here. Mandeville declared:

> if we examine every Faculty and Qualification, from and for which we judge and pronounce Man to be a sociable Creature beyond other Animals, we shall find, that a very considerable, if not the greatest, Part of the Attribute is acquired, and comes upon Multitudes from their conversing with one another. *Fabricando fabri fimus*. Men become sociable, by living together in Society.[6]

He added: 'It is hard to guess, what Man would be, entirely untaught'.[7]
For his part, Adam Smith wrote:

> Were it possible that a human creature could grow up to manhood in some solitary place, without any communication with his own species, he could no more think of his own character, of the propriety or demerit of his own sentiments or conduct, of the beauty or deformity of his own mind, than the beauty or deformity of his own face. All these are objects which he cannot easily see, which naturally he does not look at, and with regard to which he is provided with no mirror which can present them to his view. Bring him into society and he is immediately provided with the mirror which he wanted before.[8]

According to Karl Popper, the extract from Smith suggests that a child growing up to maturity in a desert 'could not develop a self'.[9] This means that 'we are not born as selves, but . . . we have to learn that we are selves'.[10] Thus, 'long time before we attain to consciousness and knowledge of ourselves, we have, normally, become aware of other persons, usually our parents'. In other words, 'a consciousness of self begins to develop through the medium of other persons; just as we learn to see ourselves in a mirror, so the child becomes conscious of himself by seeing his reflection in the mirror of other people's consciousness of himself.'[11]

To put it slightly differently, 'the child learns to know his environment; but persons are the most important objects within his environment; and through their interest in him – and through learning about his own body – he learns in time that he is a person himself.'[12]

Popper's conclusion is consistent:

> The upshot of all this is that I do not agree with the theory of the 'pure self'. The philosophical use of the term is due to Kant and suggests something like 'prior experience' or 'free from (the contamination of) experience'; and so the term 'pure self' suggests a theory which I think is mistaken: that the ego was there prior to experience, so that all experiences were, from the beginning, accompanied by the Cartesian and Kantian *I think*.[13]

What needs to be emphasised is that 'temporally, the body is there before the mind' and that 'the mind is a later development'[14], which indicates that the pure self is 'orientated and anchored' to what Popper called 'World 3' and what we can, more simply, call the social world.[15]

However, as Friedrich von Hayek clearly saw 'it is not what we know as mind that developed civilization . . . but rather mind and civilization which developed or evolved concurrently', because 'what we call mind is not something that the individual is born with . . . but something that his genetic equipment (e.g. a brain of a certain size and structure) helps him to acquire as he grows up, from his family and adult fellows, by absorbing the results of a tradition that is not genetically transmitted.'[16]

> In this sense [added Hayek] the mind consists [. . . indeed] of a testable knowledge about the world, less in interpretations of man's surroundings, more in the capacity to restrain instincts – a capacity which cannot be tested by individual reason since its effects are on the group. Shaped by the environment in which individuals grow up, mind in turn conditions the preservation, development, richness, and variety of traditions on which individuals draw.[17]

Hayek's question is: Whether 'an individual who did not have the opportunity to tap such a cultural tradition, could be said to have a mind'?[18] The same question emerges from the pages of Mandeville and Smith.

The individualistic method and the errors of psychologism

Hence, it is the absorption of tradition that transforms the brain into a mind. It is like saying that 'we cannot start afresh', that 'we must make use of what people before us have done', a datum that has often not been 'sufficiently realized by [naive] rationalists',[19] for whom there is a 'pure self' existing before the relationship with the Other.

Yet, this is what Mandeville and Smith unequivocally rejected. Their position is therefore very different from that expressed later by John Stuart Mill. In fact, he wrote:

> The laws of the phenomena of society are, and can be, nothing but the laws of the actions and passions of human beings united together in the social state. Men, however, in a state of society, are still men; their actions and passions are obedient to the laws of individual human nature. Men are not, when brought together, converted into another kind of substance, with different properties; as hydrogen and oxygen are different from water, or as hydrogen, oxygen, carbon and azote, are different from nerves, muscles and tendons. *Human beings in society have no properties but those which are derived from, or may be resolved into, the laws of the nature of individual man.*[20]

In another consistent passage Mill stated that

> Political economy concerns mankind as occupied solely in acquiring and consuming wealth . . . Under the influence of this desire, it shows mankind accumulating wealth, and employing that wealth in the production of other wealth; establishing laws to prevent individuals from encroaching upon the property of others by force or fraud; adopting various contrivances for increasing the productiveness of their labour; settling the division of the produce by agreement, under the influence of competition (competition itself being governed by certain laws, which laws are therefore the ultimate regulation of the division of the produce); and employing certain expedients (as money, credit, etc.) to facilitate their distribution.[21]

Hence, according to Mill, everything that happens in society is explicable in psychological terms.

Clearly, we are confronted here with 'the main thesis of psychologism, the doctrine that, society being the product of interacting minds, social laws must ultimately be reducible to psychological laws . . . the events of social life, including its conventions, must be the outcome of motive springing from the minds of individual men.'[22]

This is a method which inevitably falls into 'constructivism': if institutions are the direct 'projection' of what the individual mind plans, the same social order (or disorder) can be immediately attributed to the will of men; there is no social fact that cannot be traced back to the intentions interested in its taking place.

Mill's position is typical of 'philosophical radicalism', of which he was one of the greatest representatives; it is always indissolubly linked to the idea of the 'conscious' organisation of society, as we shall see in more detail in Chapter 7. Here, however, we must pause to look at his methodological inconsistencies.

Karl Popper wrote:

> Psycologism is thus forced, whether it likes it or not, to operate with the idea of a *beginning of society* and with the idea of a human nature and a human psychology as they existed prior to society . . . It is a desperate position because this theory of a pre-social human nature which explains the foundation of society – the *psychological version of the social contract* – is not only a historical myth, but also, as it were, a methodological myth. It can hardly be seriously discussed, for we have every reason to believe that man or rather his ancestor was social prior to being human (if considering, for example, that language presupposes society). But this implies that social institutions, and with them, typical social regularities or sociological laws, must have existed prior to what some people are pleased to call 'human nature', and to human psychology. *If a reduction is to be attempted at all, it would therefore be more hopeful to attempt a reduction or interpretation of psychology in terms of sociology than the other way round.*[23]

This means that *human nature* 'varies considerably with the social institutions, and its study therefore presupposes an understanding of these institutions'.[24]

Then, how do we explain the autonomy of the actor and the adoption of the individualistic method? It is opportune to follow Popper again:

> [many] argue that, since we owe our reason to 'society' – or to a certain society such as a nation – 'society' is everything and the individual nothing; or, that whatever value the individual possesses is derived from the collective, the real carrier of all values. As opposed to this attitude, the position presented here does not assume the existence of collectives; if I say, for example, that we owe our reason to 'society', then I always mean that we owe it to certain concrete individuals – though perhaps to a considerable number of anonymous individuals – and to our intellectual intercourse with them. Therefore, in speaking of a 'social' theory of reason (or of the scientific method), I mean more precisely that the theory is an inter-personal

one, and never that it is a collectivistic theory. Certainly, we owe a great deal to tradition, and tradition is very important, but the term 'tradition' also has to be analysed into concrete personal relations. And if we do this, then we can get rid of that attitude which considers every tradition as sacrosanct . . . We thus may realise that each of us (by way of example and criticism) may contribute to the growth or the suppression of such traditions.[25]

In other words, it must be pointed out that social institutions define the *situation* in which the individual finds himself placed. His actions thus become foreseeable, but they are not predetermined. The preferences of the individual can also coincide with those inherited from the past, but he can change the way in which he is prepared to compose them with those of others. This is not to say that the actor, while taking the 'costs' on himself, cannot always try to put forward completely new preferences. It is for this very reason that the problem of social order arises, i.e. the problem of the compatibility of the initiatives undertaken by each one. Order becomes a process, a permanent *to do*; it is never a given fact.

This is the point: no normative or coercive apparatus can guarantee the predetermination of individual action. There are always degrees of autonomy (cf. the hyperbola in the previous chapter) which leave open the problem of social order. Looked at from the opposite point of view, this is what makes it possible to formulate innovative proposals and to respond creatively to the new challenges of the socio-historical context.

Therefore, the individualistic method denies the existence of a 'pure self' and of a normative vacuum; it places the subject within a socio-historical context, and makes the very growth of the human personality depend on it. Yet, this does not produce a unidirectional link. There is a *feedback*: it is true that we are a product of other minds, but it is also true that once we have acquired our 'self', we are in a position to modify the work of others, 'predecessors as well as contemporaries'.[26] We live in a *situation* and our actions correspond to a 'situational logic'[27] in which a permanent dynamism takes place between us and others. Each one acts in order to assert his personal preferences and these preferences are the 'data' of the problem to be resolved. Collective living is in fact possible only if some kind of *composition* is found. Karl Popper wrote:

> [even the institutions] which arise as the result of conscious and intentional human action are, as a rule, the *indirect, the unintended and often unwanted by-products of such actions*; . . . and we can add that even most of the few institutions which were consciously and successfully designed (say, a newly founded University, or a Trade Union) do not turn out according to plan – again because of the unintended social repercussions resulting from their intentional creation.[28]

Auguste Comte: the collectivistic method and the impossibility of the 'great society'

As we have just seen, the individualistic method does not deny the social element. Instead, it creates a two-directional circuit between Ego and the Other, between the individual and society, because it recognises that individual autonomy cannot be suppressed. It follows from this that it is not possible to realise an order planned by the mind of a Legislator; another consequence is the individuation of a *process* which is produced unintentionally *beside* the objectives that individuals pursue consciously.

Yet – it needs to be repeated – the individualistic method and the 'discovery' of unintentional order have not had an easy life in sociology. Auguste Comte did not hesitate to write: 'To the eye of Positivism Man, properly so called, does not exist. It is only Humanity that can exist, since our whole development, under every aspect, is due to society.'[29] Here we see the error of considering the 'social', understood in the broad sense, that is, the actual condition of the human being, as something that exists outside individuals. This is perfectly in accord with the affirmation, also from Comte, on the basis of which 'Civilization progresses according to a necessary Law', because 'the progressive march of civilization follows a natural and unavoidable course'.[30]

The question is: Where does the law of progress come from? Let us try to reach the answer in stages. First of all, let us reflect on the opinion expressed by Comte on unintentional order. He declared:

> The essential vice of political economy, regarded as a social theory, consists in this. Having proved, as to certain matters, far from being the most important, the spontaneous and permanent tendency of human societies towards a certain necessary order, it infers that this tendency does not require to be regulated by positive institutions.[31]

He added:

> [political economy] is an essential part of the total system of critical philosophy, which during the strictly revolutionary period carried out a task which was indispensable, although only transitory . . . it has participated in an appropriate way and nearly always very honourably in this great intellectual struggle, radically discrediting the complex of industrial politics which the old social regime had been developing since the Middle Ages . . . This purely provisional function, indeed, constitutes the main social effectiveness of this doctrine. . . . The general spirit of political economy, for anyone who has properly assessed it in the totality of writings that refer to it, leads today essentially to the assertion, as a universal dogma, of the necessary absence of every *regulatory intervention*.[32]

Comte concluded as follows:

> This shows clearly the vain inability of this doctrine, in spite of its illusory claims, to limit effectively, even with the arguments most appropriate to it, the general spirit of anarchy, the development of which it has, on the contrary, powerfully supposed in this case.[33]

Thus, Comte maintained that unintentional order is impossible, because in the 'great society', about which economists theorise, the independent variable is lacking: 'Government is, thus, no longer regarded as the head of society, destined to bind together the component units and to direct their activity to a *common end*.'[34] The governors are subordinated to the control of the governed: the government 'is represented as a natural enemy encamped in the midst of our social system, against which society needs to fortify itself by the guarantees already obtained while maintaining a permanent attitude of mistrust and defensive hostility ready to break forth at the first symptom of attack.'[35] Comte said that in this social and political picture 'the dogma of Sovereignty of the People' prevails,[36] based on the 'dogma of unlimited Liberty of Conscience'.[37] Where 'the sovereignty of every individual reason' is proclaimed *'there is no society'*.[38] Comte's diagnosis displays a strong dose of naive rationalism.

In fact, he wrote:

> In astronomy, physics, chemistry and physiology there is no such a thing as liberty of conscience; that is to say everyone would deem it absurd not to place confidence in the principles established for these sciences by competent thinkers. If the case is different in politics, this arises from the circumstance that, the old principles having been abandoned while the new are yet unformed, established principles during this interregnum do not in a just sense exist. But to convert this transitory fact into an absolute and eternal dogma and treat it as a fundamental principle, evidently amounts to a proclamation that society should always continue deprived of any general doctrinal basis. It must be admitted that such a notion justly deserves the charge of anarchy brought against it by the ablest defenders of the theological system.[39]

So, what is to be done? Comte considered that it was necessary to turn one's back on the idea that society 'ought not to be organised' consciously.[40] An organic doctrine is needed, to direct the whole of society towards a common end, and a government to be 'the head of society, as the guide and agent of general activity'.[41] In order to do this, the *'scientific men ought . . . to elevate politics to the rank of a science of observation'*.[42] The 'scientific men' should be trusted for 'reorganising society'. In fact, they are:

1   by the character of their intellectual capacity and cultivation alone competent to execute these works;

2   by the nature of the case, this office is reserved for them as constituting the spiritual power of the system to be organised;

3   they exclusively possess the moral authority requisite in our day to determine the adoption of the new organic doctrine.[43]

Comte was thus going in the direction of a sophocratic Kingdom, in which politics would be legitimised by science: the binomial politics – science is the new independent variable of the social system. In societies of the past, politics was legitimised by religion. In 'positivist' society, science takes the place of religious belief and in such a way allows the re-establishment of a 'privileged point of view on the world', to which everything must be taken back. In this way, the intentional order is reconstituted through a new source of legitimation.

Now it seems clear what Comte meant when he maintained that 'man, properly so called, does not exist'. He intended to suppress the individual; he needed to do this, because he rejected the possibility of the 'great society' which to him was 'crisis', 'anarchy'. His 'law of progress' has the task of restoring the independent variable and bringing back intentional order, although it is now justified in a different way. However, we know what this is: the crystallisation of Comte's political and social personal preferences. The proof is that if such a law really existed, no one would propound the problem of order; there would be no need to give up hope for the present, nor would any effort be required to reach the solution; 'men' would be heteronomously guided towards the predetermined goal.

Nor is that all. There are some paradoxes which it is worth clarifying.

1   Comte denied the existence of the individual. But his suggestion of intentional order was based on exactly the opposite. In fact, as Hayek rightly pointed out:

> it is the theoretical collectivist who extols individual reason and demands that all forces of society be made subject to the direction of a single mastermind, while it is the individualist that recognizes the limitations of the powers of individual reason and consequently advocates freedom as a means for the fullest development of the powers of the inter-individual process.[44]

It is easy to see that here the collectivist method is none other than a psychologism in which the prerogative of occupying a 'privileged point of view on the world' is ascribed to some individuals.[45]

2   These individuals are recognised as holders of a 'superior' knowledge as representing the 'whole', the destiny of humanity; because of this, power

50

is conferred on them. Yet, Hayek reminds us that, when the truth or false-ness of a statement

> is no longer decided on the basis of logical argument and empir-ical test, but by examining the social position of the person who made it, when in consequence it becomes the membership of a class or race, and when . . . it is claimed that the sure instinct of a particular class or a people is always right, reason has been defini-tively driven out.[46]

The paradox is that 'the presumptuous aspiration that "reason" should direct its own growth can in practice only have the effect that it would set limits to its own growth, that it would confine itself to the results which the directing mind can already foresee.'[47] In other words, to the extent that intersubjective processes produce results that could not have been attained through conscious directives, 'any attempt to make them subject to such direction would necessarily mean that we restrict what social activity can achieve to the inferior capacity of the individual mind'.[48]

3   The claim that it is possible to subordinate collective life to a 'unitary direction' pushed Comte into maintaining that in a society 're-organised' in this way there is no place for chance. 'A superficial philosophy, which would make this world a scene of miracles, has immensely exaggerated the influence of chance. . . . All sensible men in our time admit that chance plays only a very small part'.[49] If this is so, then everything that happens in society should always be interpreted as the conscious result of someone's action. The consequence is that every negative result, even if produced unintentionally by the initiatives of the 'scientific class', should be attributed not to chance nor to the incapacity to control all the social variables, but to the will of an 'enemy' who is somehow installed within society. Therefore, the claim to be omnipotent has permanent need of a 'scapegoat' and a 'conspiracy theory' of collective life to give an excuse for its impotence and failures.[50]

Moreover, for clarifying further the link between the opponents of unintentional order, it is useful to add that Hegel too inveighed against chance:

> We must take into history the belief and the thought that the world of the will has not put itself into the hands of chance. That in what happens to peoples the dominating element should be an ultimate end, that in universal History there should be a reason – and not the reason of a particular person, but divine absolute reason – is a truth that we assume; its proof is the very way History is treated: it is the symbol and act of reason.[51]

51

4   Hence, at the foundation of all of Comte's structure, there is political collectivism, generated by the fear of the 'great society'. Ontological collectivism, i.e. the assertion that the individual does not exist, is the simple *justification* of the totalitarian political programme. In its turn, methodological collectivism – that is, the claim to annul individual preferences, and to give society a unitary 'organisation' – is the means of putting this political programme into effect;[52] this is why Hayek wrote that without methodological collectivism, political collectivism 'would be deprived of its intellectual basis'. If, in fact, it lacks 'the pretension that conscious individual reason can grasp all the aims and all the knowledge of "society" or of "humanity", the belief that these aims are best achieved by a conscious central direction loses its foundation.'[53] Hence, it was not without reason that William Dilthey in his time saw in Comte's ambitious programme a secularised transcription of the 'unitary plan' of theological origin.[54]

Karl Marx: between politics and science

The origins of Marx's collectivism are no different from those of Comte. Marx saw the market society as 'a desert inhabited by wild animals'[55], and added that such a society is the realisation of the function of the market, 'a born leveller and cynic . . . always ready to exchange not only soul, but body, with each and every other commodity'[56]; it brings into existence the 'time of general corruption, of universal venality'.[57]

Marx's reasoning is as follows: it was only through competition that

> civil society could separate itself completely from the life of the State, tear assunder all the species-bonds of man, put egoism and selfish need in the place of these species-bonds and dissolve man into a world of atomistic individuals with hostile attitudes towards each other.'[58] [Thus,] 'the true essence of the Jew has been realized and secularized in civil society . . . As soon as society manages to abolish the *empirical* essence of Judaism, the market and its presuppositions become *impossible*, for his mind no longer has any object, because the subjective basis of Judaism, practical need, has become humanized, and because the conflict of man's individual, material existence with his species-existence has been superseded.[59]

Therefore, Marx's problem is the suppression of the individual, the abolition of the conflict between individual existence and existence as a species. The task of resolving this problem is entrusted to '*philosophy*', to the dialectical philosopher who is the 'head' of the 'emancipation of man'.[60] The 'philosophical class' is the true proletariat, who is not 'formed by the poverty produced by natural laws, but by *artificially induced poverty*. It is not made up of the human masses mechanically oppressed by the weight of society, but of those who have their origin in society's brutal dissolution and principally the dissolution of the middle class'.[61] The objective is how to act in such a way that men move as a 'single social labour force', according to a grand 'definite plan',[62] which no longer allows the individual to express his own selfishness and shatter the unity of the species.

As can be seen, the line followed by Marx is not dissimilar to that of Comte. Both were interested in the same problem, and both pointed towards the restoration of intentional order. It is true that Comte preferred to put this trust in the 'scientific class' and Marx turned rather to the 'proletariat' originating in 'artificially induced poverty', but their political collectivism, justified through ontological collectivism and set in motion by means of collective subjects created by their own preferences and arbitrarily endowed with a monopoly of the Truth, coincides perfectly. The 'scientific class' and the 'proletariat' are, exactly as Hegel wrote, the 'universal class' which has 'the universal as the end of its essential activity'.[63]

However, the statement that these classes have the 'universal' as their goal is neither proved nor provable. The suppression of the particular and of the individual is simply a fiction produced through methodological abuse, an abuse that transforms the personal positions of Comte and Marx into those representative of a Goal, which they claimed to know, but which lies beyond proofs and confutations and which is to be attained only on the basis of a declared 'inclination' of humanity.

We have before us here a doctrine, found also in Mill, that we can call 'historicism' as Popper did: the claim to introduce a *telos* into history, to 'propound prophecies' of a historical nature and to use them in political activity.[64] However, one can ask oneself: What makes a prophecy different from a scientific prediction? The first is based on a stated 'inclination' of humanity which will inevitably be fulfilled in history; the second makes use of the individualisation of the 'conditions' which make a certain historical development possible or impossible.[65]

Marx was aware of the weakness of the prophetic position, found in Comte and also in Hegel's 'faith' in reason, which 'lies in itself and has its end in itself'. This was his motive for trying to dress up his own unconditional historical prophecy as 'scientific prediction'. In other words, he tried to derive historical development from the actions of individuals placed in a given social situation and not from generic 'tendencies' of the same individuals or external to them. This is the explanation of the reproof contained in the 'postscript' to the second edition of the first volume of *Das Kapital*:

> For Hegel, the process of thinking, which he even transforms into an independent subject, under the name of 'the Idea', is the creator of the real world, and the real world is only the external appearance of idea. With me the reverse is true: the ideal is nothing but the material

world reflected by the mind of man, and translated into forms of thought.[66]

Let us see how Marx continued.

Although Comte had accused the 'great society' of not having a 'moral bond' capable of holding its different parts together, he admitted that the economists were owed

> eternal gratitude for their successful efforts to dissipate the lamentable and immoral prejudice that propounds, whether between individuals or between peoples, the improvement of the material condition of some as if this could only be derived from a corresponding deterioration for others. This led basically to the denial or misunderstanding of industrial development, since it presupposed that the total mass of our wealth was constant.[67]

Thus, Comte gave the economists credit for having explained that from the material point of view the 'great society' is a 'positive-sum game' and is hence in a position to benefit all of the contracting parties.

Marx, on the other hand, represented the relationships of production as a 'zero-sum game'. In order to do this, he avoided comparing the initial position of the participants in the productive process with their final position, a comparison which demonstrates the improvement of everyone's position. Instead, he concentrated on the division of the results of production, showing how what goes to the workers is something that is taken from the owners of the means of production, and vice versa. To improve their own situation, the owners of the means of production choose to take out of the productive process an ever-increasing proportion of the labour force, by substituting it with the extended use of old machines and/or the introduction of new ones. The consequence is the increasing impoverishment of the working class. It also leads to the tendency of the rate of profit to fall because the increase in the 'constant capital' makes the value of work extorted from the workers diminish – i.e. it leads to a lowering of the 'exploitation' of the workers, on which, according to Marx, the rate of profit depends.[68]

In other words, Marx placed the owners of the means of production and the workers in an antagonistic social *position*. The 'situational logic' encourages the *haves* to substitute the labour force with machines so that they can pay a lower amount of wages. But this, while it fits the 'logic of the situation', leads to an *unintentional consequence*: the tendency of the rate of profit to fall. That is, the owners of the means of production are rationally led to exclude an increasing proportion of the working class from the production process. The result is to generate, alongside it, a 'perverse effect', negative with respect to its own socio-economic survival, which is the tendency of the rate of profit to fall.

In this way, the decision taken with 'good reasons',[69] to substitute the labour force with machines, produces civil war. Why?

By this time, in the intellectual proletariat, born of 'artificially induced poverty', has entered the 'human masses mechanically oppressed by the weight of society', the 'poverty produced by natural laws', on whom the process of increasing impoverishment weighs.[70] Upon the *haves*, on the other hand, weighs the fall in the rate of profit. It is a struggle for safety, it is a war between two irrevocably opposed social parties.

So, does economic life generate civil war? This is what Marx suggested. Yet, let us try to go into it in more depth. As Pitirim Sorokin[71] pointed out, in all situations – war, plague, famine – in which safety is at stake, a mechanism of polarisation is put into action which unites all those who feel threatened by the same danger. In Marx's schema, the owners of the means of production are threatened by the *have nots* and vice versa. Thus, the Marxian picture begins to become clearer. Remembering Hegel's reflections on war, Marx 'ordered' his economic formulae to deny the advantages of exchange and to divide society into two hostile parties. This means that it is not classes that determine war; it is war, created artificially by Marx,[72] that causes the polarisation into two sides opposed to each other. Given the dangerous situation, the objective of each man is safety; each wishes to preserve his own existence, an aim which, measured against individual weakness, suggests the uniting of energies. This uniting of energies gives rise to the optical illusion of the pre-eminence of class interests; but it is actually a matter of the interests of individuals caught in a situation of danger and of consequent polarisation. Therefore, individuals act, and their actions correspond to a 'situational logic'. So to say, as Marx did,[73] that it 'is not the consciousness of men that determines their being, but, on the contrary, their social being that determines their consciousness',[74] means simply rejecting psychologism, the idea – i.e. that the laws of social life can be reduced to psychological laws. Hence, the actor has to be placed in a socio-historical *situation* in which he has to measure himself against defined problems and where he will have 'good reasons' for acting in one way or another and for responding to his own 'circumstance' in a routine and foreseeable or innovative way,[75] producing, however, unintentional consequences.

Some points made by Engels confirm that this was what Marx thought. He (Engels) stated clearly:

> In the history of society . . . the actors are all endowed with consciousness, are men acting with deliberation or passion, working towards definite goals; nothing happens without a conscious purpose, without an intended aim . . . That which is willed happens but rarely; in the majority of instances the numerous desired ends cross and conflict with one another, or these ends themselves are from the outset incapable of realisation or the means of attaining them are insufficient. Thus the conflict of innumerable individual wills and

individual actions produces a state of affairs entirely analogous to that in the realm of unconscious nature. The ends of actions are intended, but the results which actually follow from these actions are not intended; or when they do seem to correspond to an end intended, they ultimately have consequences quite other than those intended.[76]

A recapitulation is, at this point, necessary. In order to dress up his 'unconditioned prophecy' as a 'scientific prediction', Marx worked out an exemplary sociological model. Someone will say, 'But the accounts do not balance'. It is true. However, that does not depend on the method adopted. It is the responsibility of the premise (the antagonistic nature of the productive process) which is false. A question arises: If it is of no use to truth, what is the use of his sociologico-economic schema? Through the mechanism of the class war, hailed as a victory and 'confirmed' by political economy, the 'bourgeois' science itself, Marx tried to reach a subtle goal. In a letter to Ferdinand Domela Nieuwenhuis, Marx wrote: 'The dream that the end of the world was near inspired the early Christians in their struggle . . . and gave them confidence in victory. Scientific insight into the inevitable disintegration of the dominant order of society . . . is a sufficient guarantee that . . . a real proletarian revolution breaks out'.[77] Thus, Marx understood what today we call Thomas's theorem: 'If men define certain situations as real, they are real in their consequences.' Therefore, Marx's is a 'self-fulfilling prophecy'[78] dressed up as a sociological model.

In other words, Marx wished for the socialist revolution, and he called in question, as guarantor of the prophecy with which he incited men to mobilise, the social sciences, through which he sought to 'prove' the inevitability of the revolutionary enterprise and its success, a success which was what he desired politically. Hence, the schema he used was a 'conditioned prediction', because it places the individual in a socio-historical *situation* which implies planned initiatives;[79] these produce unintentional consequences, beside the consciously-planned outcome. And yet Marx based his theory on a false premise: the antagonistic character of the productive processes. As a result, his analysis was simply the 'means' of formulating a 'self-fulfilling prophecy'.

However, the most important point is something else. When Marx wanted to present himself in the guise of the social scientist, he used a 'double entry account' made up of conscious individual decisions and unplanned social consequences. The same method was used by Mandeville, Hume and Smith to explore the dynamic of the 'great society' and to demonstrate that the interest of Ego is compatible with that of the Other: that there is no need for the 'privileged point of view on the world', of the 'one plan'. Nay, this cannot be realised, because it is broken by the individual initiatives and unintentional consequences, to which in fact Marx himself gave his attention.[80]

4

DURKHEIM AND THE APPLICATION OF THE COLLECTIVISTIC METHOD

Durkheim versus the 'great society'

The first subject considered by Durkheim was the relationship between the market society and social order, and this is the subject that concerns us most.

If we had to turn to a synthetic expression to describe Durkheim's attitude towards the advance of the 'great society' we would have to use terms like 'bewilderment' or 'incomprehension'. Talcott Parsons stated that Durkheim:

> directs attention immediately to the moral elements in social life. When an author insists so strongly on a proposition, it is more than likely that he holds a polemical animus against some other widely current view. One of the things that makes the interpretation of the *Division of Labor* (*Division du Travail*) difficult is that clear-cut discussion of this polemical issue is not provided until the middle of the book, after the reader's mind has already been directed into other channels.[1]

But this statement shows that Parsons was inattentive. It is in fact true that Durkheim had not hesitated to write:

> We distrust those excessively mobile talents that lend themselves equally to all uses, refusing to choose a special role and keep to it. We disapprove of those men whose unique care is to organize and develop all their faculties, but without making any definite use of them, and without sacrificing any of them, as if each man were sufficient unto himself, and constituted an independent world. It seems to us that this state of detachment and indetermination has something anti-social about it. The praiseworthy man of former times is only a dilettante to us, and we refuse to give dilettantism any moral value; we rather see perfection of the man seeking not to be complete, but to produce; who has a restricted task, and devotes himself to it.[2]

But some pages further on – in a passage deleted from the second edition of the work – Durkheim clarified the fundamental idea of his sociological thought:

> we shall say nothing of the law of ethics based upon individual interest, for that may well be regarded as abandoned. Nothing comes from nothing; it would be a *miracle of logic* if altruism could be deduced from egotism, the love of society from the love of oneself, the whole from the part.[3]

Consequently, contrary to what Parsons wrote, one has to say that in the *Division du Travail*, the 'polemical element' appears from the very first pages. It should be added that in this work the partiality with which Durkheim observed the 'great society' was kept 'under control'; it is only the tip of the iceberg. Therefore, it is worth making fully visible this partiality with the help of other writings of Durkheim.

He wrote:

> For two centuries economic life has taken on an expansion it never knew before. From being a secondary function, despised and left to the inferior classes, it passed on to one of first rank. We see the military, governmental and religious functions falling back more and more in face of it. The scientific functions alone are in a position to dispute its ground, and even science has hardly any prestige in the eyes of the present day, except in so as it may serve what is materially useful, that is to say, serve for the most part the business professions. There has been talk, and not without reason, of societies becoming mainly industrial. A form of activity that promises to occupy such a place in society taken as a whole cannot be exempt from all precise moral regulation, *without a state of anarchy ensuing*. The forces thus released can have no guidance for their normal development, since there is nothing to point out where a halt should be called. There is a head-on clash when the moves of rivals conflict, as the attempt to encroach on another's field or to beat him down or drive him out. Certainly the stronger succeed in crushing the not so strong or at any rate in reducing them to a state of subjection. But since his subjection is only a *de facto* condition sanctioned by no kind of morals, it is accepted only under duress until the longed-for day of revenge. Peace treaties signed in this fashion are always provisional, forms of truce that do not mean peace to men's mind . . . *If we put forward this anarchic competition as an ideal we shall adhere to . . . then we should be confusing sickness with a condition of good health.*[4]

Therefore, the competition on which the 'great society' is based is 'anarchy', or even, as Durkheim explicitly said, a situation in which man always lives 'on a war footing amongst his closest comrades'; he finds himself always 'in the midst of enemies'.[5]

With competition, 'from being limited and of small regard, the scope of the individual life expands . . . The individual comes to acquire ever wider rights over his own person and over the possessions to which he has title; he also comes to form ideas about the world that seem to him most fitting and to develop his essential qualities without hindrance.'[6] Consequently, competition brings about a fragmentation of culture which is not able '[to bring] men's minds into mutual understanding.'[7] It is a 'moral anarchy', accompanied by a 'tendency to political anarchy'.[8]

Let us follow Durkheim on this last point. He stated:

> It is often said that under the democratic system the will and thought of those governing are identical and merge with the will and thought of the governed. From this standpoint, the State does no more represent the mass of the individuals, and the whole governmental structure can have only the aim of transmitting as faithfully as possible the sentiments diffused throughout the collectivity, with nothing added and nothing modified. The ideal, we may say, would consist in expressing them as adequately as possible.[9]

He added:

> This way of forming an image of those governing and their functions is fairly common. But nothing can be more contrary, in some respects, to the very notion of democracy. For democracy pre-supposes a State, an organ of government, distinct from the rest of society, although closely in contact: so that this kind of view is the very negation of any State in the true sense of the term, because it re-absorbs the State in the nation. If the State does nothing other than receive individual ideas and volition to find out which are most widespread and 'in the majority', as it is called, it can bring no contribution truly its own to the life of society. It is only an offprint of what goes on in the underlying regions. It is this that stands in contradiction to the very definition of the State. The role of the State, in fact, is not to express and sum up the unreflective thought of the mass of the people, but to superimpose on this unreflective thought a more considered thought which therefore cannot be other than different.[10]

It happens, according to Durkheim, that the State is instead 'incapable of bringing a moderating influence to bear on them [individuals]'.[11] For this reason, Durkheim's conclusion was very pessimistic: 'the citizens are not restrained from without by the government, because it follows in their wake, nor from within by the state of the ideas and collective sentiments they harbour: so that, in practice as in theory, becomes a matter of controversy and division and all is in a state of vacillation.'[12]

In other words, behind Durkheim's aversion towards the 'extended society' there lies not only rejection of the competitive principle but also total incomprehension of unintentional order. He stated that 'economic functions' are one of the organs of social life and that *social life is above all a harmonious community of endeavours, when minds and wills come together to work for the same aim.*'[13] In the same way, he insisted that in democracy 'there is no firm ground under the feet of the society.'[14] 'Nothing any longer is steadfast. And the critical spirit is well developed and everyone has his own way of thinking, the state of disorder is made even greater by all these individual diversities . . . There we get an existence subject to sudden squalls, disjointed, halting and exhausting.'[15]

What we have here is nostalgia for the 'independent variable', for the 'privileged point of view on the world.' Durkheim could not have been more explicit:

> there is one defect inherent in the framing of any democratic State. Since individuals alone form the living, active substance of society, it follows that the State, in one sense, can be the business only of individuals; in spite of this, the State has to give expression to something quite different from individual sentiments. The State must derive from the individuals and at the same time it has to go beyond them. How then is this paradox to be resolved, which Rousseau in vain wrestled with?[16]

The State as independent variable

Here Durkheim was seeking a kind of 'general will'. However, he wanted to avoid Rousseau's 'antinomy'. The latter had written:

> When factions arise, small associations at the expense of the large association, the will of each of these associations becomes general in relation to its members and particular in relation to the State; there can then no longer be said to be as many voters as there are men, but only as many as there are associations. The differences become less numerous and yield a less general result. Finally, when one of these associations is so large that it prevails over all the rest, the result you have is no longer a sum of small differences, but one single difference; then there is no longer a general will, and the opinion that prevails is nothing but private opinion. It is important, then, that in order to have the general will expressed well, there is no partial society in the State, and every Citizen states only his own opinion.[17]

That is the question: If each citizen states 'only his own opinion', can the individual will ever conform to the general will? Durkheim's reply was negative. He felt the need for an 'opinion' which would rise above the reach of common man. Like Rousseau, he sought a 'functional substitute' for those decisions which 'the Lawgiver places in the mouth of the immortals, in order to rally by divine authority those whom human prudence could not move'.[18] But he did not follow Rousseau: he did not insist on a situation in which 'every Citizen states only his own opinion'. Instead, not unlike Hegel, Comte and Marx, he singled out a 'general class', bearer of a 'privileged point of view on the world'.

Durkheim said:

> The only sentiments rising above individual feelings are those that come about from actions and reactions amongst individuals in association. Let us apply this idea to political organization. If each individual, independently, comes along with his vote to set up the State or the organs which are to serve in giving it definite form; if each one makes his choice in isolation, it is almost impossible for such votes to be inspired by anything except personal and egotistic motives: these will predominate, at any rate, and an individualistic particularism will lie at the base of the whole structure. But let us suppose that such nominations were made as a result of long, collective preparation, and their character would be quite different. For, when men think in common, their thought is partly the work of the community. It acts upon them, weighs upon them with all its authority, restraining egotistic whims and setting minds on a common course.[19]

At this point, one could say in opposition to Durkheim, using however arguments dear to him, that the individual always lives among others and that what he claims is something that already exists. But Durkheim pointed towards a broader conclusion. He wrote:

> if votes are to be an expression of something more than individuals and if they are to be animated by a collective mind, the ordinary voting electorate should not be made up by individuals brought together solely for this exceptional occasion; they do not know one another, they have contributed to the forming of each others' opinions and they merely go along in single file to the ballot box. No, on the contrary, it must be an established group that has cohesion and permanence, that does not just take shape for the moment on polling day. *The guild or corporative body corresponds clearly to this desired end.* The sentiments of the members who form it are evolved in common and

express the community because they are constantly and closely in contact.[20]

In other words, as Durkheim stated in the preface to the second edition of *La Division du Travail*, a 'nation can be maintained only if, between the State and the individual, there is intercalated a whole series of secondary groups near enough to individuals to attract them strongly to their sphere of action and drag them, in this way, into the general torrent of social life.'[21] There is a paradox here. Durkheim knew that the division of labour frees the individual from the 'prison' of a single person or a few groups, allowing him to experience the continual 'intersection' of a plurality of 'social circles'.[22] Yet, he presented the 'great society' as being 'composed of an infinite number of unorganized individuals, that a hypertrophied State is forced to oppress and contain';[23] he judged all of this as 'a veritable sociological monstrosity';[24] and, to prevent society from remaining an 'aggregate of juxtaposed territorial districts', he called into being 'a vast system of national corporations'.[25] However, the corporation was not his 'general class'.

According to Durkheim:

experience in the seventeenth and eighteenth centuries goes to prove that the guild system, which kept the pattern of a municipal affair, could not be appropriate to industries that in their wide scope and importance made their mark on the common interests of the society. On the other hand, that experience demonstrates that the State was itself not able to perform this office, because economic life is too vast and too complex, with too many ramifications, for it to supervise and regulate its operations effectively. Is it not the lesson to be drawn from these facts, that the guild should assume a different character, and that it should get closer to the State without being absorbed by it? In fact, that should become something national, whilst remaining a subsidiary group and relatively autonomous.[26]

And yet the 'independent variable' is the State. There is an activity which is

neither economic nor mercantile . . . it is moral activity . . . The agency on which this special responsibility lies is the State . . . [it] does not inevitably become either simply a spectator of social life (as the economists would have it), in which it intervenes only in a negative way, or simply (as the socialists would have it) a cog in the economic machine. It is, above all, supremely the organ of moral discipline.[27]

'We can understand the better that morals are what society is and that they have force only so far as the society is organized.'[28] But how is society to be organised? 'At the present days, the State is the highest form of organized society that exists',[29] since, 'when the State takes thought and makes decision . . . [it] thinks and decides for [society]. It is not simply an instrument for canalizing and concentrating. It is . . . the organizing centre of the secondary groups themselves . . . *Strictly speaking, the State is the very organ of social thought*',[30] it is the 'social brain'.[31]

Thus, Durkheim found his 'general class' in the State, which is 'a group of officials *sui generis*; within which representations and acts of volition involving the collectivity are worked out', because the State 'is the centre only of a particular consciousness, of one that is limited but higher, clearer and with a more vivid sense of itself'.[32] In this way the condition of 'anarchy', feared by all the opponents of unintentional order, is overcome. The path to follow

> is to dispute the postulate that the rights of the individual are inherent, and to admit that the institution of these rights is in fact precisely the task of the State. Then, certainly, all can be explained. We can understand that the functions of the State may expand, without any diminishing of the individual. We can see too that an individual may develop without causing any decline of the State, since he would be in some respects the product himself of the State, and since the activity would in its nature be liberating to him.[33]

We reach a conclusion. Durkheim wrote: 'Personally, I owe much to the Germans. It is to some extent from their school that I have acquired the sense of social reality, of its complexity and its organic development.'[34] It is not out of place, then, to ask some questions. How far is Durkheim's 'solution' from that of Hegel? What is the distance between Durkheim who called for the formation of 'national corporations' and Hegel who placed the corporation next to the family and saw it as 'the second root, the *ethical* root of the State, the one planted in civil society'?[35] Between Durkheim who insisted that the State is the 'organ of moral discipline' and Hegel who judged it to be 'the actuality of the ethical idea . . . the substantial will manifest and revealed to itself, knowing and thinking itself, accomplishing what it knows and in so far as it knows it'?[36] Between Durkheim who regarded the individual as 'the product of the State' and Hegel who declared that 'man has rational existence only in the State' and that 'everything that man is he owes to the State'?[37] Between Durkheim who saw us as 'masters of the moral world', because this world, in so far as it 'is founded in the nature of things', 'is what it ought to be', is recognised 'as such', and can be accepted 'freely',[38] and Hegel who took as rational all that is real? Between Durkheim who felt himself called to be the 'tutor' of France and Hegel the creator of the 'headquarters of the *Geist*' in Berlin?[39] Consequently, Durkheim's slide towards idealistic positions was earlier than is normally believed. This was already proved by the adoption on Durkheim's part of the concept of 'collective consciousness', which belongs entirely to the romantic universe. Yet, what is most important, it confirms that there is a place at which positivism and idealism meet: that of intentional order.

Durkheim and political economy

Talcott Parsons considered that Durkheim 'had no training in economics'.[40] This is a statement that finds many points to confirm it and from which one can form the conclusion – even more important – that Durkheim lacked perception in regard to the sociological work of the founders of political economy, in particular that of Adam Smith.

On the first page of the introduction to *La Division du Travail*, we read: 'several thinkers from earliest times saw . . . [the] importance [of the division of labour]; but Adam Smith was the first to attempt a theory of it'.[41] Yet, the situation is different from what Durkheim asserted. We know, in fact, that on this subject Smith was indebted to Mandeville.

That is not all. A few lines after crying shame at the 'miracle of logic' which deduces 'altruism from egoism', Durkheim added: 'A formula widely known today defines morality as a function, not of individual utility, but of social interest.'[42] Nevertheless, he misunderstood this formula, which he attributed to, among others, Rudolf von Jhering, whose *Der Zweck im Recht* he cited. If he had known Smith's work sufficiently well, he would have had at his disposal the 'lens' through which one can see that the 'subjective purpose' and 'objective purpose' of which Jhering himself spoke set in motion a 'double entry account' in which the interest of Ego and that of the Other exist together and find a form of mutual adaptation. Hence, Durkheim would not have remained blind to the link between Jhering's juridical theory and the sociological theory of the 'great society'.

We come to some more important points. As early as the first pages of *La Division du Travail*, we can read:

> if those rules whose social utility has been best demonstrated are examined, it is seen that the services they render could not be known in advance. Thus, statistics have recently shown that domestic life is a powerful preservative against the tendency to suicide and crime; can it be said that the constitution of the family has been determined by the anticipated knowledge of these beneficent results?[43]

In other words, Durkheim claimed the existence of *unintentional consequences* and the possibly *unintentional origin* of the family and of many other social institutions. But he was unaware that the complete works of Adam Smith and the entire theory of the 'great society' are precisely based on the mechanism of unintentional consequences.

Thus, for Durkheim, it was logical to state that:

the error [of the economists] is rooted in the manner in which they conceive the genesis of society. They suppose originally isolated and independent individuals, who consequently enter into relationship only to co-operate, for they have no other reason to clear the space separating them and to associate. But this theory, so widely held, postulates a veritable *creatio ex nihilo*. It consists, indeed, in deducing society from the individual. But nothing we know authorizes us to believe in the possibility of such . . . generation.[44]

This last statement is indeed a paradox, resulting from the fact that Durkheim was used to speaking in a general way about the 'utilitarians' and the 'economists'; but he hardly ever said which 'economist' he meant. For example, in the whole of *La Division du Travail*, which is basically a work comparing the sociological theorising of the economists, he cited Adam Smith only twice, and he did so without any reference to his writings or to specific pages. But which 'economist' supposes 'originally isolated and independent individuals'? As we know, this kind of idea was alien to Mandeville, Hume and Smith. Why then attribute such an idea in a general way to the 'economists'? In the Mandeville–Smith model the problem of the *beginning* of society does not exist; on the contrary, just as Durkheim wanted, there is absent also the 'absolute personality of the monad, which is sufficient unto itself, and could do without the rest of the world'.[45]

However, by attributing to the 'economists', understood in a generic way, a position *à la* Mill, Durkheim placed a false target before himself and before those who have followed his path. This is how his deliberations often became a reply to a problem originating from *one* particular theory, rather than the reply to a problem about the market society or about the main subject of its theorising. It is right to argue against psychologism or against the idea that society is nothing but 'a jumble of juxtaposed atoms'.[46] This – it must be repeated – is the problem that arises from *one* theory, but it is not the problem of the 'great society' or of scholars like Mandeville, Hume and Smith.

The proof that Durkheim was using a false target is the frequency with which he argued not only against contractualism or what, following Popper, we have here called the 'psychologistic version of the social contract', but also against the idea that 'individuals' would be bound by a 'vast system of particular contracts'.[47] Let us follow his propositions: if such a 'system of contracts' existed, individuals

would depend upon the group only in proportion to their dependence upon one another, and they would depend upon one another only in proportion to conventions privately entered into and freely concluded. Social solidarity would be nothing else than the spontaneous accord of individual interests, an accord of which contracts are the natural expression. The typical social relation would be the economic, stripped of all regulations and resulting from the entirely free initiative of the parties.[48]

Durkheim wondered: 'Is this the character of societies whose unity is produced by the division of labour?'[49] He replied:

[I]f this were so, we could with justice doubt their stability. For if interest relates men, it is never for more than few moments. It can create only an external link between them. In the fact of exchange the various agents remain outside of each other, and when the business has been completed, each one retires and is left entirely on his own. Consciences are only superficially in contact; they neither penetrate each other, nor do they adhere. If we look further into the matter, we shall see that this total harmony of interests conceals a latent or deferred conflict. For where interest is the only ruling force each individual finds himself in a state of war with each other since nothing comes to mollify the egos and any truce in this eternal antagonism would not be of long duration. This is nothing less constant than interest. Today, it unites me to you; tomorrow, it will make me your enemy.[50]

If this were so – this was Durkheim's conclusion – 'society would solely be the stage where individuals exchanged the products of their labor, without any action properly social coming to regulate this exchange'.[51]

At this point several observations can be made.

1 Durkheim did not propound the problem of the *beginning* of society. This means that there is a 'social' in the *broad sense* that constitutes our condition, and it is the same condition of sociality that makes single and specific acts of exchange possible. Mandeville, Hume and Smith said exactly the same thing; for them, too, there is a 'social' in the broad sense that constitutes the basis of humans living together. Consequently, criticisms generically made against the 'economists' are in this case out of place.

2 Durkheim regarded exchange as a 'war'; this is totally mistaken, because exchange is a 'positive-sum game'.

3 Moreover, he insisted that interests bring individuals together only for a few moments. Thus, he failed to consider that the same interests recur, that individual life is never in a state of equilibrium and that therefore 'exchange' does not admit of solutions of continuity.

4 He did not realise that the possible and repeated substitution of the other party is not a threat to living together, seeing that the *prius* is the exchange and the normative framework which it generates, but not the

subject with which it interacts. It was not by chance that Adam Smith wrote:

> In commercial countries, where the authority of law is always perfectly sufficient to protect the meanest man in the state, the descendants of the same family, having no such motive for keeping together, naturally separate and disperse, as interest or inclination may direct. They soon cease to be of importance to one another; and in a few generations, not only lose all care about one another, but all remembrance of their common origin, and of the connection which took place among their ancestors.[52]

5   Durkheim rejected the idea that exchange could in its context have an economic and normative content, that is, that it could itself determine the 'conditions' of its fulfilment; hence, he claimed that an 'action properly social' should intervene 'to regulate' the exchange; as if to say that by 'action properly social' he meant the intervention of a *real third person*.

6   Lastly, as he was unable to see the normative content of exchange, he failed to assess the consequences that the 'social' in the *strict sense* – limitations and conditions expressed in particular contracts – imposes on 'social' in the broad sense, that is, on the more general rules of living together.

Is society a '*sui generis*' reality?

There is another problem to be weighed up. Durkheim's idea of making the state the independent variable of the social system had a further development. Durkheim wrote:

> the whole is not identical with the sum of its parts, though without the latter the former would be nothing. Thus, by joining together . . . by means of long-lasting bonds, men form a new being which has one nature and its own specific laws. This is the social being. However, collective life is not simply an enlarged image of individual life. It produces a *sui generis* character which the inductions of psychology alone do not permit us to foresee.[53]

In this extract from Durkheim, we see the criticism that he waged untiringly against positions *à la* Stuart Mill. Nevertheless, the question is this: Is society truly a *sui generis* reality? To reply to this question, it is necessary to bring the assumptions of this definition to the surface. In order to do this, it is not enough to recall Comte's influence on Durkheim, nor to recollect that Durkheim 'heartily approved the efforts of various German social scientists and philosophers who stressed the social roots of the notion of moral duty'.[54]

It is worth pausing a little on the frontier where Durkheim found himself confronting Rousseau.

Durkheim himself can explain the question to us:

> Natural man is simply man without what he owes to society, reduced to what he would be if he had always lived in isolation. Thus the problem is more psychological than historical, namely, to distinguish between the social elements of human nature and those inherent in the psychological make up of the individual.[55]

Of course, it could be objected that this 'psychological constitution' exists only in relation to the social moment. However, let us put this objection aside and, with Durkheim, let us repeat, in Rousseau's terms, that the problem is one of determining what man was like in the state of nature, and of stripping him 'of all the supernatural gifts he may have received, and of all the artificial faculties he could only have acquired by prolonged progress'.[56] Rousseau was aware that 'it is no light undertaking'; it is necessary to 'disentangle what is original from what is artificial in man's present Nature'.[57]

If one considers the objective which Rousseau proposed, the criticism that he instantly made of Hobbes is not surprising:

> [L]et us not conclude with Hobbes that because he has no idea of goodness man is naturally wicked, that he is vicious because he does not know virtue, that he always refuses to those of his kind services which he does not believe he owes them, or that by virtue of the right which he reasonably claims to the things that he needs, he insanely imagines himself to be the sole owner of the entire Universe ... Hobbes did not see that the same cause that keeps Savages from using their reason ... at the same time keeps them from abusing their faculties, as he himself claims they do; so that one might say that Savages are not wicked precisely because they do not know what it is to be good.[58]

In other words, Rousseau warned against committing the error of 'confusing Savage man with the men we have before our eyes',[59] because it is in social life that we 'accustomed to attend to different objects and to make comparisons; imperceptibly ... [we] acquire ideas of merit and of beauty which produce sentiments of preference ... Everyone began to look at everyone else and to wish to be looked at himself, and public esteem acquired a price.'[60] It is in this way that all our 'faculties' are

> developed, memory and imagination brought into play, amour propre interested, reason become active, and the mind almost at the limit of the perfection of which it is capable. Here are all natural qualities set

in action, every man's rank and fate set, not only as to the amount of their goods and the power to help or to hurt, but also as to mind, beauty, strength or skill, as to merit or talents.[61]

Rousseau concluded thus: 'Savage man and civilized man differ so much in their inmost heart and inclinations that what constitutes the supreme happiness of the one would reduce the other to despair.'[62]

Reading these extracts, all taken from the *Discours sur l'inegalité*, almost makes one feel as though one were looking at the writings of Adam Smith, where Smith insisted that as man enters society he is 'immediately provided with the mirror which he wanted before' and hence can consider 'the propriety or impropriety of his own feelings, the beauty and deformity of his own mind'. Therefore, did Rousseau influence Smith? The question is worth looking at a little more deeply.

In a letter sent to the *Edinburgh Review* in 1755, Smith spoke at length of Rousseau's *Discours sur l'inegalité*, including long extracts from the work. Here we find the answer to our question. Smith claimed that the English were superior in the fields of 'natural philosophy', 'morals' and 'metaphysics'. He wrote:

> The *Méditations* of Des Cartes excepted, I know nothing in French that aims at being original upon these subjects; for the philosophy of Mr. Regis, as well as that of Father Malbranche, are but refinements upon the *Méditations* of Des Cartes. But Mr. Hobbes, Mr. Lock, and Dr. Mandevil, Lord Shaftsbury, Dr. Butler, Dr. Clarke, and Mr. Hutcheson, have all of them, according to their different and inconsistent systems, endeavoured at least to be, in some measure, original; and to add something to that stock of observations with which the world had been furnished before them. This branch of the English philosophy, which seems now to be entirely neglected by the English themselves, has of late been transported into France. I observe some traces of it, not only in the *Encyclopedia*, but in the *Theory of agreeable sentiments* by Mr. De Pouilly, a work that is in many respects original; and above all, in the late *Discourse upon the origin and foundation of the inequality amongst mankind* by Mr. Rousseau of Geneva.[63]

Here is the passage that interests us most:

> Whoever reads this last work with attention, will observe, that the second volume of the *Fable of the Bees* has given occasion to the system of Mr. Rousseau, in whom however the principles of the English author are softened, improved, and embellished, and stript of all that tendency to corruption and licentiousness which has disgraced them in their original author.[64]

This makes it clear that Rousseau was not Smith's source because Mandeville was the source for both. Obviously, the *judgments* about the 'great society' formulated by Mandeville and Smith are different from those of Rousseau.[65] But all three authors agreed on the *social origin* of human development. Hence, they passed through a 'cross-roads' by which Durkheim also passed.

However, passing through a cross-roads does not imply that they were going in the same direction. Mandeville and Smith rejected contractualism, since the social condition does not originate in a determined programme. That is to say, the individual cannot solve the problem of collective living by means of a 'pact' because, when this problem is proposed, he already benefits from the social condition.

Rousseau, influenced by Mandeville, was fully aware of this. In fact, in criticism of Condillac, he wrote: 'the manner in which this Philosopher resolves the difficulties which he himself raises regarding the origin of instituted signs shows that he assumed what I question, namely some sort of society already established among the inventors of language.'[66] In other words, Rousseau realised that it is not possible that language had an intentional origin because that would imply its pre-existence: 'speech seems to have been very necessary in order to establish the use of speech.'[67] Nevertheless, he considered that at a certain moment in human development the 'rich', 'under the pressure of necessity' devised 'the most well-considered project ever to enter the human mind; to use even his attacker's forces in his favor, to make his adversaries his defenders, to instill in them other maxims and to give them different institutions, as favourable to himself as natural Right was the contrary to him.'[68]

Consequently, according to Rousseau, a fraudulent pact was brought into being, through which the 'rich', inventing 'specious reasons', won over others to their own 'cause':

> Let us unite – he told them – to protect the weak from oppression, restrain the ambitious, and secure for everyone the possession of what belongs to him. Let us institute rules of Justice and peace to which we are obliged to conform, which favor no one, and which in a way make up the vagaries of fortune by subjecting the powerful and weak alike to mutual duties. In a word, instead of turning our forces against one another, let us gather them into a supreme power that might govern us according to wise Laws, protect and defend all the members of the association, repulse common enemies, and preserve us in everlasting concord.[69]

These are the consequences:

> All ran toward their chains in the belief that they were securing their freedom; for while they had enough reason to sense the advantages of

a political establishment, they had not enough experience to foresee its dangers; those most capable of anticipating the abuses were precisely those who counted on profiting from them, and even the wise saw that they had to make up their mind to sacrifice one part of their freedom to preserve the other . . . Such was, or must have been, the origin of Society and of Laws, which gave the weak new fetters and the rich new forces, irreversibly destroyed natural freedom, forever fixed the Law of property and inequality, transformed a skilful usurpation into an irrevocable right, and for the profit of a few ambitious men henceforth subjugated the whole of Mankind to labor, servitude and misery . . . Societies, multiplying and expanding rapidly, soon covered the entire face of the earth, and it was not possible to find a single corner anywhere in the universe where one might cast off the yoke and withdraw one's head out of the way of the often ill-guided sword everyone perpetually saw suspended over it.[70]

Rousseau added:

When scattered men, regardless to their number, are successively enslaved to a single man, I see in this nothing but a master and slaves, I do not see in it a people and its chief; it is, if you will, an aggregation, but not an association; there is here neither public good, nor body politic. That man, even if he had enslaved half the world, still remains nothing but a private individual.[71]

Therefore, the old 'social pact' should be replaced with another. We need to 'find a form of association that will defend and protect the person and goods of each associate with the full common force, and by means of which each, uniting with all, nevertheless obey only himself and remain no less free as before.'[72] Only in this way will it be possible to produce 'a very remarkable change in man by substituting justice for instinct in his conduct, and endowing his actions with the morality they previously lacked'.[73]

Society is not a 'sui generis' reality

So, where is the frontier on which Durkheim and Rousseau confront each other and which can help us to reply to our question? We need to go some way further.

Rousseau wrote:

Man's natural force is so well proportioned to his natural needs and his primitive state that as soon as this state changes and his needs increase ever so slightly he needs his fellows' assistance, and when eventually his desires embrace the whole of nature, the assistance of the whole of mankind barely suffices to satisfy them.[74]

And yet:

The general society which our mutual needs might engender thus offers no effective help to man has become miserable, or, rather it provides new forces only to the one who already has too many, while the weak, lost, stifled, crushed in the multitude, finds no refuge to which he might flee, no support in his weakness, and in the end he perishes a victim of deceptive union from which he expected his happiness.[75]

Rousseau added:

Once one is convinced that among the motives which lead men to unite with one another by voluntary ties there is nothing which relates to the point of union; that far from seeking a goal of common felicity from which one might derive his own, one man's happiness makes for another's misery; once, finally, one sees that instead of all tending toward the general good, they come together only because they are all moving away from it; one must also sense that although such a state could subsist it would only be a source of crime and of misery for men, each one of whom would see only his interests, follow only his inclinations and heed only his passions . . . this perfect independence and this unregulated freedom, even if it is had remained associated with ancient innocence, would always have had one essential vice . . . namely *the lack of that connectedness of the parts which constitutes a whole.* The earth would be covered with men amongst whom there would be almost no communication; we would make contact at some point without being united by a single one; everyone would remain isolated amongst the rest, everyone would think only of himself.[76]

What should replace a situation such as this? Rousseau had no doubts: 'Let us conceive of *mankind* as a moral person having both a sentiment of common existence which endows it with individuality and constitutes it as one, and a universal motivation which makes every part act for the sake of an end related to the *whole.*'[77]

Here are two crucial extracts:

If the general society existed anywhere other than in the systems of the Philosophers, it would, as I have said, be a moral Being with qualities of its own and distinct from those of the particular Beings constituting it, more or less as chemical compounds have properties which they owe to *none of the components that make them up* . . . there would be a sort of *common sensorium* which would make for the concert of all the parts; the *public good or evil would not only be the sum of particular goods or evils as in a mere aggregate, but would reside in the connectedness between them; it would be greater than that sum*, and the public felicity, far from being based on the happiness of individuals; on the contrary, would be its source.[78]

There are two kinds of dependence: dependence of things, which is the work of nature; and dependence of men, which is the work of society. Dependence on things, being non-moral, does not injury to liberty and begets no vices; dependence on men, being out of order, gives rise to every kind of vices, and through this master and slave become mutually depravated. If there is any cure for this social evil, it is to be found in the substitution of law for the individual; in arming the general will with a real strength beyond the power of any individual will. *If the laws of nations, like the laws of nature, could never be broken by any human power, dependence of men would become dependence on things.*[79]

Commenting on the proposition that Rousseau had previously put forward, Durkheim declared:

If in present societies the relations fundamental to the state of nature are upset, it is because primitive equality has been replaced by artificial inequalities and, as a result, men have become dependent upon one another. If instead of being appropriated by individuals and personalized, the new forces born of the combination of individuals into societies were impersonal and if, in consequence, it transcended all individuals, men would all be equal in regard to it, since none would be in personal command of it. Thus they would depend, not upon each other, but upon a force which by its impersonality would be identical, *mutatis mutandis*, with the forces of nature. The social environment would affect social man in the same way as the natural environment affects natural man.[80]

Therefore, the accounts balance perfectly. Let us examine it in a more direct way.

1 Mandeville, Smith, Rousseau and Durkheim passed through the same cross-roads, that which sees civilisation as a social product. In spite of this, Rousseau then took the direction of contractualism; he supported an extreme form of 'constructivism'. This means that he held an instrumental

relationship with Mandeville's theory: he used it to absolve from all responsibility his 'natural men', who 'is not wicked, because he does not know what it is to be good', and to call for the remoulding of the existing situation in accordance with his own personal preferences. This is represented by his refusal to make a 'constant' readjustment and in his willingness to 'begin by purging the threshing floor and setting aside all the old materials, as Lycurgus did in Sparta, in order afterwards to erect a good Building'.[81] In other words, the objective that Rousseau had previously put forward was to eliminate the society that gives space to the 'private individual', because it has made the individual 'wicked by making him sociable'.[82] There is a paradox here: the claim to destroy established social institutions in the name of a 'state of nature' which, according to Rousseau himself, 'no longer exists . . . perhaps never did exist . . . [and] probably never will exist'.[83] *Thus, the present is delegitimised by means of the comparison with two utopias*: one past, the other future. However, this is not the most important question.

2 In his search for the 'natural man', Rousseau was able to maintain that the individual who lives in society, and who benefits from the 'products' generated by his relationship with the other, is different from what he was at first. That is: if we follow Rousseau's point of view, it is consistent to say that society is not the sum of many 'natural men'. This is the *first* meaning of the declaration that the social whole is not identical with the sum of the parts. But this declaration could not be formulated by Durkheim. He, in fact, did not pose the question of the *beginning* of society; he did not 'work' with the 'natural man'. To him, man is a being who does not acquire the social condition, but already shares it.

It is not by chance that Parsons wrote:

> Atomistic theories are in fact empirically inadequate . . . Valid objection can only be raised through what is undoubtedly a misinterpretation, but one against which Durkheim did not adequately protect himself. It is the view that the 'individual' . . . and the 'society' . . . are concrete entities, the concrete human being known to us, and the concrete group. In this sense, it is scarcely more than a truism that society is simply the aggregate of human beings in their relations to one another. But the 'individual' of Durkheim's argument, as became increasingly clear with the progress of his development, is not this concrete entity, but a theoretical abstraction. In the simplest sense it is the fictional human being who has never entered into any social relationships with other human beings.[84]

However, Parsons had slipped into an overhasty simplification. It is correct that it is a 'truism that society is simply the aggregate of human beings in their relations to one another'; but it is also a tautology to insist that the individual who lives in a presocial or asocial situation is not yet a social being. If we free ourselves from the 'fictional human being', society is not thereafter a *sui generis* reality. In other words, those who maintain that society is not a creation *ex nihilo* – and Durkheim was one of these – cannot give to social reality a value different from that of the individuals who *compose* it.

3   Next, one could emphasise the dynamic aspect and insist that society is not the sum of individuals, because interaction makes an improvement on each person's starting point. This is equivalent to saying that the inter-individual relationship makes the position of the subject at time plus one 'richer' than it was at time zero, that is at the time preceding the specific relationship. But, if we replace the word *society* with *interaction* or *co-operation*, this means precisely that the interaction and co-operation are 'convenient' for the actors involved, who benefit or gain for themselves what the relationship produces, intentionally or not.

However, Durkheim's thesis goes in a different direction. It leads one to believe that the result of the interaction of individuals is not *absorbed* by those same individuals, and that, on the contrary, it becomes *crystallised* on a *real* 'third person', separate from these subjects. Yet, such a third person, as even Durkheim admitted, is 'nothing' without 'its parts'. This leads to only one conclusion, that society is simply the synthetic expression by which we denote the only possible reality, that of individuals who interact, who give rise to a process that always remains inconclusive, by means of which the respective starting positions are intentionally, and/or unintentionally, 'enriched'. This improvement of his own position is the goal of each actor; it is what moves the individual to act. Hence, there is nothing to stop us from comparing interaction to a 'chemical reaction'; but one must bear in mind that the 'new properties' are generated and 'absorbed' by the actors, not by a 'new person' in opposition to them.

4   Nevertheless, the idea that 'the whole is not identical with the sum of the parts' can take on a more complex significance. This comes out when Rousseau writes that one should think of 'mankind as a moral person' that has a 'universal motivation which makes every part act for the sake of an end related to the *whole*'[85] or when Durkheim says that 'social life is first of all a harmonious community of forces, a communion of minds and wills for one and the same end'.[86] Here both – like all the enemies of the open society – seek to subordinate the individual actors to a 'common sensorium', which leads them to a common goal. This is how 'public good or evil' could not be 'the sum of particular goods or evils'.

Clearly, the idea that 'the whole is not identical with the sum of the parts' is here feeding on the illusion that one can find a 'privileged point of view on the world', before which what is particular or private has to recede and be annulled. This is why Rousseau did not hesitate to declare that:

to discover the best rules of society suited to each Nation would require a superior intelligence, who saw all of man's passions and experienced none of them, who had no relation to our nature yet knew it thoroughly; whose happiness was independent of us and who was nevertheless willing to care for ours; finally, one who, preparing his distant glory in the progress of time, could work in one century and enjoy the reward in another. It would require gods to give men laws.[87]

It follows from this that the 'general will' that seeks to 'annul' particular or individual will,[88] is none other than the 'functional substitute' of the divine will.

Yet, no man can take the place of God; in spite of Rousseau's ambitious aims, there is no difference between 'the will of all and the general will'.[89] We cannot get out of the swamp by hanging on to our own bootlaces. The new reality that Rousseau was seeking does not exist. The Absolute is not a human prerogative; and if someone claims that he embodies it, he is simply imposing his will, he is trying to pass off as the *whole* what still remains no more than a preference of his own. As we have seen, Durkheim was not free from the difficulties discussed by Rousseau. He stated that the 'general will' gives rise to 'antinomy' and he put his trust in corporations and in the State. However, it is not from these that one can expect the 'secretion' of superior knowledge or a new perspective. Those who act are always individuals, no different from others, and always bearers of knowledge which is partial and fallible. It follows that without the 'privileged point of view on the world' there cannot be a reality *sui generis*. This is how the collectivist method, with its conceit of defining the social Absolute, can only go as far as placing some individuals in an unjustified position of privilege.

5   If there is no 'privileged point of view on the world', Rousseau's illusion collapses – his illusion that it is possible to find a force on which men can be made to depend in the same way as they depend on nature. What we have is only the social norm, which is the product, intentional or unintentional, of the actions that individuals carry out in relation to each other; it is the result of a '*composition*' which must somehow satisfy the preferences which have motivated or motivate individuals to act. To return to Durkheim, this means that the norm 'hovers' surely 'above individuals'. The reason for this is, however, different from the one that he invoked: not because it is extraneous to the actors but because it *composes* Ego's perspective with that of the Other.

Between positivism and idealism

Durkheim himself recognised that this is how things stand. In a work written to *forestall* Tarde's criticisms, he did not hesitate to declare that the 'resultant' of interaction is 'exterior' to individuals, because 'each individual contains a part, but the whole is found in no one'.[90] Nevertheless, Durkheim was afraid to follow this path to the end. He *justified* himself with his proposal 'to free morality from sentimental subjectivism'.[91] But this covers a deeper reason: his continual preoccupation with the 'private individual', his search for a real 'third person', distinct from individuals, and in a position to 'restrain' 'selfish attitudes' and to give stability and order to society.

Yet, this attitude of Durkheim's does not stop us from showing the weakness of his thesis on the 'external' character of the 'social'. It is opportune here to pause on some points:

1   If we free ourselves from the fictional 'natural man', we free ourselves also from 'solitary consciousness'. Man's condition is always a social condition. Living together is not lost even in moments of 'solitude', since these are only a temporary 'physical' suspension of the relationship with the Other. This should have been particularly clear in Durkheim's thinking, because he did not pose the question of the beginning of society and so would always need to place the individual in a social situation in a *broad sense*.

2   When it is understood in this way, the 'social' defines the historical context and the actual life of the actors who dwell in it. Coercion, as Jean Piaget pointed out, can only be a stage on the way towards socialisation.[92]

3   A prisoner as he was of his own schema, Durkheim saw law as the social paradigm *par excellence*.[93] He extended the compulsory nature of the juridical norm to all the rules of living together; morality itself becomes a duty. Obviously, it is easy to object that not every social model is accepted because it is 'obligatory';[94] in fact there are models, higher and endowed with greater morality, which are not compulsory: these are exemplary actions which validate the choice illustrated by Max Weber as being 'value-rational'.

   That is not all. Unlike what Durkheim asserted, law is not external to individuals. Jurists have already clarified this problem, making a distinction between 'subjective law' and 'objective law'. When they use the first expression they mean the *facultas agendi*, the power attributed to the will of the subject to act in pursuit of his own goals; with the second expression they are referring to the *norma agendi*, to the 'limitations' and 'conditions' within which the action has to be carried out, in such a way that Ego's initiative does not conflict with the Other's interests. Consequently, the impersonality of law can be translated as *intersubjectivity* or *bilaterality*, so that the same law becomes a '*hominis ad hominem proportio*'. That is, law is none other than a part of the 'social' in the *strict sense*. It unites the perspectives of Ego and the Other, adjusting their actions to each other. The *facultas agendi* gives validity to the undertaking; the *norma agendi* brings together what we have called 'limitations' and 'conditions', which are then the 'faculties' that the Other enforces on Ego's action. Hence, law is not a *real* 'third person' with an existence distinct from the subjects who act. These subjects are not, as Durkheim went as far as to say, 'functionaries of society';[95] they are individuals who, recognising each other's powers and imposing 'limitations' and 'conditions' on one another, define the map of social co-operation. This means that Ego can be an 'official' to the Other and the Other to Ego. But they are not 'agents' of a distinct reality endowed with 'their own existence'.[96]

4   However, we ought to beware of the optical illusion to which we fall victim when, as we observe the evolution of law, customs and norms which rule everyday life, society seems to take on the appearance of an 'impersonal being' which puts itself 'before particularities as something which dominates them and which does not depend on the same conditions of individual life'.[97] As Georg Simmel perceptively pointed out, this 'feeling' is determined by the fact that groups often stay identical with themselves 'while their members change or disappear'.[98] That is, it can be shown that the rainbow 'persists despite the constant exchange of material of which it is composed'.[99]

In order to understand that what is involved here is 'a defect in our sight', it is sufficient to recall that, in a relationship between two people, the 'departure' of one destroys the group, in such a way that the 'life' that the individual senses as something independent of himself dies; while, in the case of a 'sociation' of three, '*a group* continues to exist even . . . [if] one of the members drops out'.[100] Consequently, the 'feeling' that there is a reality distinct from the individuals who compose the group originates from the high number of participants and from the possibility of their being continually substituted.[101]

5   If the 'social' were always external to the individual, integration would be very weak; and, in any case, the part played in collective life by consensus would be reduced. Therefore, it can be understood why Durkheim, in his *Formes élémentaires de la vie religieuse*, in the same paragraph as that where he claimed once more that society has 'a nature which is peculiar to itself and different from our individual nature', declared that 'the collective force is not entirely outside us; it does not act upon us wholly from without; . . . society exists except in and through individual consciousness . . . it thus becomes an integral part of our being'.[102]

This recognition is what prompted Parsons to say that Durkheim, in his *Formes élémentaires*, explicitly states that 'society exists only in the minds of individuals. This represents the logical outcome, and also the final abandonment of his objectivistic bias.'[103] Parsons explained in more detail:

Durkheim's substantive theory developed along lines which made the maintenance of this empiricist tendency difficult so far as the methodological implications of much of what Durkheim was doing are concerned. This implied above all that analytical categories, including that of social facts, could not be identified with any concrete entities. This interpretation was verified in the most striking manner when Durkheim finally saw that the 'individual' factor could no longer be identified with the concrete individual 'consciousness', that is, the concrete individual from the subjective point of view. The social factor was then no longer to be sought 'outside' this concrete entity, but as an element or group of elements explaining it.[104]

To put it in simpler terms, this fits in with what we have said again and again; that is, that if we free ourselves from the imaginary 'natural man', man's condition is always a social condition.

But there is more. The fifth point, which has now been dealt with, shows, sociologically, Durkheim's idealistic tendency. However, this too raises some problems. What is within concrete man is the 'social' in the broad sense, which defines the historical context and the very life of the individuals who live in it. But are the 'limitations' and 'conditions' that are imposed on individual actions, or the 'social' in the strict sense, also internal? And are they always internal? Durkheim said that morality is given to us 'in the form of an interior feeling . . . Once it is in us, it seems to belong to us . . . We have the illusion that order itself is our own work.'[105] But that precisely can be valid for the 'social' in the *broad sense*. And what about the 'social' in the *strict sense*, the 'weights' that we have to bear?

Durkheim, who, as is well known, did not make use of the distinction between 'social' in the *broad sense* and 'social' in the *strict sense*, restricted himself to writing that there is 'a given situation' of opinion '[characterised] by a given intensity . . . relating to each moral rule'.[106] He explained it in the following terms:

> In Corsica there are small clans in which the honour of the name is very strong; where the vendetta [co-exists] with an extremely weak respect for the life of the individual [*sic*]. In the same way as when, with us, the group is threatened, there is war. In a society such as Catholic society notably is, the individual is not permitted to take his life; suicide is strictly prohibited . . . [and yet] when the individual begins to free himself, he can easily arrange things for himself; then the prohibition on suicide loses its force.[107]

Durkheim was referring to 'closed' situations: the small clans of Corsica, war (with the consequent polarisation that it gives rise to), the Catholic world.

It is clear in what direction he was heading. However, if we add to this another of his statements, the question is definitively clarified: 'The average man has nothing of the hero in him . . . The average man does not dare to say out loud what he thinks within himself, sometimes more or less unconsciously.'[108] So what does this mean? Here, for Durkheim, the norm is a *prescription* which takes possession of the individual. And he is not able, and ought not, to *choose*, in the sense that the social cannot be the instrument by means of which the actor freely decides to fulfil himself or to pursue ends which lie beyond the norm; this latter is a circumstance which it is quite impossible to admit even to the actor himself. Hence, Durkheim moved in a direction contrary to that of the 'open society'.

The individual is not allowed any space. Durkheim said that 'we can investigate the nature of these moral rules, which the child receives from without, through education, and which impose themselves on him by virtue of their authority. We can investigate the reasons of their being, their immediate and remote conditions.'[109] According to Durkheim, this would make us 'masters of the moral order',[110] because to 'the extent to which the moral order is founded in the nature of things', it is 'what it ought to be', it is recognised 'as such', and 'it can be fully conformed to it'.[111] In this way 'science' is the 'wellspring of our autonomy'.[112] And yet the consequence is that the liberty of the subject does not lie in *choice*, in *innovation*; it lies in the systematic acceptance of what exists.

We can make Durkheim's position clearer by citing a very significant extract from his writings:

> to understand the world and to *order* our conduct as it should be in relationship to it, we only have to take careful thought, to be fully aware of that which is in ourselves. This constitutes a first degree of autonomy. Moreover, because *we* then understand the laws of everything, *we also understand the reason for everything*. We can then understand the reason for the universal order. In other words, to resurrect an old expression *if it is not we who made the plane of nature, we rediscover it through science*, we rethink it, and we understand why it is as it is. Hence, to the extent that we see that it is everything it ought to be – that it is as the nature of things implies – we can conform, not simply because we are physically restrained and unable to do otherwise without danger, but because we deem it good and have no better alternative. *What prompts the faithful to see that the world is good in principle, because it is the work of a good being, we can establish a posteriori to the extent that science permits us to establish rationally what faith postulates a priori.* Such conformity does not amount to passive resignation but to enlightened allegiance. Conforming to the order of things because one is sure that it is everything it ought to be is not submitting to a

constraint. It is freely desiderating this order, asserting through an understanding of the cause.[113]

It is useful to follow Durkheim further:

> To simplify the argument let us suppose that we have complete knowledge of things and that each of us has this knowledge. Thus, the world, properly speaking, is no longer outside us; it has become a part of ourselves, since we have within us a system of symbolic representation that adequately expresses it. Everything in the physical world is represented in our consciousness by an *idea* . . . Consequently, in order to know at a given moment in time what the physical world is like and how we should *adapt* to it, we no longer need to go beyond ourselves to understand physical phenomena.[114]

Thus, we are not far from Hegel's 'consciousness which has grasped its notion',[115] from philosophy as '*apprehension of the present and the actual*',[116] which produces 'absolute freedom' and which sees in the '*living ethical* world' the 'spirit in its *truth*'.[117] And, if this is how it is, then it only remains to accept 'the social', to absorb it, to be convinced that it is the truth. Consequently, Durkheim's 'collective consciousness' returns to its origins; it comes to coincide with the Romantic *Geist*, which 'takes possession' of the individual and which realises its own inexorable Destiny through 'emanation'.[118]

In his *Règles de la Méthode Sociologique*, Durkheim had criticised the separation between science and ethics; he had claimed for the 'science of man' an active function in the determining of the ends to be pursued,[119] all in perfect agreement with positivist 'constructivism'. In the culminating phase of his thinking, on the other hand, he said that science ought to reveal the 'plane of nature' and establish rationally a posteriori what faith postulates a priori. But here, too, we are outside the territory of science. The demand to give 'certainty' to the 'order of things', to declare that it is consistent with all that it should be, inevitably assigns to reason an ancillary function in relation to what exists; it becomes its instrument of *justification*. Therefore, it is a matter of 'legitimising' the real, of transforming it, in a Hegelian way, into the rational.[120] And, as in every situation when someone wants to 'decide' ends in a positivistic way, the task is that of *rationalising* – that is to give a reason to determine preferences. In both situations, science renounces its own autonomy, and the cognitive process destroys itself, manifestly violating Hume's law of the separation between facts and values.[121] It is always a continuous reasoning in circles, a tautology oriented towards justifying 'conclusions' which are already known.[122]This is why Henri Bergson, referring to Durkheim, declared:

his conversation was already nothing but . . . a series of polysyllo-gisms . . . I have always thought that he would be an abstraction-monger. I was not so mistaken. With him, one never encountered a fact. When we told him that the facts were in contra-diction with his theories, he would reply: *the facts are wrong*.[123]

This is not all. As Benrubi has mentioned, Bergson thought that Durkheim's concept of morality was that of a 'closed society'.[124]

However, in order to get out of the 'closed systems', we need to free ourselves from the pretences of 'social realism'. In the next chapter we shall see how this is possible. Meanwhile, it is not out of place to reflect on what Georg Simmel sharply wrote: 'If one seeks a fundamental fact which would be valid as a universal premise for every experience and every procedure, for every spec-ulative thought and for every joy and anxiety in life, it would be capable of expression in the formula "I and the world".'[125] As if to say that a mutual unceasing dynamism exists between us and the socio-historical context. All that is social is born and dies through this dynamism. Now it can be under-stood why Simmel himself declared:

> The destiny of the 'substance' which is 'conceived by itself' and which the concept obliges to exist, is that the demonstration either is not logically necessary or is a vicious circle. This is the inevitable tragedy of the demand that aspires to reach through thought an absolute certainty about what exists that faith no longer offers. The closed necessity of pure logic will never be able to explain the existence of things by itself: this remains a fact which can be learnt as a datum, but can never be understood with the unconditioned necessity to which this demand aspires.[126]

Hence, society cannot be 'conceived by itself' and it is not rendered 'neces-sary' by the concept. It is the name that we give to the form taken by the co-operative *life* of man, to which 'advantages' (internal to the actor and external to his counter-party) and 'costs' (external to the actor and internal to his counter-party) are connected. Without the 'social commerce' put into it by individuals, no society exists.[127]

5

IS AN 'INDIVIDUALISTIC' READING OF DURKHEIM POSSIBLE?

The elements that justify an 'individualistic' reading of Durkheim

Is it possible to find the elements of an individualistic theory in Durkheim? Parsons sought to place Durkheim's work within a 'creative-voluntaristic' schema of social action. However, as we shall see more clearly in a later chapter, Parsons' suggestion raises numerous questions.

For his part, Harry Alpert maintained, independently of Parsons, that he could free Durkheim from 'social realism' without, by that token, consigning him to 'nominalism'. According to Alpert, a 'third alternative' is possible, which can be called 'relational realism'. Because, he said, 'association itself is not so much a fact as it is a process, a procession of activities, a come-and-go of actions, interactions, reactions and counteractions'.[1]

However, what Alpert was talking about is not 'relational realism'; it is *individualistic methodology*. Alpert fell into a very common error: that of not realising that the individualistic method is indeed a 'third alternative', contrasted with psychologism and with the collectivist method. Yet, in order to put Durkheim's work back within the territory of individualism, it is not enough to go only as far as a game of 'labels'; it is necessary to do much more: to go in search of 'confessions' which Durkheim had to make, or which somehow eluded him, to set loose the results that he achieved from his preferences, from what Herbert Spencer called the researcher's 'personal equation'. Let us try to follow this path.

There are five elements that must first of all be taken into account:

1 On the subject of social groups, Durkheim went as far as to write: 'We are in contact with *those who represent them*, who are without doubt individuals, as Tarde emphasized'.[2] Hence, those who act are individuals, since the 'pressure, which is the distinctive sign of social facts, is that which *all exert upon each individual*'.[3]
2 Moreover, Durkheim maintained:

83

If one can say that, to a certain extent, collective representations are exterior to individual minds, it means that they do not derive from them as such but from the association of minds . . . No doubt, in the making of the whole, each contributes his part, but private sentiments do not become social except by combination under the action of the *sui generis* forces developed in association. In such a combination, with the mutual alterations involved, *they become something else*. A chemical synthesis results which concentrates and unifies the synthesized elements and by that transforms them.[4]

Taking account of what emerges from the preceding point, this means that the individual acts, and that this *process* enriches his original position. This is in fact the reason why Durkheim declared that our being is by society, that is, social process 'elevated and magnified'.[5]

3   Durkheim wrote:

We cannot perform an act which is not in the same way meaningful to us simply because we have been told to do so. It is psychologically impossible to pursue an end to which we are indifferent —i.e. that does not appear to us as *good* and does not affect our sensibility. . . . Thus we must admit a certain element of eudaemonism and one could show that desirability and pleasure permeate the obligation.[6]

So then, if eudaemonism insinuates itself into Durkheim's system, this is equivalent to saying that even in the closed world of *prescription*, individuals can carry out an action not because it is imperative but because it is the 'price' to which one submits in order to fulfil an aim of a personal nature.

4   Moreover, Durkheim declared:

I do not believe that we can construct [morality], in all its aspects, in the silence of a laboratory, through the forces of pure intellect alone. All the constructions . . . that the moralists normally take pleasure in, are only, in my opinion, games of logic, the uselessness of which I have, however, demonstrated. Morality is not geometry; it is not a system of abstract truths which can be devised from some fundamental notion presented as obvious. It has a quite different kind of complexity. It is of the order of *life*, not of the order of reflection. It is a collection of rules of conduct, of obligatory practices which have been instituted in history.[7]

This point completed the preceding one, which leads Durkheim out of the sphere of ethics of the formal type.

5   On several occasions, Durkheim emphasized that from 1895 he had been influenced by Robertson Smith.[8] As is well known, Robertson Smith had pointed out the existence of two aspects in sacrificial rites. The first was given by the 'prevailing tone' of the sacrifices, which was 'determined by the festive character of the service';[9] there was a 'measure of *insouciance*, a power of casting off the past and living in the impression of the moment'.[10] This was the ludic side of the rite, which gave rise to out and out entertainment. The second aspect is that of which the actors, possessed by their childish heedlessness, took less account; that is the strictly social aspect. Or rather, *besides* the entertainment, 'the act of eating and drinking together' gave 'expression' to the 'duties of friendship and brotherhood'; these were 'implicitly acknowledged in the common act'.[11] An intentionally ludic act of the individual unintentionally generated social consequences. As we shall see in more detail, Durkheim, in his *Formes elémentaires de la vie religieuse*, made use of the 'double entry account' shown by Robertson Smith.

Durkheim under the 'individualistic' lens

The arguments clarified in the points above entitle us to apply the individualistic method to some parts of Durkheim's work.

1   First of all, let us give some attention to the *Règles de la méthode sociologique*. Durkheim said, controversially: 'At the same time, as being teleological, the method of explanation followed by sociologists is essentially psychological. The two tendencies are closely linked.'[12] Let us try to reread this passage, substituting the word 'teleological' with 'intentional': 'The method of explanation usually followed by sociologists is *intentional*, and at the same time essentially psychological.' In this way the passage becomes transparent; and, in syntony with the individualistic method, and against psychologism, it suggests that human actions do not only produce intentional consequences, and that these consequences cannot be read through psychology or through the plans of the actor. Durkheim could not but agree. The proof of this is his assertion:

> Undoubtedly no collective entity can be produced if there is no individual consciousness: this is a necessary but not a sufficient condition. In addition, these consciousnesses must be associated and combined, but combined in a certain way. It is from this combination that social life arises and consequently it is this combination which explains it.[13]

Durkheim wrote again: *'The determining cause of a social fact must be sought among antecedent social facts and not among the states of the individual consciousness.'*[14]

Let us in this case substitute the expression 'social facts' with 'interaction': 'the determining cause of a social fact must be sought in the antecedent *interaction* and not among the states of the individual consciousness.' Therefore, it is interaction that produces the 'social'.

Let us give a further example. Durkheim stated, 'it is undeniably true that social facts are produced by an elaboration *sui generis* of psychological facts'.[15] Now let us substitute the adjective 'unintentional' for the expression '*sui generis*': 'it cannot be denied that social facts are produced by an unintentional elaboration of the psychological facts'. In other words, the 'social' or social order is an *unintentional* consequence of intentional actions.

2   Now we come to the question of the *division of labour*. Durkheim said that there is a 'classic' explanation in 'political economy' which seems so 'simple and so evident' that it is 'unconsciously admitted by a host of thinkers'.[16] This refers to the idea that the division of labour could be a direct consequence of the individual's search for happiness. But, as we have seen in the previous chapter, this is not the explanation given by Mandeville and Smith, who knew very well that the division of labour is not a product of human 'wisdom'. Therefore, Durkheim fell into the usual habit of blaming the 'economists' or 'political economy' in general. However, the method that he used is individualistic. Durkheim recognised this: 'the individual alone is competent to appreciate his happiness. He is happy, if he feels happy.'[17] And he saw in the division of labour 'a result of the struggle for existence', a result of its outworking in which 'opponents are not obliged to fight to a finish, but can exist one beside the other'.[18] This is equivalent to saying that the division of labour is a result of *competition*, and it is exactly what was argued by Mandeville and Smith: the individual acts eudaemonistically and that, in a *situation* in which it is possible to compete, leads unintentionally to a process of the division of labour.[19]

Directing his polemic once more in a mistaken direction, Durkheim declared, 'The division of labor appears to us otherwise than it does to economists';[20] and he added, 'For them [the economists], it essentially consists in greater production. For us, this greater productivity is only a necessary consequence, a repercussion of the phenomenon. If we specialise, it is not to produce more, but it is to enable us to live in new conditions of existence that have been made for us.'[21] Now, in the middle of the text, let us substitute the words 'unintentional consequence' in place of 'repercussion' – 'to us, its greater productivity is merely a necessary consequence, an *unintentional* consequence of the phenomenon.' When this substitution is made, the passage gains in terms of clarity.

3   As to *Suicide*, the thesis is that, 'at each moment of its history, each society has a definite aptitude for suicide'.[22] Durkheim wrote:

> The relative intensity of this aptitude is measured by taking the proportion between the total number of voluntary deaths and the

population of every age and sex. We will call this numerical datum the *rate of mortality through suicide, characteristic of the society under consideration.*[23]

What is the problem? Durkheim went on to illustrate the terms of the question:

We do not . . . intend to make as nearly complete an inventory as possible of all the conditions affecting the origin of individual suicides, but merely to examine those on which the definite fact that we have called the social suicide rate depends. The two questions are obviously quite distinct, whatever relation may nevertheless exist between them. Certainly many of the individual conditions are not general enough to affect the relation between the total number of voluntary deaths and the population. They may perhaps cause this or that separate individual to kill himself, but not give society as a whole a greater or lesser tendency to suicide. As they do not depend on a certain state of social organization, they have no social repercussions. Thus they concern the psychologist, not the sociologist. The latter studies the causes capable of affecting not separate individuals but the group. Therefore among the factors of suicide the only ones which concern him are those whose action is felt by society as a whole.[24]

As is well known, Maurice Halbwachs was the first to point out the limitations of the data used by Durkheim to demonstrate the 'social' character of suicides.[25] Basically, Durkheim's aim was to put the blame on the advance of the 'open society'. This is why he did not hesitate to declare:

We must not be dazzled by the brilliant development of sciences, the arts and industry of which we are the witnesses; this development is altogether certainly taking place in the midst of a morbid effervescence, the grievous repercussions of which each of us feels. It is then very possible and even probable that the rising tide of suicide originates in a pathological state just now accompanying the march of civilization without being its necessary condition.[26]

However, the important questions are others. From the 'procedural' point of view, we can observe, with Boudon and Bourricaud, that

many of Durkheim's conclusions should have made a greater use of 'multivariate' analysis (as we would say today). He should have introduced a higher number of control variables. But such a control on established crucial points is impracticable because of the correlation between the 'explanatory' variables. For example, Catholics are less represented in certain professions than Protestants, and much more in others. How, in this case, can one separate the effect of religious confession from that of profession? Are rates of suicide among Protestants higher only because they are Protestants or is it also because they more frequently follow stressful professions?[27]

That is not all. Durkheim's distinction between 'mechanical solidarity' and 'organic solidarity' takes Spencer's teaching on individual 'differentiation' to its extreme conclusion. Durkheim knew that 'the more primitive societies are, the more resemblances there are among the individuals who compose them.[28] In other words,

> solidarity which comes from likenesses is at its maximum when the collective conscience completely envelops our whole conscience and coincides in all points with it. But, at that moment, our individuality is nil.[29] . . . It is quite otherwise with the solidarity which the division of labour produces. Whereas the previous type implies that individuals resemble each other, this type presumes their difference . . . the activity of each is as much more personal as it is more specialized.[30]

Moreover, Durkheim knew that society based on the division of labour makes 'social roles' 'equally accessible to all citizens'.[31] This increases further the singularity of the individual personality. There are also, in Durkheim, elements which throw light on the complexity of the 'double entry account' between the actor and his own socio-historical context. It follows that suicide cannot be attributed to membership of a 'circle' or of a few social 'circles', because the individual 'intersects' very many groups; his personality draws from them different 'fragments' which are organised in a way that cannot be predetermined. This means that in the analysis of suicide, *motives* and *causes* linked to the personality of the subject cannot be excluded.[32]

4   In his *Formes elémentaries de la vie religieuse*, Durkheim wrote:

> It is a well-known fact that games and the principal forms of art seem to have been born of religion and that for a long time they retained a religious character. We now see what the reasons for this are: it is because the cult, though aimed primarily at other ends, has also been a sort of recreation for men. Religion has not played this function by hazard or owing a happy chance, but through a necessity of its nature.[33]

Durkheim tried to explain more clearly. He added:

So the world of religious things is a partially imaginary world, though only in its outward form, and one which therefore lends itself more readily to the free creations of the mind. Also, since the intellectual forces which serve to make it are intense and tumultuous, the unique task of expressing the real with the aid of appropriate symbols is not enough to occupy them.[34]

It follows from this that 'art is not merely an external ornament with which the cult has adorned itself in order to dissimulate certain of its features which may be too austere and too rude; but rather, in itself, the cult is something aesthetic.'[35]

This is not yet an explanation; we are on the merely descriptive or assertive level. Let us read this other extract carefully:

The state of effervescence in which the assembled worshippers find themselves must be translated outwardly by exuberant movements which are not easily subjected to carefully defined ends. In part, they escape aimlessly, they spread themselves for the mere pleasure of so doing, and they take delight in all sort of games. Besides, in so far as the beings to whom the cult is addressed are imaginary, they are not able to contain and regulate this exuberance; the pressure of tangible and resisting realities is required to confine activities to exact and economical forms.[36]

Let us try to make this extract clearer, using in part the same expressions as Durkheim: 'in so far as the beings to whom the cult is addressed are imaginary, they are not able to contain and regulate this exuberance'; that is, the divinities coincide with themselves, they are in a position to realise the *impossible*, they define that *extraordinary* territory in which desire and satisfaction find permanent reconciliation. 'The pressure of tangible and resisting realities is required to confine the activities to exact and economical forms.' In other words, every day men experience the constrictive dimension which encloses them within the sphere of the *possible*, on the margins of which is found what they are not humanly able to do and what is socially (and religiously) forbidden.

Now one can understand why festivity should be associated with religion. It liberates man from the restrictions, even from the religious restrictions, of daily life; hence, it gives individuals the opportunity to participate in 'out of the ordinary' life, to coincide temporarily with themselves. It fulfils man's eudaemonistic aspiration and in this way it gives *motivation* to the individual. Thus, unintentionally, new reserves of energy are created, and expectations are regenerated. And Durkheim can say that 'after we have acquitted ourselves of our ritual duties, we enter into the profane life with increased courage and ardour . . . because our forces have been reinvigorated'.[37]

In other words, the satisfaction creates new energies and makes us ready to re-enter the ambit of the impossible, of the forbidden and of everyday *ties* with new strength.

Hence, the 'individualistic' reading of Durkheim throws light on what he was trying to obscure. Even in a 'closed' universe, such as the religious universe, it is possible for cult not to be desirable in itself: and it can instead be the 'price' or the 'condition' to which individuals submit themselves for their 'recreative' purposes. That is to say, religion becomes a social 'justification', the 'weight' of an act which has quite different individual purposes. It happens, in such a way, that the temporary relaxation of everyday burdens renews one's availability towards the Other, and unintentionally provides new energy with which to confront the 'limitations' and 'social conditions'. The 'double entry account' is complete.

One conclusion stands out: the individualistic method has explanatory force both with reference to the 'open society' and in its application to 'closed systems' because it shows the attitude by which a social or religious norm tends to be accepted. For the individualistic method, this acceptance can be desirable in itself, or it can be a means towards other ends. For the collectivistic method, on the other hand, the norm is always a *prescription* which turns into subjective motivation. A well-known (and not to be neglected) consequence is that this method is not in a position to understand the change: because it annuls the motives of action, or makes them 'unconfessable', when they are different from those socially permitted, and it cannot link them to the outcomes that are produced, whether intentionally or unintentionally. Thus, as in tribal societies or, in any case, in 'closed' societies, the change has to be attributed to mysterious entities: progress, dialectical forces, structures, and so on.

Is it possible to reconcile Durkheim and Spencer?

As we have already seen, Durkheim insisted that 'it would be a miracle of logic if altruism could be deduced from egoism, the love of society from love of oneself, the whole from the part'.[38] And yet this inference is found in his pages, too, when he opens the 'double entry account' between Ego and the Other, between the actor and the socio-historical context. What has been pointed out in the previous paragraph highlights this. However, this does not prevent us from going some way ahead. To read Durkheim 'individualistically', there is a passage which we have not yet examined:

> As richly and endowed as we may be, we always lack something, and
> the best of us realize our own insufficiency. That is why we seek in our
> friends the qualities that we lack, since in joining with them, we
> participate in some measure in their nature and thus feel less incom
> plete. So it is that small friendly associations are formed wherein each

one plays a role conformable to his character, where there is a true *exchange* of services. One urges on, another consoles; this one advises, that one follows the advice, and it is this apportionment of function or, to use the usual expression, this division of labor, which determines the relations of friendship.[39]

Hence, Durkheim recognized the importance of *exchange*, and he added:

We are thus led to consider the division of labor in a new light. In this instance, the economic services that it can render are picayune compared to the moral effect that it produces, and its true function is to create in two or more persons a feeling of solidarity. In whatever manner the result is obtained, its aim is to cause coherence among friends and to stamp them with its seal.[40]

In other words, the division of labour develops unintentionally in a given socio-historical context, and produces, unintentionally in relation to the immediate benefits sought by the individual actors, a 'moral effect'. While wishing to avoid bringing up again Smith's concepts of the 'impartial spectator' and the 'invisible hand', one could say with Montesquieu that 'each individual advances the public good, while he only thinks of promoting his own interest'[41], or one could also repeat, with Hume, that each one benefits 'the public, though it not be intended for that purpose'.[42]

Therefore, we have to confirm that Durkheim himself accomplished the 'miracle of logic' of deducing 'altruism from egoism' as soon as he was willing to consider the individual and social consequences of exchange, whenever, that is, he adopted the individualistic method. Thus, in Durkheim there are two directions of thought which develop simultaneously. There is the rejection of the market society; this belongs to the area of his personal preferences, which, to be accurate, were, as Kurt H. Wolff wrote, inclined to favour 'a secular society, to be embraced [however] with sacred passion'.[43] Second, there is the recognition of the *exchange* which nourishes individual and collective life by means of a 'double entry account' of consciously pursued ends and unintentional consequences. This is the Durkheim that interests us most. And it is this Durkheim that suggests a reconciliation with Spencer (and Simmel).

Herbert Spencer is the author most fully cited by Durkheim in his *Division du travail social*. The debts owed by Durkheim to Spencer are numerous: even leaving out consideration of those relating to organicistic analogies, one should remember the theories of differentiation, of the division of labour, the distinction between mechanical and organic solidarity (in the wake of Spencer's distinction between military and industrial societies), the concepts of 'coalescence' and of 'density'. Yet Durkheim took an obstinately polemical attitude towards Spencer. This can be explained only by Durkheim's refusal to accept what Spencer, on the contrary, reckoned to be possible and already in existence: a type of society in which the individual, while 'spontaneously fulfilling his own nature, incidentally performs the functions of social unit'.[44] In other words, Spencer had clearly seen the possibility of unintentional order. Durkheim's preferences clashed with this idea, which was precisely the basis of his disagreement with Spencer. Therefore, we need to free Spencer from those 'additions' and 'extras' through which Durkheim made of him not only an easy target but also an imprudent scholar.

First, the main accusation made by Durkheim against Spencer was that, according to the latter's theory, 'higher societies' have, or tend to have 'as unique basis' the 'vast system of particular contracts which link individuals', so that they

> would depend on the group only in proportion to their dependence upon one another, and they would depend upon one another only in proportion to conventions privately entered into and freely concluded. Social solidarity would then be nothing else than the spontaneous accord of individual interests, an accord of which contracts are the natural expression. The typical social relation would be the economic, stripped of all regulations and resulting from the entirely free initiative of the parties. In short, society would be solely the stage where individuals exchanged the products of their labor, without any action properly social coming to regulate this exchange. . . . If this were so, we could with justice doubt their stability. For if interest relates men, it is never for more than some few moments.[45]

As is clear, this passage, which is taken from Durkheim's *Division du travail* but which clashes with other passages in the same work, is seriously marred by collectivistic prejudice. We have commented on it in the previous chapter. Here, instead, it is important to restore a correct view of Spencer's position:
Spencer wrote:

> Sir James Mackintosh got great credit for the saying that 'constitutions are not made, but grow' . . . Such a conception could not indeed fail to be startling when let fall in the midst of a system of thought to which it was utterly alike. Universally in Mackintosh's day . . . things were explained on the hypothesis of manufacture, rather than that of growth . . . It was held that the planets were severally projected round the sun from the Creator's hand . . . The formation of the earth, the separation of sea from land, the production of the animals, were mechanical works, from which God rested as a labourer rests. Man was supposed to be moulded after a manner somewhat akin to that in which a modeller makes a clay figure. And of course, in harmony with such ideas, societies were tacitly assumed to be

arranged thus or thus by direct interposition of Providence; or by the regulations of law-makers; or by both. Yet that societies *are not artificially put together*, is truth so manifest that it seems wonderful men should have ever overlooked it . . . You need but to look at the changes going on around, or observe social organization in its leading peculiarities, to see that these are neither supernatural, nor are determined by the wills of individual men.[46]

And again:

Plato's model republic – his ideal of a healthful body politic – is consciously to be put together by men; just as a watch might be; and he manifestly thinks of societies in general as originated in this manner. Still more specifically does Hobbes express this view. 'For by *art*' he says 'is created that great Leviathan called a Commonwealth'. And he even goes so far as to compare the supposed social compact from which a society suddenly originates, to the creation of a man by the divine fiat . . . Thus they both fall into the extreme inconsistency of considering a community as . . . an artificial mechanism.[47]

Hence, Spencer cannot be accused of 'artificialism', nor can he be reproached for seeing society as a creation *ex nihilo*. And, for just this reason, it is not possible to attribute to him the idea that the social relationship is something intermittent. The individual is always within society; and he lives by *exchanging* with others. This means that the exchanges do not bring men together for 'a few moments' because – as Durkheim himself declared – life is 'continuous'.[48]

Consequently, Spencer's emphasis on *exchange* has nothing to do with contractualism; it is an emphasis no different from that of Durkheim in the passage quoted at the beginning of this section. What Spencer meant in particular was that exchange is a 'positive-sum game': 'it became obvious that when they [men] co-operate, there must be . . . facilitation; since in the absence of facilitation there can be no motive to co-operate'.[49]

Second, Durkheim declared that the spur for social evolution is not 'as Spencer seems to believe' the need for 'greater happiness': because, if this were so, it would be 'necessary to establish that happiness grows with civilization'.[50] Nevertheless, it is arbitrary to attribute such a simplified theory to Spencer. Let us see how he really expressed himself:

The whole of our industrial organization, from its most conspicuous features down to its minutest details, has become what it is, not only without legislative guidance, but, to a considerable extent, in spite of legislative hindrances . . . *While* each citizen has been pursuing his individual welfare, and none taking thought about division of labour, or indeed conscious of the need for it, division of labour has yet been ever becoming more complete. It has been doing this slowly and silently; scarcely any having observed it until quite modern times.[51]

Therefore, it did not develop 'by the "hero as king", any more than by collective wisdom'.[52]

Spencer's conclusion was that

if these most conspicuous and vital arrangements of our social structure have arisen without the devising of any one, but through the individual efforts of citizens severally to satisfy their own wants, we may be tolerably certain that all the other less important social arrangements have similarly arisen.[53]

In other words, Spencer was calling attention to the unintentional origin of social institutions. This is why he wrote:

all actions going on in a society are measured by certain antecedent energies, which disappear in effecting them, while they themselves become actual or potential energies from which subsequent actions arise; it is strange that there should not have arisen the consciousness that these higher phenomena are to be studied as lower phenomena have been studied.[54]

Hence, it is not surprising that Spencer entrusted to sociology the task of studying the unintentional consequences of intentional human actions: 'we shall . . . find that, while the objects striven for have commonly not been more than temporarily attained, if attained at all, the permanent changes brought about have arisen from causes of which the very existence was unknown'.[55] The study of sociology, carried out scientifically, ought therefore to link 'proximate causes to their antecedents, and primary effects down to secondary and tertiary ones'.[56]

Thus, there is not − as the two points dealt with above clearly show − an impassable gulf between the positions of Spencer and of a Durkheim who declared, as we have seen in the previous section, that 'the individual alone is competent to appreciate his happiness' and who set up a systematic 'double entry account' between consciously pursued results and unintentional consequences. A Durkheim of this kind should, however, be consistent, and he should have followed Spencer further, seeing that he (Spencer) suggested limiting organicistic analogies because, in the biological organism,

consciousness is concentrated in a small part of the aggregate. In the other [social organism], it is diffused throughout the aggregate: all the units possess the capacity for happiness and misery, if not in equal degree, still in degrees that approximate. As, then, *there is no social sensorium*, the welfare of the aggregate, considered apart from that of the units, is not an end to be sought. The society exists for the benefit of its members; not its members for the benefit of the society[57]

because, when it is asserted that its members exist for the benefit of society, there is always a privileged group which hides behind the name of the whole.

Moreover, again following Spencer, a Durkheim adopting the individualistic method ought to distrust 'artificialism' totally, and should free himself from the 'current illusion' that by 'skilful manipulation' social 'evils' may be radically cured.[58] Such a Durkheim ought also to explain Spencer's disagreement with Comte, to whom must be attributed 'among other erroneous pre-conceptions, this serious one, that the different forms of society, presented by savage and civilized races, all over the globe, are but different stages in the evolution of one form.'[59] In other words, for Spencer 'social progress is not unilinear'[60]; 'social types, like types of individual organisms, do not form a series';[61] what one can say is that 'every species of organism, including the human, is always adapting itself . . . to its conditions of existence'.[62] Understood in this way, 'evolution' is a process which, to use Robert Nozick's expression, 'does not know precisely what the being he wishes to create is like'[63]; it is therefore an ateleological process.

The nearness of Durkheim to Spencer can then be seen to be more far-reaching than Durkheim's polemic would let one think. The same applies to Durkheim's relationship with Simmel.

Is it possible to reconcile Durkheim and Simmel?

In a well-known article published in *L'année sociologique,* Simmel wrote:

it is certain that only individuals exist, that human products have reality outside men only if they are of material nature, and the creations of which we speak, being spiritual, live only in personal intelligences. If only individual beings exist, how does one explain the supra-individual character of collective phenomena, the objectivity and the autonomy of social forms? There is only one way to resolve this autonomy. To understand perfectly, one has to admit that nothing else exists but individuals. If by looking it was possible to penetrate to the root of the matter, every phenomenon that seems to constitute some new and independent unity above individuals would be resolved in the reciprocal actions exchanged by individuals. Unfortunately, this perfect understanding is forbidden to us . . . It is therefore only by a process of method that we speak of the State, of law, of custom, etc., as if they were undivided beings . . . This is the resolution of the conflict that arises between the individualistic concept and what could be called the monist conception of society; the former corresponds to reality, the latter to the limited state of our faculties of analysis.[64]

It is interesting to follow Durkheim's reply. He stated:

Let us begin by laying down a proposition that should be considered axiomatic: *For sociology, properly speaking, to exist, there must occur in every society phenomena of which this society is the specific cause, phenomena which would not exist if this society did not exist and which are what they are only because this society is constituted the way it is.*[65]

However, this passage can be reread individualistically. Let us rewrite the central part, trying as far as possible to use the same words as Durkheim: 'it is necessary that in every society there should be phenomena, of which *interaction* (or social exchange) would be the specific cause, and which would not exist if there were not this *interaction*.'

On the strictly scientific level, Durkheim's preoccupation seems to have been to give a 'dominion' or territory to sociology. This is why he maintained that his own position 'clashes with an ancient sophism which still influences some sociologists who do not realize that it negates sociology itself':

this sophism says that society is formed only of individuals, and that, since the whole can only contain what is found in the parts, all that is social can be reduced to individual factors. On this basis, one would have to say that there is nothing in the living cell outside that which exists in the hydrogen, carbon and nitrogen atoms that together form it.[66]

It is not like this. As we have already made clear, the 'individualists' do not deny the 'chemical reaction'. They maintain that this reaction enriches the initial positions of individuals, but that it does not create a real 'third person'. The line of. demarcation that emerges from the comparison between Durkheim and Simmel is, hence, to be found in Durkheim's obstinate *realism*; this is a realism that satisfied Durkheim's preferences, but it is not a requirement of the sociological method. This is why it is possible, as we have seen, to make an 'individualistic' reading of some significant parts of Durkheim's work. And it is for this reason that it is possible to 'reconcile' him also with Simmel. It would be good to look at various points in Simmel's thought more clearly.

1   Simmel said:

> If we have to judge from the analogy of infant development and of many psychological phenomena of primitive peoples, the distinction between the subjective mind and the world of objects which stands in front of it must belong to a relatively late stage in the history of humanity . . . The information given by the senses, by sight and by hearing, exists as something contained, as world; but only a long spiritual effort can make the seer and the listener into a subject, can make the world thus understood into something internal, and the existing being, apart from this subjective character, to possess an autonomous character also.[67]

This means that society was not created *ex nihilo* and that the individual, when he begins to ask himself about the problem of society, is already in it.

2 Let us follow Simmel again: 'the objects confront us . . . as independent powers, as a world of substances and forces that determine their own qualities whether and to what extent they will satisfy our needs, and which demand effort and hardship before they will surrender to us.'[68] So man lives in a situation in which there is a split between desire and satisfaction. This is why he is obliged to act, to *exchange* with the Other. The result is that

> money is the expression and the agent of the relationship that makes the satisfaction of one person always mutually dependent upon another person. Money has no place where there is no mutual relationship, either because one does not want anything from other people, or because one lives on a different plane . . . and is able to satisfy any need without any service in return.[69]

In other words: 'within the practical world [money is] the most certain image and the clearest embodiment of the formula of all being, according to which things receive their meaning through each other, and have their being determined by their mutual relations.'[70] This means that the world is a 'pragmatic field', and that the social norm is none other than *a form of reciprocal life*.

3 The 'mere justice that is implied in exchange' is only 'formal and relative: any one person should have neither more nor less than any other. Over and above that, exchange brings about an increase in the absolute number of values experienced . . . The objectively stable sum of values changes through a more useful distribution, effected by exchange, into a subjectively larger amount and large measure of uses experienced.'[71]

This means that exchange is a 'positive-sum game'. And not only that. Simmel maintained: 'I consider it quite possible that the precursor of socially regulated exchange was not individual exchange but a change in ownership, which was not exchange at all but was, for instance, robbery. In that case inter-individual exchange would have been simply *a peace treaty, and both exchange and regulated exchange would have originated together*.'[72]

4   This is why man deserves, together with many other definitions already given, that of *'the exchanging animal'*.[73] This is what makes him an *'objective animal'*.[74] In the animal world, in fact, we do not find 'indications of what we term objectivity, of views and treatment of things that lie beyond subjective feeling and volition'.[75] As Simmel made clear, this produces 'the civilizing influence of culture that more and more contents of life become objectified in supra-individual forms'.[76] That is, the creation of the 'objective world' is made possible by the network of relationships that arises from exchange.

5   However, man cannot control all the outcomes of his actions:

> The following point holds especially for the web of social life: no weaver really knows what he weaves. Of course, it is true that more advanced social structure can develop only if there is a consciousness of purpose. However their development is – as this might be expressed – *external* to the individual's consciousness of purpose.[77]

In other words, a 'double entry account' exists; it is set up by individual action, and it registers, beside intentional results, a range of consequences which do not enter into the plans of the individual actors.

It is therefore possible to reconcile Spencer, Durkheim and Simmel. The 'price' to be paid is the elimination of 'social realism'. The advantages lie in the possibility of reaching a clear sociological method, and of throwing full light on the complex phenomenon that is unintentional order. This would avoid many misunderstandings. For example, Fredric Jameson has written that 'postmodernism' is 'the cultural logic of late capitalism'.[78] But things are very different from this. The fact is that modernity has not been able to give up the idea of intentional order. And while the market society was advancing, a large part of culture was incapable of decoding its sociologico-historical significance. A culture – whether called postmodern or something else – which gives up the social Absolute, or the claim to identify an End which is necessary and compulsory for all, is not the 'covering' of 'late capitalism', but what is needed to explain collective life, without resorting to metaphysical or human entities, presumed to be rulers of our Destiny.

This is why Simmel declared:

> This movement away from formal principles reaches a zenith not only in the pragmatists, but in all thinkers who are filled with the modern

feeling against *closed systems*. Earlier epochs, ruled by classical and formal considerations had raised these systems to a level of sanctity. The closed system aims to unite all truths, in their most general concepts, into a structure of higher and lower elements which extend from a basic theme, arranged symmetrically and balanced in all directions. The decisive point is that it sees the proof of its substantive validity in its architectural and aesthetic completion, in the successful closure and solidity of its edifice. This represents the most extreme culmination of the formal principle: perfection of form as the ultimate criterion of the truth. This is the view against which life, which is continuously creating and destroying form, must defend itself.[79]

6

ECONOMISTS AND SOCIOLOGISTS COMPARED

Carl Menger and Georg Simmel, Ludwig von Mises and Max Weber

Carl Menger: methodological individualism and 'marginalistic revolution'

The 'individualistic' reading of Durkheim's work enables us – as we have seen in the preceding pages – to perceive numerous points of agreement with the 'individualistic' positions of Spencer and Simmel. Other useful convergences emerge from the works of Carl Menger and Georg Simmel and from those of Max Weber and Ludwig von Mises. In this case, there is also a comparison between the positions taken in the adjoining territories of economics and sociology.

Before getting to the nub of this comparison, we should pause to consider the main contributions of Carl Menger.

Three fundamental themes can be drawn from the totality of Menger's work. Leaving out of consideration its chronological development, these are: the strictly methodological question; the theory of value; the problem of unintentional consequences.

The methodological question

In the 'open society', which is an unintentional order, events lose their teleological justification; that is to say, they are not elements of a known Destiny in gestation in what already exists. How do we understand them? How do we assess them? If the phenomena cannot be inserted in a single plan, which is ready beforehand – events can in fact go in thousands and thousands of directions – we are obliged to 'imagine' typical relationships, to prearrange a great network of hypotheses with which to isolate and capture no more than fragments of reality. This was the solution suggested by Menger. According to him, there are two fundamental moments in the cognitive process. The first is that of the study of 'forms', of types and of the typical relationships of phenomena, of the 'cognition of typical relationships'.[1] The second, on the

100

other hand, is 'the cognition of concrete phenomena', 'individual phenomena'.[2] These two moments find their meeting place in the distinction between *theoretical* and *historical* sciences.[3] 'History and the statistics of economics are historical sciences, in the above sense; economics is a theoretical science.'[4]

Obviously, what is most important to us is to know what is concealed behind Menger's idea of 'theoretical science'. Menger made a distinction between the realistic–empirical direction, which tends towards phenomenic laws (of co-existence or succession), which, not being rigorous or not exact, allow exceptions, and the *exact orientation*. This latter orientation proposes, as does any sort of enquiry in any field of the phenomenic world,

> the determination of strict laws of phenomena, of regularities in the succession of phenomena which do not present themselves to us as absolute, but which in respect to the approaches of cognition by which we attain to them simply bear within themselves the guarantee of absoluteness. It is the determination of laws of phenomena which commonly are called 'laws of nature', but more correctly should be designated by the expression *exact laws*.[5]

There is a problem that Menger clarified in an unequivocal way:

> *Exact science* . . . does not examine the regularities in the succession, etc., of *real* phenomena . . . It examines, rather, how more complicated phenomena develop from the simplest, in part even unempirical elements of the real world in their (likewise unempirical) isolation from other influences, with constant consideration of exact (likewise ideal!) measure. It does this without taking into account whether those simplest elements, or complications thereof, are actually to be observed in reality . . . without considering whether these elements could be found at all in their *complete purity*.[6]

So, four closely connected fundamental elements can be found in Menger's idea of 'exact science':

(a) research always starts off from a nucleus of initial hypotheses; therefore, it makes use of the deductive method. Menger acknowledged his debt to Aristotle, to whom he gave credit for having denied 'the strictly scientific character of induction', which, even if it were possible, would consign us to 'empirical laws' incapable to rising above 'real types' and so of attaining to the formulation of laws attributable to phenomena in their 'complete purity'.[7]

(b) there is no place for any philosophy of history nor for any analogous 'collectivistic' concept, which unfailingly *constrict* the results of human

101

activity into a finalistic design, assign to them 'values' compatible with an already given solution, which is the one and only solution permitted.

(c) scientific knowledge ought to 'reduce human facts to their original and simplest constitutive factors', to attribute to them 'the measure corresponding to their nature', and then 'to try to investigate the laws by which *more complicated* human phenomena are formed from those simplest elements, thought of in their isolation'.[8] This is the procedure which Menger defined as 'compositive' and which Menger's followers called 'methodological individualism'.[9]

(d) between the 'moral' and 'natural sciences' there is only a 'difference' of 'degree'. In fact, 'even natural phenomena in their "empirical reality" offer us neither strict types nor even strictly typical relationships'. 'Real gold, real oxygen and hydrogen, real water' provided to us by nature are not adapted to theoretically constructed types.[10] Thus, even here there is a need for a nucleus of hypotheses, for a series of theories, each of which explains to us only one side of the phenomena.[11]

The theory of value

Menger linked his own name, together with those of W. Stanley Jevons and Leon Walras, to the subjectivistic theory of value. But only the arguments used by Menger, like those used later by his successors at Vienna, lend themselves to a direct 'absorption' into the field of sociology.

For Menger, 'human life is a process',[12] in which 'man, with his needs and his command of the means to satisfy them, is himself the point at which human economic life both begins and ends'.[13] It follows that

value is . . . nothing inherent in goods, no property of them, nor an independent thing existing by itself. It is a judgment economizing men make about the importance of the goods at their disposal for the maintenance of their lives and well-being. Hence, value does not exist outside the consciousness of men. It is, therefore, also quite erroneous to call a good that has value to economizing individuals a 'value', or for economists to speak of 'values' as of independent real things, and to objectify value in this way.[14]

Menger added:

For the inhabitants of an oasis, who have command of a spring that abundantly meets their requirements for water, a certain quantity of water at the spring itself will have no value. But if the spring, as the result of an earthquake, should suddenly decrease its yield of water to such an extent that the satisfaction of the needs of the inhabitants of the oasis would no longer be fully provided for . . . such a quantity would immediately attain value for each inhabitant. This value would, however, suddenly disappear if the old relationship were re-established and the spring regained its yield of water.[15]

Menger drew a conclusion from this: 'The value of goods arises from the relationship to our needs, and is inherent in the goods themselves. With *the changes of this relationship*, value arises and disappears.'[16] This means precisely that *'goods-character is nothing inherent in goods and not a property of goods, but merely a relationship between certain things and men, things obviously ceasing to be goods with the disappearance of this relationship.'*[17]

The idea of value understood as 'relationship' leads to an emphasis on three points:

1   action and exchange arise from a situation which each person perceives as insufficient, as a disequilibrium. In other words: 'individuals strive to better their . . . positions as much as possible'.[18] It is to reach this end that they begin their activities and exchange their goods.[19]

2   'A species can have useful properties that make its concrete units suitable for the satisfaction of human needs. Different species can have decrease of utility in a given use (beech wood and willow wood as fuel, etc.). But neither the utility of a species nor the varying degree of utility of different species or subspecies can be called "value". Not species as such, but only concrete things are *available* to economizing individuals. Only the latter, therefore, are *goods* and only goods are *objects of our* economizing and of our valuation.'[20]

3   'Prices are only incidental manifestation of these activities, symptoms of economic levelling within human economies.'[21]

The force that drives them to the surface is the ultimate and general cause of all economic activity, the endeavor of men to satisfy their needs as completely as possible, to better their economic positions. But since prices are the only phenomena of the process that are directly perceptible . . . it is easy to commit the error of regarding the magnitude of price as the essential feature of an exchange, and as a result of this mistake to commit the further error of regarding the quantities of goods in an exchange as equivalent.[22]

Yet, it is possible to free ourselves from this error.

The only quantities of goods that can be called equivalents (in the objective sense of the term) are quantities which, at a given point in time, can be exchanged at will – that is, in such a way that if one of two quantities of goods is offered, the other can be acquired for it, and *vice versa*. But equivalents of this sort are nowhere present in human economic life. If goods are equivalents in this sense, there would be no reason, market conditions remaining unchanged, why every exchange should not be capable of reversal. Suppose A had exchanged his house for B's farm or for a sum of 20,000 thalers. If these goods had become equivalent in the objective sense of the term as a result of the transaction, or if they had already been equivalents before it took place, there is no reason why the two exchangers should not be willing to reverse the trade immediately. But experience tells us that in a case of this sort neither of the two would give consent to such an arrangement.[23]

In other words, behind the equality of price are hidden differentiated evaluations of the goods exchanged. Ego gives greater importance to the possession that he receives from the Other than what he has handed over; and the Other values more greatly what he obtains from Ego than what he on his part hands over. If it were not so, exchange would not be possible.

Obviously, Menger's position, as outlined above, is incompatible with other theories of value. The error of emphasising prices and of 'regarding the quantities of goods in an exchange as equivalents', has – according to Menger – caused 'incalculable damage' in economic science.[24] Scholars have dedicated themselves to seeking the causes of 'an alleged equality between two quantities of goods'.[25] Some have seen these causes in the equal amount of work involved; others, on the contrary, have identified the causes in the analogous costs of production.

In reply to the first theory, Menger objected:

[it is untenable] that the determining factor in the value of goods is the quantity of labor or other means of production that are necessary for their *reproduction*. A large number of goods cannot be reproduced (antiques and paintings by old masters, for instance) and thus, in a number of cases, we can observe value but no possibility of reproduction. For this reason any factor connected with reproduction cannot be the determining principle of value.[26]

On the theory of the cost of production, Menger wrote:

Comparison of the value of a good with the value of the means employed in its production does, of course, show whether and to what extent its production, an act of *past* human activity, was appropriate or economic. But the quantities of goods employed in the production of a good have neither a necessary nor a directly determining influence on its value.[27]

This is how Menger opened a new page in political economy, a page that indissolubly links value to individual choices. To put it in other terms, Menger introduced life and the preferences that motivate men, into economics. But, in so doing, he obtained an even bigger result. Ortega y Gasset declared that 'the profound sense of the evolution of human thought from the Renaissance onwards is nothing other than the dissolution of the category of substance into the category of relation'.[28] So then, Menger's idea of value as connection or relationship brought political economy into the fullness of this cultural evolution.

Unintentional consequences

Menger saw prices as 'incidental manifestations', the consequence, not directly intended, of the 'desire' to satisfy our needs in the best possible way. But he did not stop there. He made a more complete examination of the 'thoughtless', not deliberate, not voluntary, origin of many social institutions; and he saw in them 'a vast realm of fruitful activity'.[29] This declaration, however, does not make fully clear how valuable his insight was. If he had been more confident, Menger could in fact have said that the 'discovery' of the 'thoughtless' origin of many institutions, the 'discovery', that is, of the *unintentional outcomes* that accompany intentional human actions, lays the foundation of the social sciences. Why?

The reason is that the idea of the 'thoughtless' origin of social institutions is none other than an aspect of the wider process of secularisation, the consequence of which is that, in the territory of the profane, intentional outcomes and unintentional outcomes are attributed to human actions. This means that norms and institutions not arising intentionally are

> the unintended result of innumerable efforts of economic subjects pursuing *individual* interest. The theoretical understanding of them, or the theoretical understanding of their nature and movement can thus be attained in an exact manner . . . that is, it can be attained by reducing their elements to the *individual* factors of their causation . . . The methods for the *exact* understanding of the origin of the 'organically' created structures and those for the solution of the main problems of *exact* economics are by nature identical.[30]

There are examples of social institutions, born unintentionally, that Menger treated at length: language, law, customs, the division of labour, the state, the city, money.[31] The authors to which he explicitly referred were Montesquieu, Burke, Humboldt and Savigny.[32] However, what counts is the question that Menger asked powerfully: '*How can it be that institutions which serve the common welfare and are extremely significant for its development come into being without a common will directed towards establishing them?*'[33] The reply is not difficult. If the norm, as we have often pointed out, is a 'condition' which adjusts the action of Ego to suit that of the Other, the institutions that arise unintentionally are simply the constellations of 'conditions' which allow the carrying out of individual action; they are the 'environment' that conditions our life and at the same time makes it possible.[34]

Nevertheless, one can reproach Menger for not giving due credit to the work of Adam Smith, whom he placed in the territory of 'one sided rationalistic liberalism';[35] it would have been sufficient to be aware of the links between Smith and Burke to realise the inappropriateness of placing him there.[36] And yet, in spite of this misunderstanding, we can say today, with Hayek, that Menger was the one 'who did more than any other writer' to clarify Smith's idea about the unintentional origins of social institutions,[37] or the one who brought back to life – again Hayek's comment – 'the methodological individualism of Adam Smith and his school'.[38]

The 'convergences' between Carl Menger and Georg Simmel

When Simmel's *Philosophie des Geldes* was translated into English, David Laidler and Nicholas Rowe wondered whether, by its disregard of the results reached by Georg Simmel with this work, economic science had not suffered a serious loss.[39] Our problem is different: it is to evaluate the damage sustained by sociology by its failure to recognise Simmel's convergence with the positions upheld in economics by Carl Menger. In any case, whether the question is that raised by Laidler and Rowe, or the one we have underlined, the responsibility is to be attributed to Simmel and Menger. Simmel was responsible because, by never even citing Menger, he made it impossible to point out straight away the debts owed to the founder of Austrian marginalism. Menger was responsible because, when he called attention to the publication of Simmel's work, he restricted himself to a few lines of comment, in which he emphasised, rather than the concordances, the fact that the German sociologist did not understand economics as an economist does.[40] In this way, the opportunity for a dialogue, which would have been very useful for the development of the social sciences, was missed.

Yet, this does not mean that Simmel was not called to account by the economists, or Menger by the sociologists. Laidler and Rowe have mentioned that references to Simmel are found in German economic literature of the first three decades of the century.[41] Fritz Machlup, a pupil of Ludwig von Mises, said confidently that Simmel's work 'was well known to the Austrian economists, who . . . tended to regard it as representing a parallel development of ideas similar to their own'.[42] Then, on this side of the sociological frontier, Albion Small, who had already upheld the thesis that the successors of Adam Smith should have been found among the sociologists rather than among the economists, so great was Smith's attention to the social moment,[43] wrote that the works of Austrian marginalism gave an impetus to the 'development' of modern sociology, because the theoretical base necessary for the work of the 'general sociologists' began with Carl Menger.[44]

However, all of this has not been enough. The points of convergence between Menger and Simmel have never been transformed into a recognised territory of common problems, i.e. of questions with which both economic and sociological theory should, leaving out of consideration their specific sectorial tasks, have come to terms. Therefore, these points deserve to be clarified.

The method

The methodological question was to Menger 'the immediate need of the present'.[45] Equally, in a letter to Heinrich Rickert, Simmel declared that his true task was 'to prove that knowledge *prescribes its laws* not only to nature, but also to history'.[46] Why did the problem of methodology constitute a matter of urgency for both of these authors? It was because the still frail social sciences were subjected to continual attacks and misunderstandings.

Menger had to be measured against the 'old' (Roscher, Hildebrand, Knies), and against the 'young' German historical School of economics (Gustav Schmoller and his followers). This school dominated German economic thought from 1843, the date of the appearance of William Roscher's *Grundriss zu Vorlesungen über die Staatswirtschaft nach geschichtlicher Methode*. Roscher's conception of methodology can be summed up in his rejection of the theoretical social sciences, in the name of a historical investigation of single events, afterwards placed within the *totality* of the life of a people, in a Destiny inexorably coming to birth. The idea is, as Jacobi used to say, that we require 'a truth of which it can be said that *we* are its creations'.[47] In other words, the German historical School of economics did not know how to give up its interpretation of every human happening as the perfect emanation of a superhuman 'objective' will. In this way, the school remained firmly linked to *intentional order*.[48] To reassert this, it had to deny at all costs the possibility of the theoretical social sciences whose existence is, on the contrary, linked to an ateleological conception of social order. Thus, one understands what is the true *exchange* placed in being by the exponents of the German historical School of economics. It is true that they criticised the 'abstract' universal laws of political economy in the name of historical research. And yet, the 'abstract' universal laws were replaced with a Becoming, with a holistic vision, made out of an 'intuitive totality', which was expected to give sense to individual and collective life.

Menger, aware of this, asserted above all the primacy of theory in the construction of science. Without general understanding, that is to say, without theory, neither historical explanation nor prediction (nor the practical science of technology) is possible. Menger wrote:

The purpose of the theoretical sciences is understanding of the real world, knowledge of it extending beyond immediate experience, and control of it. We understand phenomena by means of theories as we become aware of them in each concrete case as exemplifications of a general regularity. We attain a knowledge of phenomena extending beyond immediate experience.[49]

Hence, the journey travelled by scientific research is 'essentially different from Bacon's empirical-realistic induction'.[50]

An *exact science* 'cannot provide understanding of human phenomena in their totality or of a concrete portion thereof, *but* can provide *understanding of one of the most important sides of* human life'.[51] Therefore, it should be repeated that our understanding is *partial*; we can grasp only 'fragments' of reality. This is why we ought to renounce the *whole* and to take economic and social phenomena back to their simplest elements.

This endeavour, as Menger recalled, had actually been described by the exponents of the historical School of economics as 'atomism'.[52] Yet, the 'error of this doctrine is obvious' and is 'more ultimately caused by the failure to recognize the real character of "national economy" in relation to the singular economic phenomena out of which it is constituted'.[53]

Here Menger was concentrating his attack on the holism of the historical school, on its *Begriffsrealismus*:

> The *nation as such is not a large subject* that has needs, that practices economy, and consumes; and what is called 'national economy' is therefore not the economy of a nation in the true sense of the word. 'National economy' is not a phenomenon analogous to the singular economies in the nation, to which also economy of finance belongs. It is not a large singular economy; just as little is it one opposed to or existing along with the singular economies in the nation. It is in its most general form of phenomena a peculiar complication of singular economies.[54]

Thus, the error of the historical school consists 'in the fact that "national economy" is to be viewed as a *complex of individual economies*, and is also *itself* to be viewed as a large individual economy, in which the "nation" is to represent the needing, economic, and consuming subjects'.[55]

Menger comprehended the crucial point of the question:

> Because several persons who have up to now been isolated economically and continue to pursue their *individual* aims and efforts start trafficking in goods with each other (and thus really only undertake to pursue their *individual* interests more suitably than before) their previous isolated economies do not change into *one* common

economy, nor a new one added to these. Rather, the previously isolated economies hereby merely undergo organization. They do sacrifice their character as *isolated* economies, but not their character of singular *economies*. The latter would be the case only if each economic subject gave up *his* individual economic aims and efforts, his economy.[56]

(This confirms what has already been made clear in other sections; that the reification of collective concepts serves the supporters of political collectivism for the creation of an Entity, which is presented as distinct and superior, as the delegitimator of the will of others and the depository of a 'privileged point of view on the world', of which they call themselves the delegates. Thus, *Begriffsrealismus* and the 'privileged point of view on the world' walk along side by side.)[57]

Menger's criticisms of the German historical school of economics were matched in Simmel's polemic on the subject of Leopold von Ranke's 'historical realism'. Simmel's *Probleme der Geschichtsphilosophie* begins in this way:

How does the theoretical construct that we call history develop from material of immediate, experienced reality? That question is the subject of this book. It will establish that this transformation of immediate, experienced reality is more radical than the naive consciousness usually supposes. In this sense, the book is a critique of historical realism: the view according to which historical science is simply a mirror image of the event 'as it really happened'. The error committed here seems to be no less significant than the error of aesthetic realism. According to the latter thesis, the purpose of art is to copy or reproduce reality . . . The purpose of this book, therefore, is to establish – not in detail, but only in principle the a priori of historical knowledge. For historical realism, history is a simple reproduction of event. Any discrepancy between history and the event is merely the result of an abridgment that is purely quantitative. In opposition to this standpoint, we shall establish the legitimacy of the Kantian question: how is history possible?[58]

To give a better illustration of his position, Simmel added:

It is necessary to emancipate the self from historicism in the same way that Kant freed it from naturalism. Perhaps the same epistemological critique will succeed here too: namely, to establish that the sovereign intellect also forms the construct of *mental existence* which we call history.[59]

Let us be precise: Ranke, who maintained that the calling of history is 'to say how things really happened', later shifted towards declaring that historical experiences always possess a spiritual content of their own. Yet he went too far; he even maintained that 'on the pathway of history we draw near to the task of philosophy' and that 'if philosophy were what it ought to be, if history were perfectly clear and complete, then *they would fully coincide with each other*[60] – thus, the 'anti-Hegelian' Ranke was 'near enough to Hegel'.[61] This means that the position of the historical school swings between an irrationalistic conception of history – the realm of the unique and unrepeatable fact, removed, that is to say, from the possible sway of the theoretical social sciences – and a holistic vision, in which the task of the historian consists in placing events within a providentialistic Design, in the *rationalizing* of happenings on the basis of this Design.

Like Menger, Simmel rejected both extremes of the swing of the historicist pendulum. As we have seen, he rejected its empiricism, and he rejected its constant taking refuge within 'global visions'. Our intellect, he said, 'cannot . . . produce any unity, since to perceive the whole as unity among the different directions and the various, equally demanding, aspects of reality and of its possible conceptions, would require the power of a divine spirit':[62] the 'conception of all existence as the phenomenon of one will would be only a childish anthropomorphism of the world'.[63] Hence, we must be satisfied with a *partial* knowledge.

How do we proceed?

> With the help of hypotheses and speculation, one seeks to put together the fragmentary nature of empiricism . . . Events, chaotic and accidental, are then arranged as sequences, which correspond to a certain idea or indicate the way to a determined purpose. The natural and indifferent succession of these events is questioned in order to discern in them the *sense* of what has happened.[64]

Again, in words that could not be clearer, Simmel wrote:

> the epistemological realism which explains truth as a correspondence – in the sense of a mirror image – between thought and its object, an object which is necessarily external to its corresponding thought . . . In the socio-historical sciences, however, the essential identity of knowledge and its object . . . still leads us to the same mistaken conclusion: that form of naturalism which holds that knowledge is possible as a simple reproduction of its object . . . In opposition to this view, it is necessary to make clear that every form of knowledge represents a translation of immediately given data into a new language, a language with its own intrinsic forms, categories, and requirement. In order to qualify as a science, the facts . . . must answer certain questions, questions which they never confront in

reality and in their form as brute data. In order to qualify as objects of knowledge, certain aspects of the facts are thrown into relief, and others are relegated to the background. Certain specific features are emphasized. Certain immanent relations are established on the basis of ideas and values.[65]

He added:

Consider a person who views his own life as a historical development. Here the relationship between knowledge and its objects seems to be even more intimate. Here it seems even more plausible that the forms of being and knowledge are simple ones and the same melody played in two different keys. In this case, the original data that constitute the object of knowledge are present in immediate consciousness. However this is the very case in which the following point can be made most clearly: knowledge – the synthesis of this original data – is a consequence of a priori forms.[66]

Thus, on the question of methodology, the concordances between Menger and Simmel appear to be very strong. Both rejected 'historical realism' and 'global visions'. Both declared the primacy of the theoretical moment in the construction of science, and both recognised that every scientific theory is *partial*. Menger proposed to proceed through the study of 'forms', of 'types', and of 'typical relations'[67] – that is, by means of the development of 'ideal models', as well as by the empirical direction. Simmel concentrated on the 'forms' which make it possible to 'isolate' the 'simplest and most homogeneous processes possible'.[68]

Value

We have seen that for Menger the 'goods-character of a thing' is not a property inherent in it – whether a thing can be called goods or not depends on the fact that it can be put into 'a causal *connection* with the satisfaction of human needs'.[69] Therefore, needs are what motivates man to act and to transform things into goods.

Simmel flatly rejected the labour theory of value. 'The idea, for instance, that the essential feature of value in the socially necessary labour time objectivized in it, . . . does not answer the question of how the labour power itself becomes a value.'[70] The problem is posed in a way not unlike that of Menger. Value arises from the dissociation between desire and satisfaction. 'The longing, effort and sacrifice that separate us from objects are also supposed to lead us towards them. Withdrawal and approach are in practice complementary notions, each of which presupposes the other; they are two sides of the *relationship* to objects.'[71]

Again: 'The situation, which is represented in stylized form to be the concept of Paradise, in which subject and object, desire and satisfaction are not yet divided from each other . . . is destined to disintegrate, but also to attain a new reconciliation. The purpose of establishing a distance is that it should be overcome.'[72] This means that

> the moment of enjoyment itself, when the opposition between subject and object is effaced, consumes the value. Value is only rein-stated as contrast, as an object separated from the subject. Such trivial experiences as that we appreciate the value of our possessions only after we have lost them, that the mere withholding of a desired object often endows it with a value quite disproportionate to any possible enjoyment that it could yield, that the remoteness, either literal or figurative, of the objects of our enjoyment shows them in a transfig-ured light and with heightened attractions – all these are derivatives, modifications and hybrids of the basic fact that value does not origi-nate from the unbroken unity of the moment of enjoyment, but from the separation between the subject and the content of enjoyment as an object that stands opposed to the subject.[73]

Here is the point that interests us most: 'Objects are not difficult to acquire because they are valuable; but we call those objects valuable that resist our desire to possess them. Since the desire encounters resistance and frustration, the objects gain a significance that would never have been attributed to them by an unchecked will.'[74] This was expressed by Simmel in a much more direct way, when he recognised that one should consider the 'subject, with his customary or exceptional, permanent or changing, moods and responses as the ground of valuation' – that is to say, of value.[75]

From this, it follows that the same subject can evaluate an object in different ways, depending on the circumstances. And it follows, above all, that different subjects evaluate the same objects differently; this is the premise of exchange.

Simmel rightly said:

> in exchange, value becomes supra-subjective, supra-individual, yet without becoming an objective quality and reality of things them-selves . . . The Ego, even though it is the universal source of values, becomes so far removed from the objects that they can measure their significance by each other without referring in each case to the Ego. But this real relationship between values, which is executed and supported by exchange, evidently has its purpose in eventual subjec-tive enjoyment, that is, in the fact that we receive a greater quantity and intensity of values than would be possible without exchange transactions.[76]

Hence, the need for money, which Simmel explained in these terms:

> if there is nothing to exchange, money has no value . . . money is the
> expression and agent of the relationship that make satisfaction of one
> person always mutually dependent upon another person. Money has
> no place where there is no mutual relationship, either because one
> does not want anything from other people, or because one lives on a
> different plane – without any relation to them as it were – and is able
> to satisfy any need without any service in return.[77]

In other words, value arises from the *relationship* between the subject and
the object, and is the basis of the intersubjective *relationship* made possible or
mediated by money. Here, we are well within Menger's territory.

Unintentional consequences

As has been mentioned, Menger dwelt, among other things, on the unintentional origin of money. For his part, Simmel emphasised that money is
'entirely a social institution and quite meaningless if restricted to one individual';[78] and he insisted on its character as an institution established in an
evolutionary way.

But there is more. Starting from the consideration that 'a tool continues to
exist apart from its particular application and is capable of a variety of other
uses that cannot be foreseen', Simmel explained that this

> is true not only for thousands of cases in daily life, that need not be
> exemplified, but also in much more complicated situations. How
> often are military organizations, which were intended for external
> deployment, used by a dynasty for internal political ends? How often
> does a relationship among individuals which was originally estab-
> lished for a particular purpose grow beyond this and become the
> bearer of altogether different contents?[79]

However, if it is true that the instrument 'dissociates' itself from the goal
for which it was originally conceived, in the case of money we find ourselves
before an instrument which 'is not related at all to a specific purpose', which
'acquires a relation to the totality of purposes':

> Money is the tool that has the greatest possible number of unpre-
> dictable uses and so possesses the maximum value attainable in this
> respect. The mere possibility of combined uses that money has, or
> represents, on account of its lack of any content of its own, is mani-
> fested in a positive way by the restlessness of money, by its urge to be
> used.[80]

Yet, this is what Mandeville had already pointed out: that 'to procure all the Comforts of Life' without money is like communicating without language.[81] Payment in money is the most complete form of *generic obligation*, which frees the relationship from a specific object or a specific person and which makes the condition of *means*, assumed by the *rendering of service*, absolutely clear. With reason, Simmel spoke of the obligation in money as the form of obligation 'most congruent with personal freedom'.[82] In other words, money separates the service rendered from the goals that are privately pursued by social actors; and it makes possible the 'open society', which is in fact a society that renounces a 'unitary' system of ends. This is why Friedrich von Hayek wrote:

> If it is often made a reproach to the Great Society and its market order that it lacks an agreed ranking of ends. This, however, is in fact its great merit which makes individual freedom and all its values possible . . . In the Great Society we all in fact contribute not only to the satisfaction of needs of which we do not know, but sometimes even to the achievement of ends of which we would disapprove if we knew about them. We cannot help this . . . That we assist in the realization of other people's aims without sharing them or even knowing them, and solely in order to achieve our own aims, is the source of strength of the Great Society.[83]

With his reflections on the 'abstractness' of money, Simmel threw light on the functioning of unintentional order. Hence, his contribution can be linked with those of Mandeville, Hume, Smith and Menger on this subject.

Ludwig von Mises: the theory of action in the development of Austrian marginalism

Ludwig Lachmann has written that Menger's was an 'incomplete revolution'.[84] Perhaps it would be better to say that Menger, as often happens to great innovators, did not manage to systematise his own theory or to make its premises clear. For example, to the exponents of the German historical school, who accused political economy of being affected by the 'dogma of individual interest', he replied that

> exact theory of political economy . . . has the only task of affording us *the understanding of a special side of human life, to be sure the most important, the economic*. On the other hand, the understanding of the remaining sides of it could only be attained by other theories which would make us aware of the formations of remaining propensities, i.e., from the point of view of public spirit of the strict sway of the ideal of justice, etc.[85]

But Schmoller continued to hold Menger responsible for 'schematic spectres', 'imaginary Robinson Crusoes';[86] he accused him of that 'hasty ingenuity' which sees the 'simple and ultimate elements' of action 'in the manifestation of human needs or the incentive of gain or individual profit'.[87]

Mises gave a much more cogent reply to the question than that of Menger. He wrote:

> The most general prerequisite of action is a state of dissatisfaction, on the one hand, and, on the other, the possibility of removing or alleviating it by taking action. Perfect satisfaction, and its concomitant, the absence of any stimulus to change and action, belong properly to the concept of the perfect being. This, however, is beyond the power of the human mind to conceive. A perfect being would not act.[88]

Moreover, Mises emphasised that a need cannot be satisfied without harming the satisfaction of other needs. This means that men live in a situation of permanent need. Even if all goods were 'free', it would still be necessary to economise time, one's own personal activity, one's own life as it passes.[89] It follows that 'only in a Cockaine populated by men who were immortal and indifferent to the passage of time', can need fade away.[90]

Up to this point there is nothing that was not already present in Menger. But Mises drew a very important conclusion from this. If one understands that man cannot free himself from need, it is evident that every action 'involves choice among various possibilities'.[91] All action consists in making economical use of the means available for the realisation of predetermined ends. In other words, *The fundamental law of action is the economic principle.*[92] 'For this reason', Mises added, 'no misunderstanding can be more fundamental than that of historicism when . . . it explains the economic principle as a specific feature of production in a money economy'.[93] The fact is – to quote Mises again – that monetary calculation has given life only to an economic territory in a 'strict sense', that in which it is possible by means of prices to make a quantitative comparison between costs and proceeds. And yet, even where such a monetary comparison is not feasible, and values do not have a precise quantitative determination, the individual always seeks to respect the economic principle, because in every case he has to devote his own resources (his own life, his own time) to alternative uses.

In Mises's words, all of this takes on the following tone:

> The characteristic feature of the mental tool provided by monetary calculation is responsible for the fact that the sphere in which it is employed appears to us a special province within the wider domain of action. In everyday, popular usage the sphere of economic extends as far as monetary calculations are possible. Whatever goes beyond this is called the non-economic sphere. We cannot acquiesce in this

usage . . . we can accept the terms 'economic in a narrower sense' and 'economic in the broader sense', provided one does not want to interpret them as indicating a difference in the scope of rational and economic action.[94]

That is not all. If in order to act it is necessary to economise, action has to be rational. 'The economic principle is a general principle of rational action.'[95] 'The spheres of rational action and economic action are therefore coincident. All rational action is economic. All economic activity is rational activity.'[96]

Thus, the economic problem is not a product of the market society. 'Need' is a human condition; and monetary prices are merely the instrument through which we make our valuations less approximate. It follows that the disappearance of monetary economy does not make the economic problem go away, nor does the necessity to act rationally become less strong. This is why, in contradiction to the exponents of the German historical school of economics, Mises did not hesitate to write:

> Historicism does not take its task seriously enough in being satisfied with the simple statement that the quality of human action is not supertemporal and has changed in the course of evolution. In undertaking to defend such statement, one at least has the obligation to point out in what respects the action of the allegedly pre-rational era differed from that of the rational era.[97]

However, it is necessary to come to terms with one question: If scarcity impels men to act rationally, are individual preferences also rational? On this point, Mises expressed himself with his usual clarity:

> The causes of action and the goals toward which it strives are data for the theory of action: upon their concrete configuration depends the course of action taken in the individual case, but the nature of the action as such is not thereby affected.[98] . . . These considerations have an evident bearing on the widespread tendency of the present age to appeal to the irrational. *The concepts rational and irrational are not applicable to ends at all.* Whoever wishes to pass judgment on ends may praise or condemn them as good or evil, fine or vulgar, etc.[99]

Returning to the same subject, Mises declared again:

> Modern economics, however, does not start from the action of the businessman, but from that of consumers, that is to say, from the action of everybody. In this view, therefore – and herein lies its 'subjectivism' in contrast to the 'objectivism' of the classical economists, and, at the same time its 'objectivity' in contrast to the

normative position of the older school . . . Modern economics is not and cannot be concerned with whether someone prefers healthful food or narcotic poisons; no matter how perverted may be the ethical or other ideas that govern his conduct, its 'correctness' is not a matter to be judged by economics . . . If one sees the significance of movements of market prices, as the modern theory does, in the fact that a state of rest is not reached until total demand and total supply coincide, it is clear that *all* the factors that influence the conduct of the parties on the market – and consequently, also the *'non-economic' and 'irrational' factors, like misunderstanding, love, hate, custom, habit and magnanimity – are included*. Therefore, Schelting's statement that economic theory 'assumes a society that arose only through the operation of economic factors' does not apply to modern economics.[100]

Hence, if we make *homo oeconomicus* coincide with the man who renounces his own preferences, we cannot explain 'why someone buys a better suit even though the cheaper one has the same "objective" usefulness'.[101] If, on the other hand, we accept the position of marginalist economics, we know that 'the principle of buying on the cheapest market comes into question here only in so far as the choice is between several possibilities, otherwise equal, of purchasing goods'.[102] This means that preferences come before the economic problem and constitute the data for it.[103] It follows that the scale of needs and values is not constructed rationally; only the choice of means is rational.

Thus, economics does not dictate ends. Action can originate 'from altruistic or from egoistic motives, from a noble or a base disposition'; it can be 'directed toward the attainment of materialistic or idealistic ends'; it can spring 'from exhaustive and painstaking deliberation or follow fleeting impulses and passions'.[104] Indeed, for Locke, the liberty of the individual consisted in following one's 'own will in all things, where the rule prescribes not.'[105] This is why Mises, commenting on a passage in which Max Scheler asserted that men prefer the 'pleasant' to the 'unpleasant',[106] wrote:

What Scheler says about the pleasant and the unpleasant is the fundamental law of action, which is valid independently of place, time, race
and the like. If we substitute in Scheler's remarks 'subjectively
considered more important' for 'pleasant', and 'subjectively considered less important' for 'unpleasant' this becomes even clearer.[107]

In other words: what is 'subjectively considered more important' can have a selfish or altruistic content. But economics is not responsible for that content.

The 'convergences' between Max Weber and Ludwig von Mises

The 'convergences' between the works of Carl Menger and Georg Simmel, which also make clear the common territory between economics and sociology, form a chapter of the social sciences little explored.[108] There is, however, another chapter – namely, that relating to the comparison between the theories of Max Weber and Ludwig von Mises – which seems to have been almost forgotten. It is important to recover it, to bring it back into the light, because it complements the comparison between Menger and Simmel.

As we have seen in the preceding pages, Simmel was clearly indebted to Menger, but Weber was indebted to both. In fact, the 'ideal type' of Weber owes much to Menger's 'types' and Simmel's 'forms'. Perhaps one could say that it was his adherence to the results achieved by Menger and Simmel that impelled Weber to oppose the German historical school of economics, 'among whose offspring' – as he wrote autobiographically – he was to be numbered.[109] Expressing himself clearly, Weber wrote:

> what was meant and what can be meant by that *theoretical* concept can be made unambiguously clear *only* through precise ideal – typical constructs. Those who are so contemptuous of the 'Robinsonades' of classical theory should restrain themselves if they are unable to replace them with better concepts, which in this contest means clearer concepts.[110]

Thus, Weber opposed the criticism made by his own school about theoretical economics. And he opposed the idea, this also typical of historicism, that 'in the domain of practical-political preferences, ultimately only one was the correct one'.[111] In this way, he rejected the illusion that science has the capacity to decide between different alternatives of value; he denied that the state can be considered the 'ultimate value', that 'all social actions should be evaluated in terms of their relations to its interests'.[112] He replied to Schmoller, his 'honored master', that the university is not a 'state institution for the training of "loyal" administrators. Such a procedure makes the university, not into a specialized technical school . . . but rather into a theological seminary – except that it does not have the latter's religious dignity.'[113]

In other words, Weber rejected 'historical realism' and the associated idea of the 'privileged point of view on the world'. For his part, Mises was the scholar who in the application of subjectivism pushed further ahead than any other scholar;[114] he, too, unceasingly directed his criticism against 'historical realism' and the associated 'privileged point of view on the world', which then becomes the way to delegitimise the position of the dissenter and to submit scientific thought to prescriptions of a political nature. Mises confided his preoccupations to Weber, who taught for a brief period at Vienna. Weber replied:

> You do not like the position of the *Verein für Sozialpolitik*; I like it even less. But it is a fact that it is the only Association of men in our discipline. It is useless for us to criticize it from the outside. We must work with the Association and remove its shortcomings. I am trying it in my way, and you must do it in your way![115]

A comparison between the theories of Weber and Mises allows us, therefore, to extend our examination of the convergences between sociology and economics which we began in the pages about the connections between Menger and Simmel.

To that end, it is useful to indicate some points of agreement which are obviously linked to their shared commitment, already mentioned, of opposition to *Begriffsrealismus* and to 'the privileged point of view on the world'.

Against psychologism

Weber wrote:

> [S]ociology has no closer relationship . . . to . . . psychology than to any other science. The source of error lies in the concept of the 'psychic'. It is held that everything which is not physical is *ipso facto* psychical. However, the *meaning* of a train of mathematical reasoning which a person carries out is not in the relevant sense 'psychic'. Similarly the rational deliberation of an actor as to whether the results of a given proposed course of action will or will not promote certain specific interests, and the corresponding decision, do not become one bit more understandable by taking 'psychological' considerations into account. But it is precisely on the basis of such rational assumptions that most of the laws of sociology, including those of economics, are built up.[116]

Thus, Weber was in a territory opposed to that occupied by psychologism. Mises's position is no different. He declared:

> Modern man is a social being, not only as one whose material needs could not be supplied in isolation, but also as one who has achieved a development of reason and of the perceptive faculty that would have been impossible except within society. Man is inconceivable as an isolated being, for humanity exists only as a social phenomenon and mankind transcended the stage of animality only in so far as cooperation evolved the social relationships between individuals. Evolution

from animal . . . to human being was made possible and achieved by means of social cooperation and by that alone.[117]

Economics begins where psychology ends

The opposition of Weber and Mises to psychologism is found consistently in their interpretation of the theory of marginal utility. Weber said:

> The assertion that the theory of value of the so-called Austrian School is 'psychologically' founded has been made several times . . . the most distinguished representatives of the historical school claim to have helped the theory of value to reach its present status by means of *psychology*.[118]

Moreover, taking sides against the *Kathedersozialisten*, he added:

> I do not understand the scornful way in which Brentano treats the 'Austrians'. Carl Menger expressed some excellent opinions, even if he did so in a way that was not methodologically perfect. As to 'style', today commonly overvalued at the expense of content, in this too Böhm-Bawerk, if not (perhaps) Menger, is a master.[119]

He concluded:

> The theory of marginal utility, and more generally every subjective theory of value, is not psychologically, but rather – to use a methodological term – pragmatically, founded, that is to say, founded on the use of the categories of *end* and *means*.[120]

For his part, Mises wrote:

> The expression 'Psychological School' is frequently employed as a designation of modern subjectivistic economics. Occasionally too the difference in method that exists between the School of Lausanne and the Austrian School is indicated by attributing to the latter the 'psychological' method. It is not surprising that the idea of economics as almost a branch of psychology or applied psychology should have arisen from such a habit of speech.[121]

But the situation is really quite different:

> The step that leads from classical to modern economics is the realization that classes of goods in the abstract are never exchanged and evaluated, but always only concrete units of a class of goods . . . We

derive the law of the satiation of wants from this proposition and from the further realization, . . . that, in our scales of importance, we order individual units of goods not according to the class of goods to which they belong or the classes of wants which they satisfy, but according to the concrete emergence of wants; that is to say, before one class of wants is fully satisfied, we already proceed to the satisfaction of individual wants of other classes . . . Therefore, from our standpoint Gossen's law has nothing to do with psychology. It is deduced by economics from reflections that are not of a psychological nature.[122]

Economics begins at the point at which psychology leaves off.[123] . . . The point at which the science of action begins its work is the mutual incompatibility of individual desires and the impossibility of perfect satisfaction. Since it is not granted to man to satisfy all his desires completely . . . he must choose and value, prefer and set aside – in short, to act.[124]

The postulate of scarcity

For Mises, as we have already seen, the human condition is one of need, of scarcity. Weber expressed the same concept in the following words:

Most roughly expressed, the basic element in all those phenomena which we call, in the widest sense, 'social-economic' is constituted by the fact that our physical existence and the satisfaction of our most ideal needs are everywhere confronted with the quantitative limits and the qualitative inadequacy of the external means, so that their satisfaction requires planful provision and work, struggle with nature and the association of human beings.[125]

The passage from Weber recalls also the problem of the division of labour; that is, it points out the connection between wants and social cooperation, a connection that did not escape Mises. In fact, he considered the theory of the division of labour to be 'the starting point of sociology'.[126] Contrary to what is upheld by 'collectivistic metaphysics', he underlined,

there is no irreconcilable conflict between the interests of society and those of the individual. In isolation the individual cannot attain his ends, whatever they may be . . . The sacrifices he makes for the main-tenance of social cooperation are therefore only temporary: renunciation of a momentary benefit for the sake of an advantage that endures throughout the continued existence and evolution of the division of labour. Society comes into being, and develops not by

121

virtue of a moral law imposed on mankind by mysterious powers but on forcing the individual, against his interests, into subordination to the social whole, but through the action of individuals cooperating in the attainment of ends that they severally aim at.[127]

The result of this, for Mises, is that 'every individual benefits from the existence of society and that no one would be better off as a freebooting individual in an imaginary state of isolation, searching for food on his own and engaging in the war all against all, than a member of society, though a thousand times more constrained and circumscribed'.[128]

Eudaemonism

If this is so, society is a 'positive-sum game' or, put in another way, if the world is a 'pragmatic field' from which individuals seek to draw usefulness or advantages, then the positions of Kantian ethics are untenable. This is why Weber questioned whether the ethical maxims of a 'strictly formal character' contain 'substantive indications for the evaluation of action'[129]; and he added that individualism which, strangely, is easily accepted as an expression 'strictly historically conditioned', represents, on the contrary, 'a brilliant formulation which covered an immeasurably large number of ethical situations'.[130] Here, too, we find convergence. But Mises went into it in more depth. He said:

> The weakest part of Kant's system is the ethics. Although they are vitalized by his mighty intellect, the grandeur of individual concepts do not blind us to the fact that his starting point is unfortunately chosen and that his fundamental conception a mistaken one. His desperate attempt to uproot Eudaemonism has failed.[131]

It was 'liberal social philosophy' that found the 'solution', because it discovered 'how to bring eudaemonistic doctrine into harmony with the obvious fact that moral action consists just in the individual's avoiding actions which seem directly useful to him and doing that which seems directly harmful to him.'[132]
How is this harmonisation brought about? Mises wrote:

> There is no contrast between moral duty and selfish interest. What the individual gives to society to preserve it as society, he gives not for the sake of aims alien to himself, but in his own interest. The individual, who is a product of society not only as a thinking, willing, sentient man, but also simply as a living creature, cannot deny society without denying himself.[133]

The truth, Mises explained, is that 'the power to choose whether my actions and my conduct shall serve myself or my fellow beings is not given to me –

which perhaps may be regarded as fortunate. If it were, human society would not be possible.'[134] In other words, Mises maintained that the personal interest of the individual who acts and the interests of others cannot be separated; they are two inseparable elements of that reality to which we give the name of action or social relationship. Translated into our own expressions, it means that the 'account' is either 'double entry' and it contains Ego's personal interest and his obligation to the Other, or it is not, in the sense that, if Ego withdraws from the 'payment' of the 'price' required by the Other, he has to renounce also the fulfilment of his own interests. For the actor, it is therefore convenient to 'submit' to the 'payment' in his relationship with the Other.

On this subject, Mises said again,

> [eudaemonism] proves that each single man sees in the others, first of all, only means to the realization of his purposes, while he himself is to all others a means for the realization of their purposes; . . . finally [it proves], by this reciprocal action, in which each is simultaneously means and end, the highest aim of social life is attained – the achievement of a better existence for everyone . . . society is only possible if everyone, while living his own life, at the same time helps others to live, if every individual is simultaneously means and end; if each individual's well-being is simultaneously condition to the well-being of the others.[135]

Thus, the problem posed by the antithesis between selfish action and altruistic action fades away. Action always arises from the attempt to realise a project of one's own, that is, to coincide with oneself. But it is always necessary to seek the availability of the Other, to submit to the 'conditions' dictated by him. That is, 'the social interdependence of individuals' still stands.[136]

Only the individual acts

For Weber, to act is an 'attitude' of '*individuals* in the face of the actual or potential behaviour of other individuals'.[137] In other words, sociology ought to investigate 'what happens within the threshold of intelligible meaningful behaviour, in the face of "objects" (internal or external) . . . only as conditions, or as an object of subjective reference of this behaviour'.[138] As a consequence, 'concepts such as "the State", "association", "feudalism" and so on, designate for sociology, in general, categories of determined forms of human action in society; and it is the task of sociology to relate them to "intelligible" action, and that means, without exception, to the action of the people who participate in it.'[139]

Weber expressed the same concept in another way:

For still other cognitive purposes – for instance, juristic ones – or for practical ends, it may on the other hand be convenient or even indispensable to treat social collectivities, such as states, associations, business corporations, foundations, as if they were individual persons. Thus they may be treated as the subjects of rights and duties or as the performers of legally significant actions. But for the subjective interpretation of action in sociological work these collectivities must be treated as *solely* the resultants and modes of organization of the particular acts of individual persons, since these alone can be treated as agents in a course of subjectively understandable action.[140]

However,

it is a tremendous misunderstanding to think that an 'individualistic' *method* should involve what is in any conceivable sense an individualistic system of *value*. It is as important to avoid this error as the related one which confuses the unavoidable tendency of sociological concepts to assume a rationalistic character with a belief in the predominance of rational motives, or even a positive valuation of rationalism. Even a socialistic economy would have to be understood sociologically in exactly the same kind of 'individualistic' terms; that is, in terms of the action of individuals, the types of officials found in it, as would be the case with a system of free exchange analysed in terms of the theory of marginal utility.[141]

For his part, Mises stated:

For the purposes of science we must start from the action of the individual because this is the only thing of which we can have direct cognition. The idea of a society that could operate or manifest itself apart from the action of individuals is absurd. Everything social must in some way be recognizable in the action of the individual. What would the mystic totality of the universalist be if it were not alive in every individual? Every form of society is operative in the actions of individuals aiming at definite ends. What would the German national character be that did not find expression in the Germanism of individuals? . . . That one is a member of a market society, a party comrade, a citizen, or a member of any other association must be shown through his actions.[142]

Mises replied to Othmar Spann, who allotted to sociology the sphere of those spiritual facts that cannot be drawn from experience because they possess, 'by virtue of their *a priori* character, a pre-empirical and supra-empirical existence', that sociology understood in this way 'it is not at all *a priori* reasoning, but intuitive insight into a whole'.[143]

Mises's conclusion was that a theory that rejects rationalism, individualism and eudaemonism 'can say nothing about human action'.[144]

> To be sure, it tells us that men love and hate, that they are garrulous and taciturn, that they are cruel and compassionate, that they are sociable and that they shun society. But it can say nothing about the fact that they act, work, labor, and toil to achieve goals ... If one wants to explain society without reference to the action of men, the only expedient that remains is to view it as the outcome of mysteriously operating forces.[145]

Without prices, economic calculation is not possible

In 1912, Ludwig von Mises published his *Theorie des Geldes und der Unlaufsmittel*, which Weber judged to be the 'most acceptable'[146] theory of money. And that was not all. In 1919, Mises gave a lecture on 'Die Wirtschaftsrechnung im sozialistichen Gemeinwesen', the text of which appeared later in the *Archiv für Sozialwissenschaft und Sozialpolitik*.[147] Weber was able to cite it just in time;[148] he agreed with its contents. Mises's thesis was that without prices, determined by the market, economic calculation is not possible; this is the consequence to which socialist planning is subject. And Weber maintained:

> Money accounting attains the highest level of rationality, as an instrument of calculatory orientation of economic action, when it is applied in the form of capital accounting. The substantive precondition here is a thorough market freedom ... The competitive struggle for customers, which is associated with this state, gives rise to a great volume of expenditures, especially with regard to the organization of sales, advertising, which in the absence of competition – in a planned economy or under complete monopolization – would not have to be incurred.[149]

Thus, the agreement between Mises and Weber here is complete.[150]

Mises's criticism of Weber's quadripartition of meaningful action

The convergences in the topics mentioned above did not prevent Mises from harshly criticising Weber's theory of rationality. What is the point here? As we have seen, for Mises action is always rational. In his polemic against historicism, he said that anyone who maintains those positions has 'the obligation to point out in what respect the action of the allegedly pre-rational era differs from that of the rational era', just as they are also obliged to clarify 'how, for example, action other than rational could take place or would have been able to take place'.[151]

Mises added: 'Max Weber alone felt this obligation'[152] and, 'in the realm of "meaningful action" he distinguishes four types'.[153] It is opportune to explain Weber's fourfold division:

> Social action, like all action, may be oriented in four ways. It may be:
>
> 1 *instrumentally rational*, that is, determined by expectations as to the behaviour of objects in the environment and of other human beings; these expectations are used as 'conditions' or 'means' for the attainment of the actor's own rationally pursued and calculated ends;
>
> 2 *value-rational,* that is, determined by a conscious belief in the value for its own sake of some ethical, aesthetic, religious, or other form of behaviour, independently of its prospects of success;
>
> 3 *affectual* (especially emotional), that is, determined by the actor's specific affects and feeling states;
>
> 4 *traditional*, that is, determined by ingrained habituation.[154]

Moreover, Mises recalled that for Weber there was also a 'merely reactive behavior, to which no subjective meaning is attached' and that the line between such 'behavior' and a meaningful action cannot be, according to Weber, 'sharply drawn empirically'.[155] Mises's criticism took off from just this point.

He wrote:

> When we say that an instance of human behavior is merely reactive, instinctive or conative, we mean that it takes place unconsciously. It must be noted, however, that where we deem it inexpedient to conduct ourselves in such a way, we meaningfully set about to eliminate merely reactive, instinctive, or conative behavior. If my hand is touched by a sharp knife, I instinctively draw it back; but if, for example, a surgical operation is intended, I will endeavor to overcome reactive behavior through conscious action. Conscious volition controls all spheres of our behavior that are at all accessible to it by tolerating only that reactive, instinctive or conative conduct which it sanctions as expedient and would itself have carried out. Consequently, from the point of view of the investigation proper to the science of human action, which aims at something quite different from that proper to psychology, the boundary between meaningful

and merely reactive behavior is not at all indeterminate. As far as the will has the power to become efficacious, there is only meaningful action.[156]

Having clarified this, Mises singled out the reasons for Weber's fourfold division of meaningful action. Weber fought against the 'misunderstanding that identifies "rational" action with "correct" action'.[157] In other words, he was opposed to the idea that the scale of subjective preferences could be constructed rationally. And yet he fell into an ambiguity: he did not take account of the autonomy attributed by Austrian marginalism to individual preferences. It is not by chance that he declared:

> The theory of marginal utility, in order to reach specific objectives of knowledge, considers human action as if it took place, from beginning to end, under the control of a *commercial calculation* – a calculation carried out on the basis of *all* the conditions that have to be considered. It considers individual wants and goods, both for production and for exchange, to be available for their satisfaction as 'sums' and as mathematically calculable 'quantities' in a continuous process of book-keeping. It considers men to be like actors who constantly carry out an economic undertaking, and considers their life to be the object of their 'enterprise', which is carried out according to calculation. This way of seeing things connected to commercial book-keeping is, more than anything else, the point of departure for the construction of the theory of marginal utility.[158]

Nevertheless, as we have already seen, that is what Austrian marginalism refuses to be. As Mises said, economics explains how market prices are set:

> prohibitionists see a serious failing of mankind in the consumption of alcoholic beverages, which they attributed to misunderstanding, weakness of character and immorality. But in the view of catallactics, there is only the fact that there is a demand for alcohol. He who has to explain the price of brandy is not concerned with the question whether it is 'rational' or moral to drink brandy. I may think what I will about motion picture dramas, but as an economist I have to explain the formation of the market prices for the cinema, actors and theater seats, not sit in judgment on the films. Catallactics does not ask whether or not the consumers are right, noble, generous, wise, moral, patriotic, or churchgoing. It is concerned not with why they act, but only with how they act.[159]

Thus, he ends, 'neither require nor are capable of rational justification'.[160] Marginalism, therefore, does not construct the scale of preferences rationally. This is equivalent to saying that Weber's accusations were wholly out of place. And yet the question is: Is Weber's fourfold division of meaningful action valid? Let us see what conclusions Mises reached.

If the 'economic principle' is valid, all that we consider as human action is rational. Let us examine action determined affectively.

> Under the impulse of passion, the rank order of ends shift, and one more easily yields to an emotional impulse that demands immediate satisfaction. Later, on cooler consideration, one judges differently. He who endangers his own life in rushing to the aid of a drowning man is able to do so because he yields to the momentary impulse to help, or because he feels that duty to prove himself a hero under such circumstances, or because he wants to earn a reward for saving the man's life.[161] . . . In each case, his action is contingent upon the fact that he momentarily places the value of coming to the man's aid so high that other considerations . . . fall into the background. It may be that subsequent consideration will lead him to a different judgment. But at the moment – and this is the only thing that matters – even this action was *rational*.[162]

Let us move on to action which is determined traditionally. Mises wrote:

> When an aristocratic landowner rejects the proposal of his steward to use his name, title and coat of arms as a trade mark on the packages of butter going to the retail market from his estate, basing his refusal on the argument that such a practice does not conform to aristocratic tradition, he means: I will forego an increase in my income that I could attain only by the sacrifice of a part of my dignity.[163]

That is to say, he values family customs more than the potential increase in his own income. Therefore, his action is 'rational'.

Let us give some attention to 'instrumentally rational action' and 'value-rational action'. Mises declared:

> If I simply want to buy soap, I will inquire about the price in many stores and then buy the cheapest one. If I consider the trouble and loss of time which such shopping requires so bothersome that I would rather pay a few cents more, then I will go into the nearest store without making any further inquiries. If I also want to combine the support of a poor disabled veteran with the purchase of soap, then I will buy from the invalid peddler, though this may be more expensive. In this case, if I want to enter my expenditure accurately in my household accounts book, I should have to set down the cost of the soap at its common selling price and make a separate entry of the over

payment, in the one instance as *for my convenience* and in the other *for charity*.[164]

Weber declared that 'examples of pure value-rational orientation would be the action of persons who, regardless of possible cost to themselves, act to put into practice their convictions of what seems to them to be required by duty, honor, the pursuit of beauty, religious call, personal loyalty, or the importance of some "cause" no matter in what it consists.'[165] And Mises's conclusion is that Weber 'employs an inappropriate mode of expression to describe this state of affairs. It would be more accurate to say that there are men who place the value of duty, honor, beauty, and the like so high that they set aside other goals for their sake.'[166]

It follows that, in the first place, it is not exact to say that someone, who acts in a 'value-rational' way, does not take account of the 'possible cost'; he does take account of it, but he is prepared to put up with it. Second, Weber's fourfold division of meaningful action does not strictly refer to action. This is rational in every case, because it is a 'means' considered suitable for the attainment of an end. Weber himself showed that he was convinced of this, when he insisted that 'even the empirically "free" actor – i.e. who acts on the basis of his *deliberations* – is teleologically bound by the means for attainment of his own ends';[167] and when he wrote that, in the presence of an objective decided in 'value-rational' way, 'action is instrumentally rational only in respect of the choice of a means'.[168]

Therefore, Weber's typification needs to be related not to the 'context' of action, but to that of motivation, which can obviously be of various kinds. Weber, as an 'offspring' of the historical school, used this to demonstrate, by means of 'value-rational' action, 'affectual' action, and 'traditional' action, that preferences are not formed rationally; and to declare, moreover, that the same 'instrumentally rational' action is 'only a limiting case' of essentially constructive character.[169]

To uphold all of this against Austrian marginalism is, however, out of place. It is instead relevant to mention that preferences ought always to be in subjection to the means available. If they survive, even in spite of the negative verdict of economic in the 'strict sense' or of the immediate 'conveniences' (think of the person in the condition of avoiding his obligations, and yet he respects them), it means that they have – to use the same language as Weber – a 'value for its own sake'.[170] As a result, Weber's four types can be reduced in number and summarised under the heading of 'value-rational' actions and 'instrumentally rational' actions. Choices determined affectively or on the basis of tradition can, in fact, overcome the negative judgement of economic calculation in the 'strict sense', or of immediate 'conveniences' only if they have a value in themselves, if therefore they gratify the actor in some other way. Thus, we have confirmation that 'value rationality' and 'instrumental rationality' cannot be referred to action pure and simple, but to the motivation of the person who acts. They can indeed be brought back respectively to the 'ethics of ultimate end' and the 'ethics of responsibility'.[171] And this is a further proof of the fact that – exactly as Mises made plain – they refer to the importance of the objective to be attained, to the type of relationship carried on by the subject with his own purposes: a relationship which can be one of identification with them or merely of using them as an instrument.

It is a situation well described by Alfred Schutz:

> Any end is merely a means for another end; any project is projected within a system of higher order. For this very reason any choosing between projects refers to a previously chosen system of connected projects of a higher order. In our daily life our projected ends are means within a preconceived particular plan – for the hour or the year, for work or for leisure – and all of these particular plans are subjected to our plan for life as the most universal one.[172]

When the hierarchy of ends has been defined, the rationality of action can only be one thing – that is, it refers exclusively to the choice of means.

7

THE EARLY PARSONS
Between sociology and economics

The 'death' of Spencer and the expulsion of Simmel

In Chapter 3, we have seen how methodological collectivism is, in the works of Comte and Marx, made to serve political collectivism. In the following chapter, we have pointed out how the same phenomenon occurs in Durkheim. But we have also shown how Marx and Engels, when they wanted to give scientific appearance to their writings, used methodological individualism. And we have also illustrated how it is possible to read Durkheim's work 'individualistically', in such a way as to shed light on its original scientific inadequacy.

This shows that genuinely sociological results are not the prerogative of methodological collectivism. And it shows that the adoption of this method serves only the person who, wishing to carry out political preferences of a collectivistic character, tries to maintain the impossibility of the 'open society'; this is expressed in the elimination of individual autonomy and creativity, and in the prohibition of understanding the genesis and development of norms and social institutions.

There is no link of this kind in the case of methodological individualism; it does not serve political individualism. As Joseph Schumpeter wrote, *political* individualism and *methodological* individualism 'do not have even the most insignificant element in common';[1] the individualistic method does not decree a priori the impossibility of a social system of a collectivistic type; it only shows that it is based on the 'privileged point of view on the world', on an economy that is not competitive and that is therefore inefficient, and so on.

We have also seen in the previous two chapters how it is possible to reach, by means of the 'individualistic' reading of Durkheim, a convergence between the results that he achieved and those reached by 'individualistic' sociologists such as Spencer and Simmel. In addition, we have pointed out how the 'convergences' can be extended to Max Weber and, moreover, can refer to economics and sociology: Menger and Simmel, and Weber himself, and Mises. Thus, a methodological accord can be suggested that links Mandeville, Hume and Smith and that can be extended to include the 'individualistic' reading of

131

Durkheim and the other scholars, economists and sociologists already mentioned.

We have recalled, too, in previous chapters, the importance attributed to Smith and Menger by Albion Small. Small, like Simmel, tried to give sociology a 'firm methodological foundation'.[2]

All these 'convergences' could have been collected on this side of the sociological frontiers by Talcott Parsons, the scholar, who after the demise of the 'founding fathers', dedicated himself to identifying a point at which the different 'traditions of sociological research' and political economy could be gathered together. In his *Structure of Social Action*, and in other writings related to it, he made himself the long-winded interpreter.[3] But Parsons, who reached the right 'cross-roads' at the opportune moment, embarked on a path not unlike Durkheim's 'sociologistic' one. He did not succeed in 'purging' Durkheim's work of holism, and he created a 'convergence' between Marshall, Weber and Pareto, in which the common denominator was supplied by Durkheim. In this way, he made himself responsible for a series of alterations and distortions (of which more later). And what is more serious, he 'skipped' or threw out authors who would have demonstrated most conspicuously the inadequacy of his own theoretical program.

The 'coup de théâtre' by which Parsons freed himself from Spencer is well known: 'Spencer is dead'.[4] But the one who knowingly killed him was in fact Parsons himself, when he attributed to him ideas such as: 'He and those who thought like him were confident that evolution would carry the process on almost indefinitely in the same direction cumulatively',[5] or: 'Spencer believed that religion arose from the pre-scientific conceptions of men about the empirical facts of their own nature and their environment. It was, in fact, the product of ignorance and error. Religious ideas would, with the progress of knowledge, be replaced by science'.[6] And yet we know quite well, as pointed out in Chapter 5, that for Spencer 'social progress is not unilinear'[7]; and we know he thought that the 'Universe is an insoluble problem' and that he drew a clear line between the boundaries of science and those of the 'unknowable'.[8]

The fate that befell Georg Simmel is not dissimilar. He was in fact one of the authors whom Parsons excluded from his *Structure of Social Action*. He had originally drawn up a chapter, the first part of which contained a brief treatment of Simmel. But this was later omitted, and in the *Structure of Social Action* only the second part of this chapter was included under the heading of *A Note on Gemeinschaft and Gesellschaft*.[9]

It is well known that when Jeffrey Alexander asked a specific question about the missing pages on Simmel, Parsons offered several explanations. He first of all referred to the lack of space;[10] and yet this could not have been the reason, since it is clear that such a problem would not have been resolved by the omission of these few pages, the value of which we shall consider later. Instead, the fact is that he did not consider Simmel to be one of 'his' authors. At any rate, in his answer to Alexander, Parsons added:

It is true that Simmel's programme does not fit my convergence thesis. Not only was this the case, but his position had been used, as relatively few people are still aware, as the take-off for an attempt to build a social system theory which I considered to be fundamentally mistaken. This began in Germany with a large work by Leopold von Wiese, with the title *Beziehungslehre*.[11]

Again, Parsons said:

I am not personally very clear just why there is a Simmel *revival* . . . There is a general search for alternatives to what I still regard as the 'main line' of development, which goes back to Weber and Durkheim. Furthermore, I am entirely settled in my conviction that the attempts to disprove the convergence in that area have failed miserably.[12]

And referring to Simmel's *Philosophie des Geldes*, Parsons explained that he was 'unable to make any serious use of it', because it 'seemed' to him 'off on quite a different track'.[13]

These 'confessions' about the 'individualist' Simmel throw light also on the 'sentence of death' pronounced on the 'individualist' Spencer. These authors did not 'adapt themselves' to Parsons' plan and it was necessary to avoid them somehow. This is a conclusion that would make an examination of the omitted pages on Simmel completely superfluous. However, they are recommended as a preliminary example of the alterations and distortions for which Parsons was responsible in his attempt to square the circle of his own theoretical proposal. For the moment, it is worthwhile considering two points.

The non-contractual elements of the contract

Under the obvious influence of Durkheim, Parsons wrote:

Hence, for there to exist contractual elements in the relations of individuals on a large scale there must exist in the same social system other elements of a different order not formulated in the conception of the contractual relation. These have been found to lie, above all, in the institutional framework within which these relations are formed. And, just in so far as this institutional framework is important for the concrete situation, the latter will not be accounted for *solely* as a resultant of the *ad hoc* interests of the contracting parties . . . Some mode of differentiation between the resultant aspects of form of relationship and other elements of it must be found. This Simmel's conceptual scheme entirely fails to provide.[14]

And yet, as we have already mentioned, for Simmel 'exchange and regulated exchange' emerged 'together'.[15] Hence, there are also 'non-contractual' elements. This is why Simmel himself said:

> It is a prejudice to assume that every socially regulated relationship has developed historically out of a similar form which is individually and not socially regulated. . . . Exchange transcends the subjective forms of appropriation such as robbery and gifts . . . and so exchange is socially regulated in the first possible form of supra-subjectivity alternative.[16]

Sociologism

Despite the criticisms mentioned above, Parsons recognised that in Simmel

> the institutional aspect of social systems . . . was clearly thought of as something analytically separable from the immediate 'motives' of individuals . . . It was something which could be thought of as 'canalizing' their actions in certain directions which would not have been taken without its existence. It was a 'mold' into which the pliable material of action is poured. And this emergent quality arises through the process of interaction as such. This, and this only, is the grain of truth in the 'organic' theories of society.[17]

Parsons added in a note: 'On this basis Simmel can quite legitimately be placed within the "sociologistic" school'.[18]

By insisting here that the 'emergent quality', which cannot be anything other than unintentional consequences, 'arises through the process of interaction as such', Parsons contradicted his own declaration, referring back to the preceding point, according to which this 'quality' cannot be the 'resultant [what sort of resultant?] of the *ad hoc* interests of the contracting parties'. What counts, however, is another aspect of the matter: this is the carelessness with which Parsons placed Simmel in the 'sociologistic school'. Did Parsons not know about the dispute between Simmel and Durkheim? Was he not aware of Simmel's interminable and harsh criticism in his confrontations with 'social realism'? Did he not recall Simmel's refusal to consider society as something different from the 'sum' of its parts?[19] Above all, can a scholar 'push around' or exclude 'data' that refute or falsify his own theory?

The misunderstanding of the rational construction of preferences

In the previously quoted letter to Jeffrey Alexander, Parsons showed regret that insufficient importance had been attached to the questions he had raised on the *status* of economic theory.[20] He also made a declaration that lends itself to acting as a key to the interpretation of his intellectual journey:

> There is a very important sense in which the fundamental formulation of the problem was derived from Weber and it was this that motivated my study of Marshall as an 'orthodox' economist and led me to devote a great deal of attention to Pareto.[21]

But what is there in Parsons' criticism of economic theory that he derived from Weber? That is soon answered. As can be recalled from the previous chapter, Weber battled against the idea that the scale of subjective preferences can be constructed rationally. In doing this, however, he went too far, because he believed that political economy – including marginalism in all its versions – was responsible for the notion of the life of men as 'the object of their "enterprise", which is carried out according to calculation'.[22] We already know Mises's comment on this statement. Here we can add – it was Mises himself who recalled it – that Weber, despite holding a professorial chair of economics, lamented 'the extreme limitation of his knowledge of modern and classical economics' and expressed the fear that 'time would not permit him to fill these regrettable gaps'.[23] Obviously, it is not a question of the level of Weber's training in economics. It is rather the fact that Parsons took as his point of departure the misunderstanding into which Weber fell. Could Parsons have freed himself from this misunderstanding?

Mises's 'Soziologie und Geschichte', which appeared originally in 1929 in the *Archiv für Sozialwissenschaft und Sozialpolitik*, was cited in the bibliography at the end of *The Structure of Social Action* with an explanation that pages 470–97 were devoted to Weber. For our purposes, however, it is useful to mention that there was more about Mises. Restricting ourselves to the works most directly concerned with the problem, we should recall the pages dedicated to Weber in the *Kritik des Interventionismus* of 1929, the first and second editions of *Gemeinwirtschaft* (1922 and 1932, respectively), and the *Grundprobleme des Nationalökomie* of 1933 which, among other things, includes 'Soziologie und Geschichte'.[24]

Thus, Parsons had enough elements to enable him to free himself from Weber's misunderstanding. But he did not do it. He even 'projected' the misunderstanding on to Lionel Robbins's *Essay on the Nature and Significance of Economic Science*, to which he devoted a harsh comment.[25] Let us proceed step by step.

Robbins's essay, although not lacking methodological uncertainties, was written partly under the influence of Mises.[26] Therefore, it is not surprising that, on the subject of preferences, Robbins wrote:

> In my purchase of bread I may be interested solely in the comparison between the bread and the other things in the circle of exchange on

which I might have spent the money. But I may be interested too in the happiness of my baker. There may exist between us certain liens which make it preferable for me to buy bread from him, rather than procure it from his competitor who is willing to sell it a little cheaper. In exactly the same way, in my sale of my own labour or the hire of my property, I may be interested only in the things which I receive as a result of the transaction; or I may be interested also in the experience of labouring in one way rather than another, or in the prestige or discredit, the feeling of virtue or shame, in hiring out my property in this line rather than in that.[27]

The passage from Robbins does not move far from the analogous positions, already described, that were taken by Mises in 'Soziologie und Geschichte'. To back this up, Robbins then cited in a note Wickstead's *Commonsense of Political Economy* and referred to Marshall; in particular, he placed the latter author with others, among them Smith, considering them all to be 'a representative sample of what would be regarded as the more hard-boiled English tradition'.[28]

Of Smith, Robbins cited the tenth chapter of the first book of the *Wealth of Nations*, from which we have already discussed, among others, the following passage:

> Pecuniary wages and profit, indeed, are everywhere in Europe extremely different, according to the different employments of labour and stock. But this difference arises partly from certain circumstances in the employments themselves, which, either really, or at least in the imagination of men, make up for a small pecuniary gain in some and counter-balance a great one in others.[29]

But, even without this reference, we know very well that Mandeville, Hume and Smith never theorised about constructing the scale of individual preferences rationally.

However, this going back to Smith is by no means useless: Parsons did not only disagree with Robbins, he also extended his criticism – not unlike Max Weber – to the whole of political economy. In order to do this, he leant heavily on Elie Halévy, whose work *La formation du radicalisme philosophique* he judged as 'the most penetrating account available of the aspects of utilitarian thought which are important for this discussion' in which he found himself involved.[30] And yet, in doing this, Parsons established a false equality: that between political economy and philosophical radicalism. This shows that he did not know enough about Smith and his cultural collocation; nor did he manage to perceive the differences, to some extent indicated also by Halévy, between the evolutionistic positions of Mandeville, Hume and Smith and the 'constructivistic' positions of Bentham, James Mill and Ricardo.[31] It also shows that

Parsons was not able to grasp the sociologico-economic significances of Austrian marginalism.[32]

The similarity between philosophical radicalism and political economy is the crucial point of Parsons' criticism of economic theory. Parsons identified in this a scheme of action characterised by three elements (we shall speak later of a fourth element, the 'randomness' of ends): atomism, rationality, empiricism.[33] If we give some attention to what he meant by 'rationality' and 'empiricism', we can take the argument a useful step forward.

Parsons wrote:

> the position taken by political economy represents the polar type of case where rationality is maximized. It is the case where the actor's knowledge of the situation is, if not complete in any ultimate sense, fully adequate to the realization of his ends. Departures from the rational norm must be associated with falling short in some respect of this adequacy of knowledge. Now the significant thing in this connection is that . . . there is no other, alternative type of norm in relation to which such departures from rationality may be measured. Their characterization must be purely negative. There are two current terms which quite satisfactorily describe this – 'ignorance' and 'error' . . . The explanation must be that they are due to intrinsically understandable factors which the actor has either failed to understand or positively misunderstood . . . It follows directly from these considerations that if and in so far as the actor comes to know these elements in action, and is able to act rationally relative to them, it must be in the form of acquiring scientifically valid knowledge of them, of eliminating the ignorance and error. *Being rational consists in these terms precisely in becoming a scientist relative to one's own action. Short of the ultimate boundaries of science, irrationality, then, is only possible so long as actors are not in possession of the logically possible complement of knowledge affecting human affairs.*[34]

The definition of rationality that Parsons ascribed to political economy brings us to Descartes. He had in fact stated:

> Those long chains of reasons, all quite simple and quite easy, which geometers are wont to employ in reaching their most difficult demonstrations, had given me occasion to imagine that all the possible objects of human knowledge were linked together in the same way, if we accepted none as true that was not so in fact, and kept to the right order in deducing one from the other, there was nothing so remote that it could not be reached, nothing so hidden that it could not be discovered.[35]

Commenting on this passage, Ortega y Gasset wrote:

> Man . . . can know the truth about everything. It is enough that he should not be afraid in the face of the complexity of the problems, that he should not let his mind be clouded by his feelings: if he uses his intellect with serenity and self-control, particularly if he uses it in an orderly way, he will find that his faculty of thought is *ratio*, reason, and that with reason man has an almost magic power to throw light on everything, to make what is opaque become crystal clear, penetrating it with analysis and in this way clarifying it. *Thus the world of reality and the world of thought are two cosmoses that coincide*, each of them compact and continuous, in which nothing remains fragmentary, isolated and unreachable.[36]

The reference to Descartes, and Ortega's comment, help us to draw a conclusion. The rationality that Parsons attributed to economic theory is, to use Hayek's well-known expression, of a 'constructivistic' type; this is confirmed by the fact that Parsons himself picked out in Hobbes's system 'almost a pure case' of that utilitarianism on which he considered political economy to be based.[37]

Now we can see what Parsons meant by 'empiricism'. The schema of action present in philosophical radicalism is characterised, not only by rationality, but also by the fact that the ends to be sought are of an exclusively 'empirical' character. And yet Parsons wrote: 'the fact that empirical reality can be modified by action shows that this empirical reality . . . is not a closed system but is itself significantly related to the other aspects of reality'.[38] There are, Parsons added, finalities that exist 'outside the realm of empirical observability' and that can be called 'transcendental ends'.[39] In particular, one can think of 'the actor as attempting to attain only a subjective state of mind – happiness, for instance'.[40] Parsons explained in more detail: 'I wish to distinguish "objective" empirical ends from "subjective" empirical ends. The attainment of both is verifiable, but in different ways. This is to assume . . . the anti-behavioristic position, that scientific observation of an individual's subjective state of mind is possible and valid'.[41]

Thus, accounts balance perfectly. The rationalism that Parsons attributed to political economy is precisely that 'constructivism' which is accompanied by a 'tendency to dispose of all values as things which do not refer to facts (and are therefore "metaphysical"), from a tendency to treat them as pure matters of emotions and therefore not justifiable, or meaningless'.[42] This is what gives life to 'objectivity', to the scientific demand to suppress the 'personal' element of action, a demand which is found in Comte's position, in 'behaviourism' and 'physicalism'.

If this is so, we can share Parsons' criticism of the attempt by philosophical radicalism to define preferences rationally by means of the 'maximization of rationality'; Bentham proposed the creation of a mathematical science of pleasure and pain. Moreover, we can level the same accusation of 'constructivism' at the economic theory of general equilibrium. Here, as Parsons himself emphasised,[43] the time variable is suppressed and one is directed towards the achievement of a predefined 'optimum'. In fact,

in the typical models of general equilibrium, prices are initially unknown. And the theory serves precisely to calculate the prices required in order to attain the harmony of individual equilibria with the general equilibrium . . . [so that] the final optimum condition [the Paretian optimum] is actually pre-arranged: one already knows where one wishes to arrive. Rationalism is teleological, reason knows *a priori* what the optimum is like, and it is a matter of persuading the maximizing individuals to go towards it simultaneously.[44]

In other words: the 'optimum' is rationally predetermined, and subjects act rationally in order to achieve it.

This is why Israel Kirzner wrote:

If we are to assume that all economizing decisions are indeed 'correct', we have necessarily to confine ourselves to a fully coordinated, equilibrium world – something imaginable only on the basis of universal mutual omniscience concerning what market participants can and will choose to do. To *confine* ourselves and our economic analysis to the context of full mutual omniscience means is not merely to accept a wildly unrealistic assumption; it is to confess that our model of the economizing world is *unable to throw light upon any process of adjustment* . . . in the real world of imperfect knowledge.[45]

However, as we have anticipated, considerations of this kind are not applicable to Smith's theory or to Austrian marginalism. Here the actor does not seek the 'optimum' but 'points' of convenience, of 'possible co-living'; he is never in a state of equilibrium (and it is for this reason that he acts) and nor is society in equilibrium. It follows that the individual is not an 'atom' which adapts irreversibly to the situation. On the contrary, he is an actor who contributes to determining the situation by means of creative 'challenges' or 'responses'; the same reading of the expectations of others involves the creative element. Therefore, individual ends are not endured mechanically or passively; they form part of a choice in which the pre-rational or creative moment cannot be suppressed and upon which weighs the uncertainty of attainment.

In search of the 'voluntaristic-creative' element

In the theories formulated by Weber, Marshall, Pareto and Durkheim, Parsons picked out a 'voluntaristic-creative' element of action with which he proposed to pursue two objectives contextually:

a   to overcome the positions of philosophical radicalism, by demonstrating that the individual is an 'active subject';
b   to make the 'voluntaristic-creative' element into the variable for the resolution of the problem of social order.

Max Weber

Parsons wrote:

> In the 'economic' aspect of modern life [he] attempts to demonstrate the existence of a non-economic, ethical element, the idea of selfless, disinterested devotion to a 'Calling', i.e. any ordinary occupation, as an end in itself. This attitude towards work, conspicuous for the absence of calculation of personal advantages, Weber finds to be both a most prominent element in the modern economic world and indispensable to its functioning. This attitude toward acquisitive occupations, and not any avaricious interest in gain as such, is what Weber calls the *spirit of capitalism*.[46]

The first questions are these: Are choices made 'rationally with respect to value' absent in Mandeville and Smith? Certainly not. Had Smith not said that 'difference arises partly from certain circumstances in the employments themselves'? Had he not written that 'honour makes a great part of the reward of all honourable professions'?[47] And again, had he not asserted that 'Disagreeableness and disgrace affect the profits of stock in the same way as the wages of labour'?[48] And so on.

However, Parsons did not wish to demonstrate only the existence of a 'creative' element in action; he wished also to make of it, as we have already said, the 'non-egoistic' variable which is able to give order to collective living. This is why he insisted on the 'selfless' of the 'Calling'. But this raises other questions: Can the 'Calling' be disinterested? Does it not coincide with the existential project that each of us is? Indeed, this project is not 'constructed' rationally, but do we not have an interest in fulfilling it? Have we not seen in the previous chapter that, even in the case of 'value-rational' decisions, the actor assesses the 'possible cost' and is inclined to put up with it? Above all, do we not need, for the fulfilment of our project, the 'availability of the Other'? The fact is that in Parsons' position there is a strong dose of Kantism, an ethical formalism incompatible with Weber's actual position and with the whole content of 'non-formal ethics'.

It is as well to make this point clear. There is no doubt that we need to leave behind philosophical radicalism and its 'calculus of pleasures and pains'. But the alternative cannot be the 'mysticism of duty',[49] because this too is the child of intellectualistic exasperation. That is to say, if philosophical radicalism uses reason to make the calculus of pleasures and pains, and in this way also to define preferences, Kantian ethics resorts to reason in the presumption that by this it can take itself out of the calculus. But it is setting out on a road that does not exist: seeing that in action it is only given to man, after the autonomy of the existential project has been made clear, to choose between what is *immediately* convenient (to take advantage of favourable circumstances to free himself from social 'burdens') and what is convenient in the *medium or long term* (to respect norms, in spite of the pressure of favourable circumstances, in order to be able to develop the relationship and obtain more in the future). It follows that however noble the individual objectives may appear to be which each person is interested in pursuing, actions we consider to be exemplary or endowed with lofty morality are simply those in which the 'convenient' result is deferred. Hence, exemplarity, extension of the period of 'waiting' and uncertainty go along at the same pace.

So, it is not out of place here to recall what Max Scheler wrote: Kant constructed 'a colossus of steel and bronze' which 'obstructs the way of philosophy toward a concrete and evidential *theory of moral values*': if 'Kant's terrifyingly sublime formula, with its emptiness, remains valid . . . we are robbed of the clear vision of the fullness of the moral world and of its qualities as well as of the conviction which we might have that this world is something *binding*'.[50]

Alfred Marshall

Parsons recognised Marshall as a child of philosophical radicalism, an exponent of the doctrine of 'maximum satisfaction'. This is perfectly relevant. As it happens, Marshall, who had also detected the 'cracks' in this doctrine, had concluded:

> they show that much remains to be done, by a careful collection of the statistics of demand and supply, and a scientific interpretation of their results, in order to discover what are the limits of the work that society can do towards turning the economic actions of individuals into those channels in which they will add the most to the sum total of happiness.[51]

However, in his attempt to project on to it the idea of 'Calling' or *Beruf*, Parsons read Marshall's work through Weberian 'lenses'. The opportunity was offered by what Marshall described as 'needs in relation to activities'.[52] To what does this refer? Marshall wrote:

> while wants are the rulers of life among the lower animals, it is to changes in the forms of efforts and activities that we must turn when in search for the keynotes of the history of mankind.[53]

And he added:

> Speaking broadly therefore, although it is man's wants in the earliest stages of his development that give rise to his activities, yet afterwards each new step upwards is to be regarded as the development of new activities giving rise to new wants, rather than of new wants giving rise to new activities . . . It is not true therefore that 'the theory of consumption is the scientific basis of economics'. For much that is of chief interest in the science of wants, is borrowed from the science of efforts and activities. These two supplement one another; either is incomplete without the other. But if either, more than the other, may claim to be the interpreter of the history of man, whether on the economic side or any other, it is the science of activities and not that of wants.[54]

Parsons commented:

> Marshall has introduced a factor quite outside the scope of the ordinary utility theory . . . Concretely the activities and qualities of character he had in mind are those embodying the virtues . . . of energy, initiative, enterprise . . . In such activities, these virtues . . . are thought of . . . strictly . . . as ends in themselves without thought of reward.[55]

It is clear: Parsons projected on to Marshall the Weberian idea of 'Calling'. Therefore, it must be repeated that, unlike what he appeared to think, those who feel themselves 'called' are, precisely because of that, 'interested' in the accomplishment of their projects and always need the 'availability' of others in order to attain this. And furthermore, is the 'thought of reward' absent? Parsons wrote that 'the wealth acquired during the process is not the purpose but rather the by-product'.[56] Is that really how things stand?

Smith had declared: 'nobody but a beggar chuses to depend chiefly upon the benevolence of his fellow-citizens'.[57] In other words, the gain is subordinate to the services that one renders to others; exactly as in the 'vocation' on which Parsons insisted, the person who feels himself called to produce or innovate can take on greater risks,[58] but his objective is always that of being able to serve 'his fellow citizens'. Thus, profit is not an accidental 'by-product'. It is rather the measure of the capacity to satisfy the demands of others; it is the demonstration that our 'Calling' is not impossible, that it can overcome the 'limitations' and the 'conditions' imposed by the socio-historical context. A 'vocation' external to the world of production has to endure economic 'limitations' and 'conditions' in a broad sense. A productive project, on the other hand, has to be measured against economic 'limitations' and 'conditions' in a strict sense – that is to say, expressed in monetary terms. This is why Parsons was constrained to recognise that the 'virtues' of the 'Calling', 'as much as . . . the other "utility" elements, characterise the modern system of *free enterprise*'.[59]

Therefore, it is not worth emphasising, as Parsons did, the critical position taken by Marshall towards Jevons. As is well known, marginalism rejects the theory of the 'cost of production' and makes the value of goods depend on consumer demand. Marshall 'reinterpreted' Ricardo and sought to give new life to the theory of the cost of production. In doing this, he challenged Jevons's criticisms of Ricardo and those of 'Professors Walras and Carl Menger, who were contemporaries with Jevons and [of] Professors von Boehm-Bawerk and Wieser, who were later'.[60]

Parsons wrote on this subject:

> It becomes evident, then, that the real basis of Marshall's discontent with pure utility theory is something other than a conviction of the importance of the other factors in the positivistic repertoire. The fact is that his 'activities' have no place there at all. They constitute rather a 'value' factor . . . They are an expression of ends or wants but not in the same sense as the wants of utility theory. For the latter are, for the purposes of utility analysis, significant only as constituting the ultimate basis of demand functions. Marshall's activity values are, on the other hand, directly embodied in specific modes of activity, essentially independent of demand.[61]

Parsons believed that in this way he could give greater force to the idea of productive activity as an end not interested in gain. What we have already said about Weber refutes this idea. And yet we can follow a further itinerary to be found in the pages of Marshall himself.

Marshall regarded the 'stationary state' as a simple instrument of analysis.[62] Talking about the future, he wrote:

> On every side further openings are sure to offer themselves, all of which will tend to change the character of our social and industrial life, and to enable us to turn to account vast stores of capital in providing new gratifications and new ways of economizing effort by expending it in anticipation of distant wants. *There seems to be no good reason for believing that we are anywhere near a stationary state in which there will be no new important wants to be satisfied*; in which there will be

no more room profitably investing present effort in providing for the future, and in which the accumulation of wealth will cease to have any reward. The whole history of man shows that his wants expand with the grow of his wealth and knowledge.[63]

This means that for Marshall the life of man is in a permanent state of disequilibrium. But, if this is so, 'activities' cannot be, contrary to what Parsons claimed, 'disinterested' or 'essentially independent of demand'; instead, they are an attempt, never crowned with complete success, and always being renewed, to bridge this disequilibrium, without which even the discovery of new needs would be totally inexplicable. Hence, Marshall's polemic against the theory which makes the value of goods depend on consumer demand, is misplaced.

This conclusion can be supported further. If it is recognised that individual and collective life are in permanent disequilibrium, one has to give up the illusion that it is possible to reach an 'optimum', a static concept that does not take into account the continual changing of individual projects. Marshall could therefore have given up the doctrine of 'maximum satisfaction': individuals economise, but the very fact that they live in a condition of disequilibrium indicates that they can improve their position and, moreover, can never reach any 'optimum'. Parsons should have noted well that Mises, a harsh critic of the idea of equilibrium, had written some time before:

> In any economic system which is in process of change all economic activity is based upon an uncertain future ... Economic activity is necessarily speculative, because it is based on an uncertain future. Speculation is the link that binds isolated economic action to the economic activity of society as a whole.[64]

Consequently, 'speculation' is a risky attempt to foresee uncertain future, namely the future actions of the Other. But why do we try to foresee the actions of Others? The answer is simple: to save our own actions from failure; this demonstrates that 'activities' cannot be 'disinterested.'

Vilfredo Pareto

In order to isolate the 'non-economic' elements of action, Parsons dwelt in the first place on what Pareto called logical actions and non-logical actions.[65] In this way, he took a path which can cause confusion: because the rationality contained in Pareto's logical action, unlike what happens in Weber or Mises, has to be such not only for the person who acts but also for those 'who have more extensive knowledge'.[66]

Parsons would have done better to point at once in another direction, a direction, moreover, that was not unknown to him.[67] By doing this, he could have made his task easier. In fact, Pareto maintained that the concept of utility is affected by 'vagueness' (indetermination).[68] In other words:

> if we take a state of material prosperity as our limit state for a people, our utility will not be greatly different from the entity that practical man designate by that name, but it will differ widely from the ideal envisaged by the ascetic. Conversely, if we take the state of perfect asceticism as the limit state, our 'utility' will coincide with the entity to which the ascetic aspires, but will differ altogether from the ideal of the practical man.[69]

Pareto drew a conclusion from this:

> a society determined exclusively by 'reason' does not exist and cannot exist, and that not because 'prejudices' in human beings prevent them from following the dictates of 'reason', but because the data of the problem that presumably is to be solved by logico-experimental reasoning are entirely unknown.[70]

This is equivalent to saying, to return to terminology already used here, that the scale of preferences cannot be constructed rationally. But this was very clear to Smith and to the exponents of the Austrian School; and it was clear to Robbins himself, however criticised by Parsons.

Let us look into the other aspect of the question. As in the case of Marshall and Weber, Parsons used the 'creative' element pointed out by Pareto, in order to seek to orient socially individual action. It was for this reason that he transformed (aided in this by the 'residues' of sociality) the Paretian 'residues' into a normative framework, capable of conferring order on the actions of individuals.[71] If, with Schumpeter, however, we consider the 'residues' as the 'objective determinants of actual behavior',[72] we have to conclude that in some way they represent what moves the actor and what gives rise to, but does not solve, the social problem; instead, 'derivations' are social 'justifications'. This leads towards the articulation of an unintentional order, very different, as we shall soon see, from what Parsons theorised.

Émile Durkheim

Parsons wrote about him:

> Durkheim's primary concern is with the understanding of a society characterized by 'economic individualism'. He chooses the division of labor as his subject because of the central place occupied by that conception in individualistic economic thought. His fundamental thesis is that a highly differentiated economic order cannot be

understood as resting entirely upon 'contractual relations' . . . that is, on the determination of the concrete relations of the individuals alone by the direct and immediate economic interest of each. There is, on the contrary, present in all *concrete* contractual relations a qualitatively different element which we can call the *institution* of the contract, a body of rules and norms, both legal and informal, determining the conditions according to which contracts are and may be entered to . . . In Durkheim's view, it is only by virtue of the presence of this 'non-contractual' element that a *system* of contractual relations is possible at all.[73]

Here, however, Parsons' attitude is reversed. Parsons did not start from the 'creative' elements of a 'disinterested' type to make them into the resolutive variable of the problem of social order. He singled out the 'normative' elements and made their validity essential for the possibility of social life. We ought to give some attention to this schema because it leads to the 'extinction' of individual autonomy. Action is no longer free and even though, in a debatable way, 'disinterested', it is imposed from above.

The problem of the 'common system of ultimate ends'

We should make the question of social order more explicit. Parsons said:

> An optimum is essentially a static concept: it is an optimum adjustment to certain fixed factors.[74] . . . But then . . . [the] independence [of ends] disappears and they are assimilated to the conditions of the situation . . . action becomes determined entirely by its conditions.[75]

Nevertheless, there is an alternative. 'In conformity with the voluntarism of the Christian background', utilitarianism never doubted the 'reality of the agency of the actor'.[76] Thus, 'the active agency of the actor in the choice of ends is an independent factor in action – and the end element must be random'.[77] And yet, if '[ends] may be held to vary at random', the utilitarians failed 'to consider the relations of ends to each other':[78] the problem of their compatibility, of social order, arises. In this way, one falls into the 'utilitarian dilemma': either ends have no independence, and 'action becomes . . . a function of its conditions',[79] or the randomness of ends is assumed and the problem of social order is opened up.

Parsons put the problem of order in the following terms:

> It is logically possible to conceive a society composed of a plurality of individuals . . . each thinking of and related to the others only in the capacity of means to each others' ends or hindrances to them. Such a society is, to be sure, logically conceivable, but there are sound

reasons for believing it is not empirically possible . . . there is no reason to believe that the ultimate ends of individuals should be automatically compatible with each other. In the absence of some positive factor bringing them into coherence, such a society would be a mere chaos of conflicting individuals – would in fact be Hobbes's celebrated state of nature. But of course in such a state human life would be impossible.[80]

Parsons added:

There are three logical possibilities of escape from this dilemma. One is Hobbes's own solution, that the ends are not integrated and brought into harmony at all, but that coercive authority restrains the actions of individuals . . . so as to prevent the conflict being fatal to order and security. The second is the assumption that in somehow, for some unknown reasons, ends are not in conflict – that there is a 'natural identity of interests'. This is of course a strictly inexplicable pre-established harmony attributed to a metaphysical 'nature'. It has in fact lurked in the background of much . . . economic theory. There is a third possibility, that men's ends should be not separated, and either forcibly restrained or miraculously compatible, but in fact, in a given society, held in common.[81]

We should look more closely at the 'solution' that Parsons judged 'lurked in the background of much . . . economic theory', and at the 'third possibility' to which he clearly linked his own name and in which 'men's ends' are not 'separate' but are 'held in common'.

The natural identity of interests

Here Parsons was once again indebted to Elie Halévy.[82] In fact, it was he who declared that Mandeville and Smith had based their ideas on the principle of the 'natural identity of interests' and that 'political economy, ever since Adam Smith, has rested entirely' on that principle.[83]

However, things are not as simple as that. The 'natural identity of interests' was defined by Halévy in such a way: 'By the mechanism of exchange and of the division of labour, individuals, without desiring or knowing it, and while pursuing each his own interest, are working for the direct realisation of the general interest'.[84] Parsons skipped the expression 'without desiring or knowing it', and spoke of a 'rational recognition' of the 'natural identity of interests'.[85] Above all, he put philosophical radicalism under the heading of this theory; and so he altered Halévy's position even more. Halévy had explained:

> According to the principle of the natural identity of interests, every individual is the judge . . . of his own interests . . . According to the principle of the artificial identification of interests, it is the benevolence and the competence of the legislator that is counted on to establish the harmony of interests, by means of limitations imposed on individual liberties.[86]

Halévy had pointed out, with reference to Bentham, that 'the primitive and original form in which in his doctrine the principle of utility is invested is the principle of the artificial identification of interests'.[87] Moreover, he had emphasised that Bentham only 'occasionally' applied the principle of the 'fusion of interests'; Halévy also added that in philosophical radicalism the 'artificial identification of interests' serves precisely to 'refute' the 'natural' identification.[88]

Some clarification is necessary. As Friedrich von Hayek perceived, Halévy's expression 'the natural identity of interests' is misleading: individuals compose their interests 'without desiring or knowing it'.[89] Hence, there is no 'natural identity of interests'; there is a process that produces unintentional order. However, Parsons made some greater mistakes. In fact, he was rigidly linked to a superficial acceptance of Halévy's formula; he obstinately rejected the possibility that it could indicate a social process, a permanent *to do*, rather than a 'strictly inexplicable pre-established harmony attributed to a metaphysical *nature*'.[90]

Instead, 'harmony' is closely connected with the positions of philosophical radicalism. But this harmony – it is as well to make this quite clear – is not in such a case established metaphysically; it is constructed artificially. This is the reason for Herbert Spencer's polemic against Bentham,[91] a polemic that Parsons, even though his understanding came through Halévy,[92] should have known and assessed the consequences of.

Not only that. It was widely known that philosophical radicalism was a paradigmatic expression of social 'constructivism'. J. M. Guyau had written:

> Bentham's disciples compared their master to Descartes. '*Donnez-moi la matière et le mouvement*', said Descartes, 'et je ferai le monde'. Bentham could say, in his turn, 'Give me human affections, joy and sorrow, pain and pleasure, and I shall create a moral world. I shall produce not only justice, but also generosity, patriotism, philanthropy, and all the amiable and sublime virtues in their purity.'[93]

This brings us to Descartes' extolling of Sparta, ruled by a single lawgiver and led towards a single end,[94] and it shows us that philosophical radicalism is closely linked to the idea of an order given intentionally. That is, it presupposes an omniscience which, as Friedrich von Hayek explained, is 'never satisfied in real life and which, if it were ever true, would make the existence of those bodies of rules which we call morals and law not only superfluous but unaccountable and contrary to the assumption'.[95]

However, what had the most serious effects on Parsons' schema is not the inability to see the link between philosophical radicalism and social artificialism – both in the case of an authentic natural identity of interests and in that of artificial identity, the individual has in fact to bow to an order that pre-exists life. What produces the most distorting results in Parsons is his inability to 'isolate' the position taken by Mandeville and Smith and to explore the evolutionist tradition.

The voluntaristic solution

As we have seen, Parsons bestowed on the formula of the natural identity of interests the meaning of a 'rigorously pre-established harmony' of a 'metaphysical' nature. And yet he added that it was 'basically a fortunate error' to believe that

> the identity of interests was 'in the nature of things' and that never under any circumstances was there occasion to question the stability of such an order . . . This fact may serve as a lesson to those who are overly puristic in their scientific methodology. Perhaps it is not always wise to discard even methodologically objectionable elements so long as they can serve a useful scientific function, unless one has something better to substitute. Of course the fact is that, however untenable in other respects, the postulate of the natural identity of interests was a way of stating a crucially important fact, that in some societies to an important degree there does exist an order which makes possible an approximation to the conditions required by the assumptions of classical economic theory.[96]

Thus, the question is: 'How is it possible, still making use of the general action schema, to solve the Hobbesian problem of order and yet not make use of such an objectionable metaphysical prop as the doctrine of the natural identity of interests?'[97]

Parsons' reply was based on the idea that, in order to be compatible, the actions of individuals ought to be directed by a 'socially integrated system of ultimate ends'.[98] He wrote:

> Partly *a priori* and partly empirical considerations lead to view that these ultimate ends do not occur in random fashion, but that both in the case of the individual and of the social group, they must be thought of to a significant degree integrated into a single harmonious *system*'.[99] This system is endowed precisely with 'coherence';[100] 'individuals shares a *common* system of ultimate ends'.[101]

Of course, this raises the question: Where does the 'common system of ultimate ends' come from? Parsons said that social norms 'bear directly the stamp of their origin in the common system of ultimate ends'.[102] But, if this is so, the 'ultimate ends' pre-exist norms and actions; the individual is exclusively a *rule taker*, action is heterodetermined. In such a way, we are dangerously close to the idealistic position in which the *Geist* comes about by emanation. Parsons slipped into idealism whenever he spoke of the system of ultimate ends as an entity 'hanging in the air' that heterodetermines individual actions.[103]

Hence, the 'common system of ultimate ends' coincides with Durkheim's 'collective consciousness', which is precisely, as Parsons did not fail to emphasise, 'the totality of the beliefs and sentiments common to average citizens of the same society' which 'forms a determined system which has its own life'.[104] This is why the American sociologist added:

> Durkheim was calling attention to an aspect of the normative regulation of action which is relatively 'external' to the acting of the individual. It can to a point readily be treated as a set of *given* conditions of action. But . . . it concerns not only the conditions under which men act in pursuit of their ends but enters into the formulation of the ends themselves.[105]

Again, Parsons said: 'Durkheim's main stress is on the existence of a body of norms which . . . are socially *given*'.[106]

How does one get out of this situation? Parsons took two paths. To save himself from the heteronomy of action, he did not hesitate to admit that individual ends are 'the specification, the fixing in certain forms and directions of something vaguer, less determinate, which is, however, of the order of a value-element'.[107] These words of Parsons' raise a question: Is it possible that a *vague* and *indeterminate* system should be 'the only alternative to a state of chaos'?[108] It seems clear, then, that to give an answer to the question of order, Parsons resorted to the 'common system of ultimate ends'; and yet, in extracting himself from the heterodetermination of action, he weakened the 'system' and made it *vague* and *indeterminate*.

It was at this point that he was forced to take a second direction, that of the 'mysticism of duty'. The 'common system of ultimate ends' is not imposed on individuals, but they take it on themselves 'voluntaristically', Parsons wrote:

> there is the possibility that while the norm constitutes one structural element in the concrete action it is only one. There are obstacles and resistances to its attainment which must be overcome and are, in fact, only partially overcome. Hence the failure of the actual course of action to correspond exactly with that prescribed by the norm is not proof that the latter is unimportant, but only that it is not alone

important. The existence of this resistance and its (even partial) over-coming implies another element, *effort*.[109]

There is a good deal of 'orthopaedics' in Parsons' position. He was attempting to transplant the categorical imperative into romantic idealism, which leads to a result not unlike that obtained by Hermann Cohen and his followers. In fact,

> in spite of the hatred they displayed towards Schelling and Hegel, the men from Marburg were, without realizing it, motivated by a firm resolve: they intended to raise Kantism to the same level as post-Kantian idealism, while enclosing speculative idealism firmly within Kant's *naturalistic*, Newtonian frontiers.[110]

In other words, 'romantic idealism had reproached the transcendental method for not knowing how to raise itself out of subjective thought and of being, therefore, incapable of grasping the Truth, which is accessible only to the absolute or speculative method.'[111] In order to escape from this accusation, Cohen absolutised logic, believing that he was objectifying knowledge;[112] but, in doing this, he cancelled every link between reflection and the spatio-temporal collocation of the individual. Culture remains rootless, it 'claims to be free from space and time, to be utopian and achronistic'.[113] With the categorical imperative, Cohen proposed to bring about 'ethical socialism';[114] Parsons intended to set up a 'common system of ultimate ends' which is 'hanging in the air'. For both – in the one case, socialism, in the other, social order – they were to be achieved voluntaristically.

And yet the voluntarism of action cannot hide the fact that, in Parsons' proposal, order is predefined and that the individual merely 'adapts' to it;[115] the social *process* is missing. Therefore, we have before us a false theory of action and we are in a position diametrically opposed to that which characterises the 'open society', in which order is obtained unintentionally, through agreements which concern means and not ends.

The 'sociologistic theorem'

We have seen how the 'common system of ultimate ends', to which Parsons entrusted the task of resolving the problem of social order, is a clear emanation of the concept of 'collective consciousness' used by Durkheim. Parsons also agreed with Durkheim's idea of society understood as a *sui generis* reality, a whole that is greater than the sum of its parts.

However, as we know, Parsons wrote:

> Atomistic theories are in fact empirically inadequate . . . Valid objec-tion can only be raised through what is undoubtedly a

misinterpretation, but one against which Durkheim did not adequately protect himself. It is the view that the 'individual' . . . and society . . . are concrete entities, the concrete human being known to us, and the concrete group. In this sense, it is scarcely more than a truism that society is simply an aggregate of human beings in their given relations to one another. But the 'individual' of Durkheim's argument, as became increasingly clear with the progress of his development, is not this concrete entity, but a theoretical abstraction. In the simplest sense it is the fictional human being who has never entered into any social relationship with other human beings.[116]

This means that, if we free ourselves from the 'fictional human being', society cannot be a *sui generis* reality, greater than the sum of its parts.

Even if the question is put in dynamic terms, the judgement does not change. In fact, one can say that interaction produces a new position within which are both intentional and unintentional consequences; but those who benefit from this 'new position' are the same social actors, who heap up on themselves what they produce, intentionally or not. The 'emergent' effects are above all the 'conditions' that make the relation possible and that therefore form part of the action seen in its completeness – that is to say, in which, through his own initiative, Ego adds up the 'limitations' and the 'conditions' demanded by the Other and that Ego himself decides to accept.

This is why Ludwig von Mises, emphasising the social interdependence of individuals, declared that the actor does not have the 'power' to choose what is useful for himself and to leave out what is useful to others.[117] This is true: he who plans something does not know exactly what 'price' he will have to pay for the collaboration of others. But in the action that he completes there is the 'double entry account': the objectives attained by Ego with the Other's co-operation, and that which Ego does for the benefit of the Other, in order to obtain his collaboration.[118]

However, let us return to the problem. What must be remembered here is what Parsons knew very well: that society, if we take the 'concrete' human being into consideration, cannot be a *sui generis* reality. Consistency would have forced Parsons to take a path different from Durkheim's. But he did not do so. And he kept alive the 'sociologistic theorem', the idea that society can be considered a *sui generis* reality.

It is not difficult to pick out the reasons for this inconsistency. Parsons was not able to articulate even the slightest dynamic between the individual moment and the strictly social moment. There are two conclusive variables in this inability of his. The first is his 'moralism', namely the claim to make social *justification* the grounds for action. The second in his 'hermetism' towards the unintentional consequences of intentional human actions; suffice it to say that when speaking of Weber he made only an occasional reference to the 'unanticipated indirect effects of action'.[119] If he had been sufficiently aware of the explicative power of the theory of the unintentional origins of social institutions, he could have toned down his 'moralism' and his 'subjection' towards Durkheim; or perhaps, if his 'moralism' had been less rigid, he could have been more open towards the idea of the unintentional consequences of intentional human actions, and could have realised that one can do 'good' unintentionally and live within order, without being constrained to endure any 'common system' of ends.

None of these hypotheses was worked through and so it was that, while Parsons was arguing with philosophical radicalism because of the lack of autonomy to which it condemns the individual, he proposed an equally 'lame' solution: all that remains for the individual is that he should conform to a series of ends which are imposed on him; he does not act but is 'acted upon', and order, to use a favourite expression of Friedrich Hayek and Michael Oakeshott, is of the 'teleocratic' type.[120]

Here is the point we are interested in. If we think that individuals can regulate their co-living through a network of 'conditions', everyone must have the liberty to choose his own ends; if we think that individuals cannot produce spontaneously the norms and institutions capable of regulating collective life, we are saying, as Parsons did, that society 'has properties not derivable from those of its constituent units by direct generalization';[121] and, as a result, it is necessary to convey the life of each person towards a hierarchized system of collective ends. In its turn, this produces the demand for a standard, a norm or a 'privileged point of view on the world', to which the hierarchisation of these same ends is entrusted. This was Parsons' perspective. He did not suspect that the adoption of a 'privileged point of view on the world' determines the birth of intentional order and of a closed system; and he sought to find the application of the 'sociologistic theorem' also in Pareto and Weber.

First, let us consider Pareto. Here, Parsons overlooked a significant situation – the fact that Pareto himself, probably arguing directly against the positions taken by Durkheim, had declared:

> It is a banal and often-repeated observation that a society is not a simple juxtaposition of individuals, and that by the mere fact of living in society they acquire new characteristics. So, if we could observe men living in isolation and men living in society, we would have the opportunity of learning in what way they differ . . . But the first term of this comparison is missing and only the second is known to us.[122]

Hence, for Pareto, there is no 'sociologistic theorem'. And yet Parsons believed that, somehow or other, he could see its existence in the work of the Italian sociologist. Pareto wrote:

When the community stands at a point, Q, that it can leave with resulting benefit to all the individuals, procuring greater enjoyments for all of them, it is obvious from the economic standpoint it is advisable not to stop at that point, but to move on from it as far as the movement away from it is advantageous to all. When, then, point P, where that is no longer possible, is reached, it is necessary, as regards the advisability of stopping there or going on, to resort to other considerations foreign to economics – to decide on grounds of ethics, social utility, or something else, which individuals it is advisable to benefit, which to sacrifice. From the strictly economic standpoint, as soon as the collectivity has reached point P, it has to stop. That point therefore plays in the situation a role analogous to the role of the point where the maximum of individual ophelimity is attained and at which, accordingly, the individual stops. Because of that analogy it has been called point of maximum ophelimity *for* the community.[123]

Pareto had also added:

In pure economics a community cannot be regarded as a person. In sociology it can be considered, if not as a person, at least as a unit . . . So, in pure economics there is no danger of mistaking the maximum of ophelimity *for* a community for a non-existent maximum ophelimity *of* a community. In sociology, instead, we must stand watchfully on guard, since they both are there.[124]

The first observation to be made is that the points of maximum ophelimity of which Pareto wrote do not exist. The individual and society find themselves in a permanent state of disequilibrium; preferences are subject to a process of incessant change; and this means that one does not know what ought to be maximised. To follow Parsons, we can disregard this situation. But we should add that the attainment of the maximum *for* society (point P above) and of the maximum *of* society is incompatible with the principles of a free society.[125]

Let us concentrate on the maximum *of* society, in which Parsons saw an application of the 'sociologistic theorem'. Pareto thought that this 'maximum' was possible on condition that society was considered as a person – that is to say, on condition that 'some hypothesis' should be introduced which makes 'heterogeneous' individual preferences comparable and sets them in order.[126] This leads to the suppression of the principle of equality before the law on which the 'great society' is based. Why? Because it is necessary to place part of society in a privileged position and to give it the task of hierarchising preferences, and, as Pareto did not fail to perceive, this part of society then pursues its own interests.[127]

Parsons stated that in this way society is worth more than individuals, because a hierarchised system of ends has been introduced.[128] But what we can say with certainty is that it is the 'privileged' group that is worth more than the rest of society. And that is the result of an abuse, of a fall into methodological collectivism and into the myth of the Lawgiver or Planner.

The distortions to which Parsons resorted in the case of Weber are no less serious. As is well known, Weber had tried in various ways to free himself from the holism of the German Historical School, of which he was an 'offspring'. Thus, it would have been wholly inconsistent if, after having argued with the 'revered master' Schmoller, and with the positions of his own cultural tradition, he had accepted Durkheim's holism. And he did not do so. On the contrary, in a letter to Robert Liefmann in March 1920, Weber wrote:

> If I have finally become a sociologist (as my appointment indicates), it is essentially in order to bring to an end these exercises based on collective concepts, the spectre of which is always lying in wait. In other terms, sociology itself can only proceed from the actions of a single individual, of several individuals, or of numerous separate individuals. This is why sociology ought to adopt strictly *individualistic* methods.[129]

After leaving romantic 'constructivism' behind him, Weber tried not to get bogged down in positivistic 'constructivism'. Hence, his criticism of the rational 'construction' of preferences, and his insistence, also beyond the call of duty, on the fourfold division of action (to which we gave attention in the previous chapter).

Nevertheless, Parsons accused Weber of having fallen into 'methodological atomism',[130] an accusation that he justified thus:

> His pluralism tends, by hypostatization of ideal types, to break up . . . the organic unity both of concrete historical individuals and of the historic process. In the reification phase it issues in what may be called a 'mosaic theory' of culture and society, conceiving them to be made up of disparate atoms.[131]

This did not stop him from also saying:

> Weber ruthlessly discarded from his work all nonempirical entities. The only *Geist* with which he will have anything to do is a matter of empirically observable attitudes and ideas which can be directly related to the understandable motivation of action. *But in spite of this fact, he definitely took a sociologistic position.*[132]

And here is the reason: because 'one of the most fundamental results [of Weber's work] is that of the dominant social role of religious ideas and value attitudes . . . which are *common* to the members of a great social movement or a whole society'.[133]

But the presence of 'religious ideas' and 'value attitudes' does not lead to the resumption of a holistic position. Nor does it imply that order is attained intentionally, based on an 'organized' and 'consistent' system of ends. Indeed, Weber had written:

> Anyone who lives in the world cannot but experience in himself a struggle between a plurality of values, each of which taken by itself appears to be binding: he will have to choose which of these gods he wishes and ought to serve, but he will always find himself in conflict with some of the other gods of the world.[134]

That is not all. Weber had spoken harshly about what he called 'ethical paradoxes', which he illustrated in this way:

> Let us confidently take the present as an example. He who wants to establish absolute justice on earth by force requires a following, a human 'machine'. He must hold out the necessary internal and external premiums, heavenly or worldly reward, to this 'machine' or else the machine will not function. Under the conditions of the modern class struggle, the internal premiums consist of the satisfying of hatred and the craving for revenge; above all, resentment and the need for a pseudo-ethical self-righteousness: the opponents must be slandered and accused of heresy. The external rewards are adventures, victory, power and spoils. The leader and his success are completely dependent upon the functioning of this machine and hence not on his own motives. Therefore he also depends upon whether or not the premiums can be *permanently* granted to the following . . . The following can be harnessed only so long as an honest belief in his person and his cause inspires at least part of the following, probably never on earth even the majority. This belief, even when subjectively sincere, is in a very great number of cases really no more than an ethical 'legitimation' of cravings for revenge, power, booty and spoils . . . Emotional revolutionism is followed by the traditional routine of everyday life; the crusading leader and the faith itself fade away, or, what is even more effective, that faith becomes part of the conventional phraseology of political Philistines and banausic technicians.[135]

All of this shows that there is not a common system of ends; instead, there is a common *justification* for different personal ends. Various subjects go through the same cross-roads; that is to say, they render reciprocal 'services', but aim at different personal destinations. And yet, for Parsons, it was as if

Weber had written nothing about this, and he looked for a 'teleocratic' order.[136]

However, the interesting point here is this: the attempt to demonstrate the presence of the 'sociologistic theorem' in Pareto and Weber helped Parsons to link the work of these authors with that of Durkheim. But 'methodological individualism' rejects the idea of society as a *sui generis* reality. Individualistic method reveals the danger and arbitrary nature of 'sociologistic theorem', and articulates the 'passing' from the personal moment to the social moment by means of the theory of the unintentional consequences of intentional human actions. As we have already mentioned, Georg Simmel wrote: '[exchange] is a form of socialization. It is one of those relations through which a number of individuals become a social group, while "society" is identical with the sum of these relations.'[137]

The missing solution

As we have noted in the preceding pages, for Parsons the individual is exclusively a *rule taker*. This position prevented him from formulating a real theory of action, which originates in the moment in which each person is also – whether he wants to be or not – a *rule maker*. In fact, it is only in this way that the regulatory norms of social life are subjected to continual change – and order is not predetermined, but is a permanent task.

The first question is: In relation to what do social norms change? The answer is simple: They change in relation to personal ends. This is what is suggested by the 'methodological individualism' of Mandeville or Smith, of Menger or Simmel, of Mises or Weber; and, furthermore, it suggests that norms are 'conditions' which make possible the achievement of personal ends. Thus, what makes individual actions compatible is an exclusive network of 'conditions'. This is what Parsons, following Durkheim, refused to accept. It was not by chance that, arguing against the 'individualistic' explanation of social order, he wrote:

> But all these – life, health, liberty and possessions – are to be regarded as the universal conditions of the attainment of individual ends, not as the ultimate ends in themselves. They are the things which all rational men want as conditions or means, regardless of the character of their ultimate ends.[138]

And yet, contrary to what Parsons thought, 'methodological individualism' has shown that social order is made possible by a network of 'conditions' and not by a 'common system of ultimate ends'. It is true. Generalising this network and putting it at the service of everyone produces an optical illusion; it seems to be a consistent collection of ends, rather than of means. But we are always concerned with 'conditions'. Without them, collective life would be impossible, and we are therefore led to describe them, at a raised level of abstraction, as ultimate values.[139]

The validity of this assessment comes out also from what Parsons maintained. In fact, he wrote that this 'system of rules, fundamental to any society . . . is what . . . [we] call its institutions'; and he explained:

> conformity to the norm may, apart from any moral attitude, be in the given concrete situation a means for the realization of the actor's private ends . . . This type may in turn be divided into two main types – where conformity is due to the positive advantage attached to it . . . and where it is due to the desire to avoid unpleasant consequences of non-conformity – its sanctions.[140]

Since Parsons was concerned, not only with 'institutions' but also with 'ultimate ends of non-empirical nature' and with 'religious action', we can take these further modalities of acting back to the schema discussed above. Let us ask ourselves: When the objective that we pre-arrange for ourselves is determined by a moral attitude, is not the action (as we have seen in the preceding pages) a way to coincide with ourselves, to accomplish that existential project that each of us is? And is it not necessary, in every case, even when our calling directs our conduct 'altruistically', to respect the 'conditions' that the Other imposes on us? As to 'religious action', can it not be, as we have shown in the chapter about the 'individualistic' reading of Durkheim, a means for private ends? And can it not be undertaken with the sole intention of avoiding possible earthly or heavenly sanctions?

As we shall see in more detail, it is possible to find in Parsons the elements for constructing a true theory of social action. But it must at once be said that the achievement of such an objective is incompatible with the presence of a 'common system of ultimate ends'. As James Coleman has correctly written, this system is in fact 'a *reductio ad absurdum* that had more than one unfortunate consequence for Parsons. It led him to fail in making the micro to macro transition';[141] it led him to abandon the attempt 'to found a social theory on the basis of a theory of rational action';[142] it pushed him towards 'sterile' classification schemes;[143] and it imprisoned him within a theory that 'emphasizes equilibrium and consensus'.[144]

Here could we ask: Why did Parsons fatally link himself to the 'common system of ultimate ends'? The reply is simple and it allows us to clarify the most important error in Parsons' theory. Jeffrey Alexander has stated: 'There is a profound moralism at the heart of Parsons' theory . His actors are imbued with the desire to be good, and they are understood as trying to conform with principles that express this moral aspiration.'[145] It is precisely this 'moralism' that, by reducing the terms on which one can work, places Parsons in a blind alley. Why?

The 'individualistic' theory makes it possible to read every action in two ways. Action can be *explained* by means of the personal objective of the actor, and it can be *justified* through socially accepted 'reasons', in which the 'conditions' imposed on Ego by the Other are reflected; a 'double-entry account', which has already been discussed at length, is in force. In order to combat behaviourism, Parsons recognised the 'personal' element of action; and yet, to give a solution to the problem of order, he tried to make this element coincide with the specifically social element through 'moralism' or individual participation. This is why he reduced the terms of the question; that is to say, he claimed that the *justification* for action coincides with the *explanation*, and this led him fatally to suppress precisely the term that he wished to accentuate, the 'creative' element.

The result is that this schema is not even able to take into account the order present in a 'closed society'. In fact, here too there exists, even if it cannot be admitted, an explanation of action that is different from its social justification. This – whether the actors are 'imbued with the desire to be good' or not – condemns Parsons' schema to powerlessness. Parsons should have kept in mind what Simmel had repeatedly emphasised: human life 'is not entirely social' in the 'strict sense', because we construct our reciprocal relations with the 'negative reservation of a part of our personality so as to prevent this part from entering into interaction'.[146] As a result, groups are 'structures which consist of beings standing inside and outside [them] at the same time'.[147]

If Parsons had taken this into account, he would have had to abandon the idea that social order can be intentionally constructed by 'actors', who are directed towards it by a previous 'common system of ultimate ends' and that they are in fact 'made to act' by this system; and he should have recognised that if human life 'is not entirely social' in the 'strict sense', order removes itself from any sort of plan and can be brought about only unintentionally, through the simple instrumental co-adaptation of individual projects. This would have allowed Parsons to formulate the 'subjective' theory of social institutions to which he aspired,[148] and which was clearly present in the theorists of order understood as an unintentional consequence of intentional human actions.

This would have required, among other things, acceptance of the fact that 'Darwin is the culminating of a development which Mandeville more than any other single man had started'.[149] In other words, Parsons should not have considered Adam Smith's position to be equivalent to that of philosophical radicalism; he should not have passed judgement, with Crane Brinton, on the scientific death of Herbert Spencer; and he should not have dismissed Darwin so hastily.

We have repeatedly spoken of Parsons' inability to separate Smith from philosophical radicalism; we have also pointed out the inappropriate assessments that he made of Spencer. What we have not yet done is to clarify the 'treatment' that he reserved for Darwin. Here Parsons declared that he had followed Pareto. Let us see to what extent he did so.

Parsons justified his rejection of radical utilitarianism, *à la* Bentham, with the fact that 'action becomes an exclusive function of its conditions'; this is already known to us and is perfectly acceptable. However, Parsons added that positivism, when it is not expressed in the rationalist form, takes an anti-intellectualistic position. Parsons himself wrote:

Thus the utilitarian dilemma is broadened into a more inclusive form. It may, in this form, be stated in the following proposition: In so far as the utilitarian position is abandoned in either of its two major tenets, the . . . alternative . . . lies in the conditions of the situation of action objectively rather than subjectively considered, which for most practical purposes may be taken to mean in the facts of heredity and environment in the analytical sense of biological theory.[150]

Parsons explained further:

Precisely in so far as this 'biologizing' tendency, which in fact took primarily the Darwinian form, gained ascendancy, there was an abandonment of the utilitarian position in favour of radical anti-intellectualistic positivism. In so far as the conditions of the environment are decisive it does not matter what ends men may think they pursue; in fact, the course of history is determined by an impersonal process over which they have no control. It should be noted that in the shift the subjective category of ends disappears and with it the norm of rationality. Darwinian variation constitutes an entirely objective element requiring for its theoretical formulation no subjective reference. Even though rational action might have, empirically, a place as one mode of adaptation to the environment, the point is that it falls out of the general framework of the theoretical system altogether and becomes a contingent phenomenon, an unimportant fact in the strict sense.[151]

Pareto had stated on this subject:

The form of the society is determined if given the sentiments and the external circumstances (environment) in which the society is situated; or if the circumstances only are given, but the sentiments are regarded as determined by circumstances. Darwinism carried to the extreme, gave the complete solution of that problem with its theory of the survival of the individuals best adapted to the environment.[152]

Parsons, welcoming this Darwinism 'pushed to its extreme', said:

Along with this disappearance of the normative aspects of the utilitarian system, ends and rationality, goes another most important consequence; the problem of order . . . evaporates. Without the normative elements of action order in the normative sense becomes meaningless. The only order which concerns the scientist of human action is a factual order from both the subjective and objective points of view. Indeed, ironically enough, the order which is found to dominate this factual world is precisely that which had played the part of antithesis to social order in utilitarian thought – the 'state of war'. It has changed its name to the 'struggle for existence' but is in all essentials the Hobbesian state of nature.[153]

Here, however, Parsons went much further than he should. Pareto had also written, relevantly, that 'the element of truth in the Darwinian solution' is that 'forms and residues cannot stand too openly in conflict with the conditions in which they are evolved'.[154] This, translated into terms more familiar to us, means that individual ends cannot lead to the distortion of 'conditions' or social norms, which are thus a 'filter' that eliminates some of the actor's objectives, but are not the mould that heterodetermines personal ends. Parsons, who also examined Pareto's interpretation given above,[155] did not draw the obvious conclusions: if conditions are only a 'filter', the action is not suppressed; the individual remains an actor, and with his acting he is, whether he likes or not, the producer of the same 'conditions' in which action is fulfilled;[156] competition is not the 'war of all against all' but the meeting that takes place on the basis of rules that every actor contributes towards determining;[157] individual ends are not 'random', because the 'conditions' define what is 'impossible' at a particular moment and come together to make a range of possibilities that is open – subject, that is, to continual reformulations.[158]

Thus, the alterations and distortions to which Parsons subjected the 'materials' on which he worked are by no means negligible. Yet, these extreme measures did not succeed in excluding the elements of a theoretical schema of 'individualistic' type from his own treatment of social action. We shall restrict ourselves to three points:

1 As we have already made clear, Parsons interpreted in Kantian terms the 'Calling' of which Weber spoke. If we abandon the categorical imperative and accept that each person has an interest in realising the existential project that is his own life, we ought to recognise that the interest of the actor, however much it may be directed to the benefit of the Other, has to be subject to the conditions that the latter dictates. If we add that Parsons could not but admit that the 'conditions' are respected for the sake of attaining objectives of a personal nature and in order to avoid the sanctions inflicted in the event of violation,[159] we have the activation of a

'double entry account' between the objectives of Ego and the 'prices' imposed by the Other. Thus, we leave the 'common system of ultimate ends' and the idea of a social order obtained 'voluntaristically', and we enter the territory of unintentional order.

2   The abandonment of the 'voluntarism' of order is not equivalent to falling back into the rationalistic schema of philosophical radicalism. Indeed, it means recognising that the person who acts has an autonomy that the 'common system of ultimate ends' is not able to grant him; in particular, it means coming out of the logic of intentional order, which dominates both the idealistic and the positivistic approach.

With reference to Alfred Marshall, Parsons declared: '[he] refuses to take wants as given; his central doctrine is that of a progressive growth of wants generated by new activities'.[160] It follows that individuals reach their own innovative purposes only if they know how to overcome the 'conditions' that they themselves share in determining; conditions which, however, cannot be planned, because each one 'will discover what he knows or can find out only when faced with a problem'.[161] This should have made clear to Parsons that what confers autonomy on the individual and order on a society is exclusively a network of 'conditions' which acts as a 'filter' to objectives of a personal character and which changes in relation to the 'challenges' and 'responses' of the social actors – that is to say, on the basis of variables that no 'participant' can overcome. Therefore, order is unintentional, and the process is of an evolutionistic nature, since 'innovation is to society what mutation is to biology. Not all mutations are good. Some are just unfortunate experiments. Only natural selection (which is not rational although *ex post* it can be rationally explained) will tell over time which are good and which are bad mutations'.[162]

3   The same logic that presents 'conditions' and order as unintentional results of intentional human actions can obviously be extended to institutions. Here, too, Parsons came near to a solution. Following Durkheim, he wrote that exchange is made possible by the 'institution of contract', 'a whole set of conditions which may be regarded as *involuntary* and obligatory'.[163] If he had put aside his voluntarism and had at least given some attention to Carl Menger's *Untersuchungen über die Methode der Sozialwissenschaften*, he would have been brought to that theory of social institutions he had failed to formulate and which, contrary to his belief, could not be found in a 'highly unsatisfactory state'.[164]

The three points set out above show that in Parsons himself we can find elements that contradict his voluntaristic theory of social order and are incompatible with his criticisms of the market society.[165] These elements can well be used in a vision of social order seen as an unintentional process devoid of a 'stable endpoint toward which the process must lead' and devoid of 'a single path that it must follow'.[166] And yet, to enter completely into the territory of unintentional order, one has to turn one's back unequivocally on the 'moralism' to which Parsons was a victim. Let us make it clear: this does not mean that actions cannot be decided 'rationally with respect to value' (they certainly can); nevertheless, order does not depend on the way in which we take our position towards past 'conditions', but rather on the fulfilment, accepted by the Other, of what is dictated by the new 'conditions' that our initiative, finalised for purely personal ends, shares in defining. Only thus is it possible to make action into something different from a form of *adaptation* to a pre-existing order, to remove it from those passive patterns of behaviour that in Parsons' schema are just like 'philosophical radicalism'.[167] In other words, one must realise that

> the premise that the initial . . . [situation] is given and remains stable at least until the final situation is inferred, is misleading. In reality, the initial . . . situation is not given, but is constructed, and constructed at great cost. This construction is practically continuous, because we are continuously acting, learning and inventing. Even the utility of future results, which is only imagined, and uncertain, evolves little by little as our knowledge changes. If even the initial . . . situation has not changed in the meantime, the final situation could possibly not please us once it is realized, and precisely because it is now realized.[168]

Economic cost and social obligation

As we have emphasised several times, Durkheim based the validity of the 'sociologistic theorem' on a 'fictional human being', who does not yet benefit from the 'social' element. Nevertheless, anyone who does not pose the question of the *beginning* of society cannot operate with a schema such as this, because the individual is already a *social being*; he benefits from what, in Chapter 3, we have called 'social in the broad sense'. This is a condition that Vilfredo Pareto described in the following terms:

> The adjectives individual and social are vaguer than the corresponding substantives. Since man lives in society, from a certain point of view it can be said that all his characteristics are individual, and considering the same phenomenon from another point of view, it can be said that all his characteristics are social. In short, there is no sure way to separate these two kinds of characteristic from each other. And when we think that we can effect this separation, we let ourselves be carried away by considerations of a completely different kind.[169]

How is it possible to break away from this situation? We have also dealt with this aspect of the problem in Chapter 3. There we pointed out that there is a 'social' in the 'strict sense', which is given by the 'conditions' that the Other imposes on Ego's initiative. This means that the 'social' in the proper sense coincides with the network of 'limitations' and 'conditions' which makes 'commerce' between individuals possible and which is often a result not planned by the actors. In this way, it is possible to state that the purpose which the actor plans in advance is individual, but that the 'conditions' which the pursuit of that purpose cuts across are social.

This clarification enables us to tackle a final problem, that of the collocation of the economic moment in action and the object of the social sciences.

We have seen that in the theories of Mandeville and Smith, Menger and Mises, Simmel and Weber, action is economic. It involves 'costs' which affect the limited resources of the actor; consequently, it is always economic action, even if its purposes are non-economic. The costs constitute a way of doing, a service to be rendered to the advantage of the Other; that is, they are what we have frequently called 'conditions'. This is equivalent to saying that the elements that 'bind' the actors of a 'great society' are of an economic nature.[170]

Yet, Talcott Parsons wrote that sociology should 'be thought of as a science of action – of the ultimate common element, *in its relations* to the other elements of action'.[171]

Let us examine the question in more detail. When Parsons sought to give autonomy to the actor, ultimate-values became 'emergent properties', which anyway he was not able to reach through interindividual action. Thus, ultimate values remain 'hanging in the air' and become the 'common system of ultimate ends', which triumphs over the individual and which he realises 'voluntaristically.' This means that it is the inability to pass from the individual to the social in the 'strict sense' that makes the 'sociologistic theorem' possible and makes of sociology the science that concerns itself with 'ultimate ends'. Here we are within the ambit of Durkheimian holism.

It is possible to break away from this situation and to reach a conciliation with the 'individualistic' approach. If we recognise that interaction is able to produce the 'conditions' of social exchange, '*emergent properties*'[172] are not a mysterious entity 'hanging in the air'. They are the non-intentional result of individual action. While attaining its own purpose, individual action intersects non-planned 'conditions'; the lack of respect for them renders it impossible to obtain the voluntary collaboration of others, that is, to carrying our project through to a positive conclusion.

It follows that ultimate values are themselves 'conditions',[173] which arise from interaction and which make the individual into a *price* or *rule taker* and, at the same time, into a *price* or *rule maker*. The price to which we submit ourselves in the monetary economy, and which we share in determining, is thus no different from the social obligation that we agree to respect and that we, in one way or another, contribute towards defining by our preferences. In both cases, we are in the presence of a 'cost' to which the fulfilment of our personal ends has to be subject.

In other words, the payment of a monetary price and the fulfilment of a social obligation have the same nature of 'counter-item' for the co-operation of others. It is not by chance that Smith's 'invisible hand' was represented by a network of prices, and the 'impartial spectator' was constituted by a network of norms. In both cases, we find ourselves – if we like to use a Durkheimian expression – confronted by 'moral' facts. Thus, 'methodological individualism' enters the sphere of morality without needing to resort to *Geist*, the 'collective consciousness', or to other metaphysical entities. And it can also be reconciled with Durkheim when he said that the 'social fact' is a *'way of acting, whether fixed or not, capable of exerting over the individual an external constraint'*.[174] A 'condition' is actually external to the individual's project; it is what the Other claims for his co-operation with Ego's action. We spoke of it at length when we discussed 'subjective law' and 'objective law' in Chapter 4.

This allows us to conclude that if we free ourselves from methodological collectivism, the task of the social sciences is clearly that of studying the unintentional origin of the 'conditions', namely of the norms and institutions that make collective life possible.

8

CONCLUSIONS

'Let us learn to be selves'

We have seen that Durkheim identified political economy with psychologistic positions *à la* John Stuart Mill. And we have pointed out that Parsons, taking this identification to its extreme conclusion, put economic theory on the same level as 'philosophical radicalism'.

The criticisms levelled at psychologism or radical rationalism are not without foundation. However, one must not go too far and think that political economy and philosophical radicalism are *dii consentes*, Dioscuri born together and destined to live together. There are ways of escaping from this idea. Within economic theory there is a very different 'tradition of research', initiated by Mandeville, Hume and Smith and extended in the Austrian school of economics. It is a tradition which has always opposed the idea that human life can be pure psychology or its 'constructivistic' projection .

Therefore, let us consider a recurrent misunderstanding. When political economy is spoken of, it is said to make use of 'methodological individualism'. Thus, the question is: Does 'methodological individualism' apply indiscriminately to the whole of economic theory? From what we have been saying so far, it is already evident that the individualistic method fosters, in a specific way, the 'tradition of research' that reaches from Mandeville to Austrian marginalism. Nevertheless, what philosophical radicalism makes use of is not methodological individualism; in philosophical radicalism 'the characteristic institution which economists call "the market", and whose functioning is the main object of their studies, can be derived in the last analysis from the psychology of the "economic man", or, to use Mill's phraseology, from the psychological phenomena . . . of the pursuit of wealth'.[1]

Karl Popper wrote:

> [The] doctrine which teaches the reduction of social theories to psychology, in the same way as we try to reduce chemistry to physics, is . . . based on a misunderstanding. It arises from the false belief that this 'methodological psychologism' is a necessary corollary of a

methodological individualism – of the quite unassailable doctrine that we must try to understand all collective phenomena as due to the actions, interactions, aims, hopes and thoughts of individual men, and as due to traditions created and preserved by individual men. But we can be individualists without accepting psychologism. The 'zero method' of constructing rational models is *not* a psychological, but a logical method.[2]

On the other hand, Joseph Schumpeter, who coined the expression 'methodological individualism', declared: 'relations do *not* exist between economics and psychology, neither methodological nor material relations, of the sort that would be necessary in order to attain our results'.[3] Ludwig von Mises, as we have already emphasised, stated that 'economics begins at the point at which psychology leaves off'.[4] And Lionel Robbins wrote:

It is well known . . . that certain of the founders of the modern subjective theory of value did in fact claim the authority of the doctrines of psychological hedonism as sanctions for their propositions. This was not true of the Austrians. From the beginning Mengerian tables were constructed in terms which begged no psychological questions. Boehm-Bawerk explicitly repudiated any affiliation with psychological hedonism; indeed, he went to infinite pains to avoid this kind of misconception.[5]

However, there is one point that separates methodological individualism from psychologism more clearly than any other. It is the idea, to express it in Popper's terms, that 'we have to learn that we are selves'.[6] This means that methodological individualists do not work with a *beginning* of society. When man discovers himself, he is already united with others by a social bond; he does not need to create it. In this sense, as we already know, Mandeville declared that 'if we examine every Faculty and Qualification, from and for which we judge and pronounce Man to be a sociable Creature beyond other Animals, we shall find, that a very considerable, if not the greatest Part of the Attribute is acquired, and comes upon Multitudes, from their conversing with one another'.[7] And Smith wrote: if a human being 'could grow up to manhood in a solitary place, without any communication with his own species, he could no more think of his own character, of the propriety or demerit of his own sentiments or conduct, of the beauty or deformity of his own mind, than of the beauty or deformity of his own face'.[8]

We have commented on passages such as these in Chapter 3, where we said, with Popper, that we are not born as selves but have to learn to be selves. This concept was expressed on many occasions by Ludwig von Mises, and at this point it is useful to quote the following passage from his writings:

Nothing is more false than to assume that man first appeared in history with an independent individuality . . . All history, evidence and observation of the life of primitive peoples, is directly contrary to this view. Primitive man lacks all individuality in our sense. Two South Sea Islanders resemble each other far more closely than two twentieth-century Londoners. *Personality was not bestowed upon man at the outset*. It has been acquired in the course of evolution of society.[9]

In a note on this passage, Mises cited Durkheim. It is an apposite citation, because the methodological individualists, whether they operate primarily on the economic side or whether they place themselves on the more strictly socio-logical side (Spencer, Simmel, Weber), share the idea of the self as a 'conquest' or 'discovery'; an idea which is rightly central also in Durkheim's work and which serves to set one free from psychologism, or, to quote Popper, to realise that 'if a reduction is to be attempted at all, it would . . . be more hopeful to attempt a reduction or interpretation of psychology in terms of sociology than the other way round'.[10]

That is not all. The anti-psychologism of the individualistic method is found also in Schutz.[11] Having to choose between the position of Husserl and that of Scheler and Mises, Schutz took the side of the latter two and declared that the sphere of 'we' is 'given to each of us prior to the sphere of the I'.[12]

Consequently, methodological individualism should not be confused with psychologism. From this derives the unacceptability of the theses, such as that of George Homans, according to which 'sociology *is* a corollary of psychology at least in the sense that social phenomena require general psychological propositions for their explanation';[13] nor is it possible to follow Homans himself when he maintained, in a controversy with Popper, that methodolog-ical individualism 'entails' psychologism.[14]

However, the boundaries of methodological individualism should be marked out on another side also. That is, it needs to be repeated, with Schumpeter, that *political* individualism and *methodological* individualism 'do not have even the most insignificant element in common'.[15] It is true that, just to mention a few names, Menger, Mises, Hayek and Popper linked polit-ical individualism with methodological individualism. But Engels, too, was a methodological individualist when he maintained, in a rare moment of honesty, that 'in the history of society . . . the actors are all endowed with consciousness, are men acting with deliberation or passion', and when he added that actions 'have consequences quite other from those intended'.[16] The result of this is, exactly as Mises stated, that we ought to begin with the indi-vidual, because only he 'thinks', 'reasons', 'acts'[17]; and not for other motives. It is not by chance that Ferdinand Toennies did not hesitate to write: 'Religious faith makes the most important corporations appear as real organic, mystic and even supernatural beings. Philosophical criticism is right in discovering and explaining that all are creations of man and that they exist except insofar as human intellect and human will are embodied in them.'[18]

This does not mean that 'nations, States, municipalities, parties, religious communities' are not 'real factors determining the course of human events'.[19] But the life of a collectivity exists 'in the actions of the individuals constituting its body'.[20] And this is

> the meaning that marks one action as the action of an individual and another action as the action of the State or the municipality. The hangman, not the State, executes a criminal. It is the meaning of those concerned that discerns in the hangman's action an action of the State. [And so, if] a group of armed men occupies a place . . . is the meaning of those concerned which imputes this occupation not to the officers and soldiers on the spot, but to their nation.[21]

Sociology and economics

Thus, there is an error that does not need to be committed. It is the error into which Durkheim and Parsons fell in their attempt to point out the gaps in economic theory; they identified political economy with philosophical radicalism.[22] The same error is committed by anyone who, in an attempt to emphasise the superiority of the economic explanation, does not realise that in political economy there is a 'constructivistic' element, which is precisely what harms economics itself and which cannot be 'imported' from sociology. Consequently, it is true, as Raymond Boudon says, that there is no 'reason' to leave the paradigm of action to 'economics';[23] but it is also true that it is necessary to put 'constructivism' aside. In other words, one must be careful not to throw out the baby with the bath water; and yet it is also necessary to avoid taking the bath water with the baby.

What does the 'bath water' represent? There are three closely connected elements in 'constructivism', from which the social sciences should free themselves. They are psychologism, the rational construction of preferences and the maximisation of results, or the *optimum*. We have turned our attention to all three of these elements on several occasions at several points in this discussion. We have also returned to psychologism in the preceding section; however, it is useful to repeat, with Popper, that 'ideas such as (a) imitation, (b) language, (c) the family, are obviously social ideas . . . Thus psychology presupposes social ideas . . . What we cannot, in principle, explain psychologically, and what we must presuppose in every psychological explanation, is man's social environment.'[24] It follows that, if there were no social variable, we would not even be able to speak of the psychological dimension;[25] this is tantamount to saying that it is wholly illusory to think of a life reduced to pure psychology.

As we have explained in the preceding section, 'man learns to be a self'; and this experience of learning is carried out through the process of primary socialisation. In other words, man learns to be a self, after settling within himself the models, norms and beliefs that he absorbs from the socio-historical context into which he is born. Georg Simmel wrote 'that words and deeds are the corresponding expression of convictions and obligations – all this signifies not so much a value that we have, but a value that we are';[26] and again, referring to normative orientations, he added : 'We do not *possess* them . . . but rather we *are*' these orientations.[27]

It follows that reason never operates in a void, but that it works within that social and normative continent which is the source of the problems of our life and of the information through which we seek to resolve those same problems. This is why Adam Smith spoke of 'certain circumstances' which 'in the imagination of men', 'make up for a small pecuniary gain' in some cases and 'counterbalance a great one in others'.[28] Here, Smith was referring to individual preferences which pre-exist monetary calculation. For his part, Ludwig von Mises, reacting to Weber's accusation against political economy including Austrian marginalism, in believing that it was possible to make a rational construction of the scale of preferences, declared that ends 'neither require nor are capable of a rational justification'.[29]

We have not called on Smith and Mises at random. We have done so in order to prove that the 'tradition of research' which goes from Mandeville to the Austrian school of economics demonstrates the impossibility not only of psychologism but also of the rational construction of the scale of preferences. And it rejects the idea of equilibrium because there is action only where there is disequilibrium.[30]

Is it possible to reconcile this 'tradition of research' with sociology? We have seen the strong convergences that emerge from the works of Menger and Simmel and from those of Weber and Mises. These convergences make it clear that the 'bath water' that prevents the two disciplines from 'co-operating' comes from philosophical radicalism and its constructivistic claims. When he reached the end of his conversations with economists and sociologists, Richard Swedberg emphasised how on the part of the latter criticisms were levelled particularly against the idea of *maximization*;[31] criticisms which are, as has also emerged here, wholly legitimate. But the point is that political economy is not exhausted in philosophical radicalism, nor in the theory of equilibrium and the maximisation of rationality. This means that political economy outlives 'constructivism'. Consequently, the question is another: Ought not we also, from this side of the sociological frontiers, free ourselves from constructivistic claims?

The authors, from the sociological side, who have principally made it possible for us to clarify the convergences between sociology and economies are Georg Simmel and Max Weber. Both can be placed within the mainstream of methodological individualism; both opened a 'double entry account' between intentional actions and unintentional consequences which makes social order possible; both conducted an intense dialogue with political economy. Durkheim's position was very different. In it the predominating idea was that, in the end, order is entrusted to a 'social brain.' This position is pervaded by 'constructivism', by a continuous polemic towards political economy, identified, moreover, with its most rationalistic version, and it is a battle between two types of constructivism.

In the case of the theories of Menger and Simmel and of Weber and Mises, one finds co-operation between economics and sociology, because both free themselves from the temptation of constructivism. This leads to the emergence of a series of points that are common to both:

1   Action arises from a situation of disequilibrium, which man attempts to make good and which, nevertheless, he keeps alive by continually bringing his own existential project up to date. Therefore, disequilibrium cannot be eliminated.
2   Action is always social, conscious and responsible. Man is set within a social (and normative) framework, from which he can never get free and which he actually needs in order to attempt the fulfilment of his objectives. Edmund Burke said that 'no man could act with effect, who did not act in concert'.[32]
3   Social action is always economic action. Taking a position not unlike that of Mises, Parsons wrote:

> Because of the finitude of human life span it is strictly impossible for everyone ever to 'find the time' to do everything he might want to do. [This] precludes the notion sometimes put forward that we are on the verge of an 'economy of abundance' where scarcity in the economic sense would come to be in principle meaningless.[33]

Parsons then added: 'The most fundamental limitation, however, is the directly relational . . . The relational limitation rests upon the fact that it is inherent in the nature of social interaction that the gratification of ego's needs-dispositions is contingent on alter's action and vice versa'.[34] This means, as we have already pointed out in Chapter 2, that the Other asks in the first place 'not to do' or to leave aside part of our plan; hence, Ego's project has to be multiplied by a coefficient k, given by the measure – from zero to one – of the Other's 'availability'. Not only that. In exchange for the co-operation that is demanded of him, the Other asks also 'to do' for his own benefit. Ego's project is therefore subject to 'limitations' and 'conditions'. And we cannot act without a scale of priorities which 'distributes' our resources, and without paying 'costs'.

4   The limited nature of the means available obliges man to economise. However, if the means have to be economic, this is not to say that the ends are. Lionel Robbins wrote: 'to speak of any end as being itself "economic"

is entirely misleading. The habit, prevalent among certain groups of economists, of discussing "economic satisfactions" is alien to the central intention of economic analysis.'[35] And Hayek added: 'ultimate purposes are always non-economic. The task of all economic activity is to reconcile ends by deciding for which of them the limited means are to be used'.[36]

5   As we have shown with the line of the hyperbola presented in Chapter 2, the inter-individual relationship produces *places of possible co-living*; that is to say, the relationship is possible only if the 'cost' is acceptable. Thus, in order for the exchange to take place, it is not necessary for the actors to attain the *maximum*. On the other hand – as we have already pointed out several times – the very idea of maximisation is incompatible with action understood as permanent *to do*, as a process in which the subject's knowledge is partial and fallible, subject to new flows of information, which modify the ends and the judgement on them. If this is so, we can only look for acceptable solutions – 'good solutions'.[37]

6   To say that social action is economic action signifies making it clear that the use and acquisition of means, which are the specific of the economic dimension, are included within action in its totality. The economic moment defines the 'limitations' and the 'conditions' to which action has to be subject. Therefore, it is found within action. Georg Simmel wrote, 'inter-individual exchange' is no more than a 'peace treaty', and 'exchange' and socially 'regulated exchange' have emerged as a unitary fact.[38]

This makes it clear that within rules is also found the modality (market or plan) through which economics in the 'strict sense' is articulated.[39]

7   We have several times declared that the social norm is the relationship in which one service rendered is exchanged with another. This leads to the statement that the norm is a 'price' or even that the price is a norm. One must then ask oneself: Which is the field of sociology and which is that of political economy?

Both are concerned with human action, which is always social and economic. But political economy 'is mainly concerned with the analysis of the determination of the money prices of goods and services exchanged on the market'.[40] This is 'the field of the catallactics or of economics in the narrower sense', which is thus concerned with actions in which the economic moment is expressed on the basis of monetary calculation.[41] Where prices, that is to say the norms of social exchange, are not expressed in a monetary form, we find ourselves instead in the territory of sociology. Consequently, the two share the task of studying the unintentional origin of the 'conditions' that make collective life possible.

The task of the social sciences

Robert K. Merton wrote: 'the problem of the unanticipated consequences of purposive action has been treated by virtually every substantial contributor to the long history of social thought'.[42] And yet, in the light of what has emerged so far, the question here is not that of seeing whether one scholar or another has been concerned with the unintentional consequences of intentional human actions. The problem is to establish what is the relation between the social sciences and the unintentional consequences of intentional human actions.

Friedrich von Hayek, who can be considered as the scholar who led the research of the Austrian school of economics to a higher level of awareness, did not hesitate to declare that the problems that the social sciences 'try to answer arise only insofar as the conscious action of many men produce undesigned results, insofar as regularities are observed which are not the result of anybody's design';[43] and again: 'If social phenomena showed no order except insofar as they were consciously designed, there would be indeed no room for theoretical sciences of society and there would be, as is often argued, only problems of psychology'.[44] As we know, Karl Popper, with whom Hayek conducted an intense dialogue, wrote:

> It must be admitted that the structure of our social environment is man-made in a certain sense; that its institutions and traditions are neither the work of God nor of nature, but the results of human actions and decisions, and alterable by human actions and decisions. But this does not mean that they are all consciously designed, and explicable in terms of need, hopes, or motives. On the contrary, even those which arise as the result of conscious and intentional human actions are, as a rule, *the indirect, the unintended and often unwanted by-products of such actions* . . . we can add that even most of the few institutions which were consciously and successfully designed (say, a newly founded university, or a trade union) do not turn out according to plan – again because of the unintended social repercussions of their intentional creation.[45]

Popper's conclusion is consistent: '*the main task of the theoretical social sciences . . . is to trace unintended social repercussions of intentional human actions*'.[46] It is to this conception of the social sciences that we ought to turn to understand that society is an 'inner bond'.[47] In other words, 'Society is not an absolute entity which must first exist so that all individual relations of its members . . . can develop within its framework or be represented by it: it is only the synthesis or the general term for the totality of these specific interactions.'[48] That is, relationships generate the 'conditions' that make their development possible. Or, as Bernard de Mandeville put it, '*fabricando fabri fimus*'.[49]

NOTES

PREFACE

1 Salvemini (1964: 2). I use the original Italian version of Salvemini's book, because the English translation does not contain some of the passages quoted here.
2 Ibid.: 2–3.
3 In such a case, as Böhm-Bawerk (1962: 61) had pointed out, there is a 'flagrant error of duplication'. Reality is duplicated.
4 Simmel (1978: 175).
5 Popper (1990: 24–5).

1 INTRODUCTION

1 Hayek (1960: 148), my italics.
2 Ortega y Gasset (1966a: 497).
3 Ibid.
4 Hayek (1979).
5 Hayek (1978: 3). For a comprehensive philosophical view of social 'constructivism', see Baldini (1994).
6 Hayek (1978: 5).
7 Ibid.
8 Hayek (1982: 22). On this point, cf. Sombart (1923) and Mongardini's writings (1970: 77–132) on Sombart.
9 Smith (1976b I: 26–7).
10 Mandeville (1924 I: 60).
11 Ortega y Gasset's expression (1969: 146).
12 Mandeville (1924 II: 335).
13 Ibid.: 333.
14 The expression comes from the followers of Saint-Simon, quoted by Hayek (1979: 269).
15 Saint-Simon (1877–8 XX: 59).
16 Comte (1974a: 123).
17 Durkheim (1964: 172).
18 Ibid.
19 Saint-Simon (1877–8 XXI: 16).
20 Comte (1974b: 224).
21 Durkheim (1952: 364–5).
22 Marx (1977a: 52).
23 Marx and Engels (1969 I: 183).

24 Saint-Simon (1877–8 XVIII: 186).
25 Comte (1970: 216–21).
26 Marx (1973: 69, 107).
27 Nisbet (1967: 7).
28 Schumpeter (1954: 27).
29 Nisbet (1967: 16).
30 Ibid., cf. Nisbet (1975).
31 Descartes (1960: 45). The extract is also frequently referred to by Hayek.
32 Hayek (1978: 5).
33 Hayek (1982 I: 29).
34 Popper (1966 II: 302).
35 Hayek (1978: 179–90).
36 Hayek (1979: 368).
37 Hegel (1977: 292).
38 Hegel (1942: 36, 148).
39 Hegel (1977: 288.
40 Hegel (1942: 129.
41 Quoted by Hayek (1979: 372).
42 Ibid.
43 Ibid.
44 Op. cit.: 371.
45 Ibid.: 369.
46 Ibid.
47 Hegel (1942: 155).
48 Hegel (1977: 289).
49 Boudon and Bourricand (1986: 82).
50 Mises (1969).
51 Hume (1923 II: 167–78). For a more extensive treatment of this point, see also Antiseri (1989: 41, 69–70).
52 Weber (1991b: 148).

2 BERNARD DE MANDEVILLE AND ADAM SMITH

1 Mandeville (1924 II: 132).
2 Ibid.
3 Ibid.: 199.
4 Ibid.: 222–3.
5 Ibid.: 285.
6 Ibid.: 223.
7 Op. cit.: 189.
8 Ibid.
9 Op. cit.: 223.
10 Op. cit.: 168.
11 Ibid.
12 Ibid.: 169.
13 Ibid.: 296.
14 Smith (1976a: 85, 1976e: 398).
15 Smith (1976a: 110). The mirror of which Smith spoke can clearly be connected with Jacques Lacan's (1949).
16 Smith (1976a).
17 Op. cit.: 160.
18 Ibid.: 111.

19 Ibid.: 110.
20 Mandeville (1924 II: 121).
21 Ibid.: 182–3.
22 Op. cit.: 183.
23 Op. cit.: 350, my italics.
24 Ibid.: 349.
25 Ibid.
26 Op. cit. I: 221.
27 Ibid. II: 284.
28 Smith (1976b I: 26), my italics.
29 Op. cit.: 37.
30 Op. cit.: 30. On the subject of Smith's debts to Mandeville on the division of labour, Karl Marx spoke of a passage 'copied almost *word for word*'. Marx (1976 I: 374, note 33).
31 Mandeville (1924 I: 234). It is useful to recall also what David Hume stated (1963: 40–1):

> Political writers have established it as a maxim, that, in contriving any system of government, and fixing the several checks and controls of the constitution, every man ought to be supposed a *knave* and to have no other end, in all his actions, than private interest. By this interest we must govern him, and by means of it, make him, notwithstanding his insatiable avarice and ambition, co-operate to public good.

Hayek (1949: 11), expressed himself as follows on the subject:

> [the] point about which there can be little doubt is that Smith's chief concern was not so much with what man might occasionally achieve when he was at his best but that he should have as little opportunity as possible to harm when he was at his worst. It would scarcely be too much to claim that the main merit of the individualism which he and his contemporaries advocated is that it is a system under which bad men can do least harm.

Cf. also Magri (1987). So it is clear why Popper (1966 I:.121) insisted that the old question 'Who should rule?' must be replaced by the question: 'How can we so organize political institutions that bad or incompetent rulers can be prevented from doing too much damage?'
32 Mandeville (1924 I: 234).
33 Smith (1976a: 86).
34 Op. cit.: 63.
35 Mandeville (1924 II: 335).
36 Op. cit.: 333.
37 Op. cit.: 335.
38 Op. cit. I: 190, my italics.
39 Smith (1976a: 86).
40 Op. cit.: 175–6.
41 Mandeville (1924 II: 349).
42 Ibid.
43 Ibid. II.
44 Op. cit. I: 80.

45 Smith (1976a: 160).
46 Smith (1976b II: 630).
47 Ibid.
48 Op. cit. I: 456. As we shall see more clearly in the concluding paragraph of this chapter, this does not mean that Smith believed in the possibility of an individual and social *best*; instead, he believed in the necessity of continually reformulating productive projects, that is, to correct past errors without, however, being able to avoid them in the future. The competitive allocation of resources – as Hayek wrote (1982 III: 68–9) – is like 'experimentation in science, first and foremost a discovery procedure . . . It therefore cannot be said of competition any more than of any other sort of experimentation that it leads to a maximisation of any measurable results. It merely leads, under favourable conditions, to the use of more skill and knowledge than any other known procedure.' Cf. also Ricossa (1988: 7–14).
49 Smith (1976c: 49).
50 Smith (1976b I: 116).
51 Here I use an expression of Hayek's (1978: 265). On Smith as an evolutionist before Darwin, cf. Huxley (1893: 78, note 1). On Darwinian evolution understood as ateleological development, cf. Kuhn (1962: 170–1).
52 Smith (1976b I: 25).
53 Mandeville (1924 II: 285).
54 Smith (1976a: 233–4).
55 Smith (1976e: 402). However, it must be added that the conclusions to be drawn on the political level received 'their magnificent formulation from the great seer Edmund Burke' (Hayek, 1982 I: 22).
56 Sartori (1979: 201–2).
57 Mandeville (1924 I: 184).
58 Op. cit. II: 274.
59 Ibid. I: 333.
60 Ibid.: 379.
61 Ibid.: 56.
62 Ibid.: 142.
63 Op. cit.: 166–7.
64 Ibid. On Mandeville's debts to Bayle, cf. Jones (1975: 43–65) and Scribano (1980: 21–46).
65 Mandeville (1924 vol. I: 52).
66 Ibid.
67 Op. cit: 68.
68 Op. cit.: 210.
69 Op. cit.: 168.
70 Op. cit. II: 90.
71 Ibid.
72 Op. cit. I: 71–2.
73 Ibid.: 72, 221.
74 Smith (1976a: 113).
75 Op. cit.
76 Ibid.: 114.
77 Ibid.
78 Op. cit.: 16–7.
79 Op. cit.: 19.
80 Op. cit.: 158.
81 Ibid.

82 Op. cit.: 159.
83 Op. cit.: 168.
84 Op. cit.: 50.
85 Op. cit.: 12.
86 Ibid.: 158–9.
87 Salomon (1945: 28–9).
88 Smith (1976a: 135).
89 Op. cit.: 161–2.
90 Op. cit.: 147.
91 Ibid. Hence, the 'impartial spectator' can be compared, to the extent that he exercises control over the actor, with the 'generalised other' of Mead (1934) and, to the extent that he becomes an 'interior companion', with Freud's Super-I (1949).
92 Smith (1976a: 137).
93 Ibid.: 170. Which, as we shall see, coincides with Karl Popper's 'logic of the situation'.
94 Op. cit.: 163.
95 Weber (1968 I: 24–5).
96 Smith (1976a: 308).
97 Op. cit.: 309.
98 Op. cit.: 50.
99 Ibid.
100 Sombart (1923: 10).
101 Smith (1976a: 312).
102 Halévy (1928: 90). We can add: the fact that Mandeville and Smith denied an innate moral sense does not mean that they denied innate 'expectations and anticipations' as Popper expressed it (1979: 258).
103 Cannan (1904: xlvi), cf. also Schumpeter (1914: 52).
104 Viner (1937: 99, note 87). Viner's ideas are shared by Colletti (1975: 57). A thesis analogous to Viner's is supported by Hirschmann (1977: 18–19) and Hollander (1973: 312–14).
105 Hayek (1982I: 145).
106 On the supporters of the *Umschwungstheorie*, cf. D. D. Raphael, A. L. Macfie *Introduction* to Smith (1976a: 20–5). Unfortunately, the theory of the impossibility of reconciling the *Moral Sentiments* with the *Wealth of Nations* was shared also by Viner, as seen in his commemorative lecture given in January 1927: cf. Viner (1927: 201).
107 Mandeville (1924 I: 52). We can say, using Berger and Luckmann's expression (1967), that for Mandeville, Hume and Smith reality is truly a 'social construction'.
108 Hume (1923: 273–4). On this subject, cf. Morrow (1923a: 64–70), Preti (1957: 55–6), Lecaldano (1976: 60–73).
109 Hume (1923 II: 82–3).
110 Smith (1976a: 184–5).
111 Hence, Morrow's thesis (1923b: 32) is not acceptable. According to him, utility is an individual concept, which applies only to individual experience, while the concept of morality is social. When we determine the utility of one of our actions we cannot leave out of consideration the 'prices' which we have to pay to the other; this is equivalent to saying that in order to define what is useful, one must take into account the 'conditions' that others impose on us, exactly as happens in the moral field. Thus, Wilhelm Windelband (1893: 518) hit the nail on the head when he saw 'in the mechanism of sympathetic transfers of feeling an adjustment

of individual interests similar to that which [Smith] believed himself to have discovered in the realm of the exchange of external goods'. On the contrary, Amartya Sen (1987: 28) declares that 'the support that believers in, and advocates of, self-interested behaviour have sought in Adam Smith is, in fact, hard to find on a wider and less biased reading of Smith'. Sen reintroduces, therefore, the *Umschwungstheorie*, an idea which clearly differs from Smith's text and which annuls the debt owed by Smith to Mandeville.

112 Mandeville (1924 I: 181).

113 Smith (1976c: 244).

114 Lujo Brentano (1891) laid great stress on Smith's stay in Paris in order to emphasise the influence of Helvetius' materialism on the *Wealth of Nations*. However, not to mention other issues, Smith had already declared in his Glasgow lectures that the logic of the market is 'Give me that which I want and you shall have this which you want'. He had already formulated the paragraph in which he stated that men are moved not by benevolence but by selfishness (1976e: 493). The origin of this paragraph can be seen in the *Fable of the Bees* (1924 I: 87) where Mandeville speaks of thieves and pickpockets, the victualler and the brewer.

115 Here Smith (1976a: 320) was in complete agreement with Mandeville, and with Hume who had written (1923 II: 220): 'All morality depends upon our sentiments, and when any action, or quality of mind pleases us after a certain manner, we say that it is virtuous'.

116 On 'non-formal ethics' cf. Scheler (1973), Morra (1987), Infantino (1990) The 'non-formal' character of Smith's ethics means that, unlike August Oncken (1897: 445), we do not see Smith as a 'precursor of Kant', whose ethics are formal, that is, rationalistic. Smith's ethics conflict both with Kant's and with Bentham's naive rationalism.

117 Mandeville (1924 I: 135).

118 Smith (1976a: 219).

119 Smith (1976b II: 674).

120 Op. cit.

121 Smith (1976a: 233–4).

122 Tocqueville (1967: 259–60).

123 Taylor (1967: 91). On this subject, cf. Halevy (1928: 266–70), Scott (1937: 124), Bryson (1945: 145).

124 Smith (1976e: 492).

125 Smith (1976b I: 456).

126 Scheler (1980: 139–49); Ortega y Gasset (1946a: 15–21, 1946b: 231–41). The 'perspective' of which Scheler and Ortega spoke can be equated with Alfred Schutz's 'world within my reach' (1962d: 224).

127 Stephen (1902 II: 75).

128 Obviously, just as the level of individual autonomy influences change in the normative and institutional network, in the same way this network influences individual autonomy. Marx's debts towards the 'Scots' on this latter point are considerable. Cf. Forbes (1954), Meek (1954), Lehmann (1960).

129 Thus, historical development represents the product of actors interacting. This places Mandeville, Smith and the 'Scots' far from Turgot and Comte, who had, on the contrary, separated historical phases on the basis of psychological categories. Cf. Burrow (1974: 10–23).

130 This means that norms, however much they are perceived as 'objective', cannot assume an ontological status independent of the activity that has given rise to them. Here it is opportune to add that when economists refer to the relationship in which goods are exchanged for other goods, they speak of *relative prices*; they

define the relationship expressed in monetary terms as an *absolute price*. However, given that money too is a 'good', different from other goods because it functions as the common denominator of exchange, it is right to point out that, despite the usages of economists, prices are always *relative*.

131 Nozick (1974: 314). On this point, cf. the lucidly expressed support of Antonio Martino (1994: 31–3).

132 Smith (1976b I: 116). Therefore, Winch (1978: 70) rightly says that 'the *Wealth of Nations* can be accurately . . . described as an extended treatise on the reciprocal relationship between commerce and liberty'. See also Haakonsen (1981: 139), West (1990: 101).

133 Ibid. II: 687.

134 Jhering (1924: 102) declared that 'the egoism of the seller who tries to force too high a price is paralysed by the egoism of another who prefers rather to sell for a moderate price than not to sell at all, and the egoism of the buyer who offers too little is paralysed by that of another who offers more–*competition is the social self-adjustment of egoism*'. Moreover, Jhering pointed out the existence, in 'cases or peculiar relations in which competition is temporarily or even permanently excluded', of an 'individual self-regulation of egoism' (op. cit.: 103). In fact 'the egoistic exploitation of the present is opposed by a regard for the future. The egoist balances the two possible advantages against each other, and sacrifices the advantage of the moment, no matter how great it is, in order to secure the smaller but permanent advantage for the rest of his life. Concern for the future is the individual self-regulation of egoism' (ibid.).

135 The idea expressed here coincides exactly with the theory formulated by Bruno Leoni (1980: 236) that 'juridical norms correspond . . . to market prices'. Cf. Downie (1976: 102).

136 Smith (1976b II: 687–8).

137 Smith (1976a: 187). Thus, Smith was hostile to legislative artificialism. On this point, cf. also Hayek (1960) and Leoni (1961); for a fair treatment of Bruno Leoni's original theoretical journey, cf. Cubeddu (1922a).

138 Nevertheless, political pressures force the sphere of 'public goods' to expand. Coase (1960, 1974) has underlined all of this and the high cost of any state administration. Therefore, Rothbard (1970 II: 884) rightly says that the 'very concept of "collective goods" is a highly dubious one', and he also adds: 'even if only one agency must supply the good, it has not been proved that the *government*, rather than some voluntary agency, or even some private corporation, cannot supply that good'.

139 Hayek (1988: 14). Cf. Hayek (1937, 1945, 1978: 179–90). Hayek's position obviously recalls the teaching of Mises (1981a: 183) who had controversially stated on the subject of the planner: 'His vision must include everything which is of significance to the community. His judgement must be unfailing; he must be able rightly to weigh the conditions of distant parts and of future centuries.' Alfred Schutz (1962a: 14) was inspired by Hayek to work out his concept of the 'social distribution of knowledge'.

140 For a fuller treatment, cf. Ricossa (1982: 167–9), Kirzner (1994: 101–9).

141 Criticisms of the 'commercial society' were made also by Adam Ferguson, who was an exponent of the Scottish School. As is well known, the publication of Ferguson's *Essay on the History of Civil Society* (1966) was advised against by Hume and the book was considered by Smith to be in part a plagiarism of his own lectures. Marx (1976 I: 219–20, note 29; 483, note 47) on the other hand, emphasised Ferguson's importance. Schumpeter (1954: 184, note 10) rightly

spoke of it as a case of 'undeserved fame'. On Ferguson, cf. Lehmann (1930), Kettler (1965).
142 Viner (1937: 99).
143 Smith (1976b I: 456).
144 Hayek (1978: 58).
145 Hayek (1982 II.:114, 323).
146 Op. cit.: 114–5.

3 WHICH METHOD?

1 Jhering (1924: 46), my italics.
2 Ibid.: 40.
3 Hayek (1988: 111).
4 Forbes (1966: xxiv).
5 Boudon (1984: 268).
6 Mandeville (1924) vol. II: 189.
7 Ibid.
8 Smith (1976a: 110).
9 Popper (1977: 111, note 7).
10 Ibid.: 109.
11 Ibid.: 109–110.
12 Op. cit.: 110.
13 Op. cit.: 111.
14 Op. cit.: 115.
15 Ibid.: 131.
16 Hayek (1988: 22–3).
17 Ibid.
18 Op. cit.: 23.
19 Popper (1949: 129).
20 Mill (1892: 531), my italics.
21 Op. cit.: 546. The passage had already been expounded in Mill (1967: 322).
22 Popper (1966 II: 90). The same observation had been made about Mill by Gabriel Tarde (1899: 28–9).
23 Popper (1966 II: 93), my italics.
24 Popper (1960b: 158).
25 Popper (1966 II: 226).
26 Popper (1977: 144).
27 cf. Popper (1966 II: 96–7; 1960b: 148–9).
28 Popper (1966 II: 93).
29 Comte (1903: 117–8).
30 Comte (1974a: 143).
31 Comte (1974b: 240, note 2).
32 Comte (1970: 217–8), my italics.
33 Op. cit.: 219, note 1.
34 Comte (1974a: 115).
35 Ibid.
36 Ibid.: 116.
37 Ibid.: 115.
38 Ibid., my italics.
39 Op. cit.: 116.
40 Comte (1974b: 217).
41 Comte (1974a: 115).

42 Op. cit.: 134.
43 Op. cit.: 133.
44 Hayek (1979: 152).
45 For Comte, the 'scientific class' was a 'general' or 'universal class', the only depositary of Truth. This is a restating of the Platonic idea which entrusted power to the philosophers, because of their 'superior' knowledge; and it is a fore-runner of the privileged position entrusted by Marx to the dialectical philosopher. The thesis was taken up again by Mannheim (1954) with his theory of *freischwebende Intelligenz*; criticisms against this can be seen in Schumpeter (1954), Stark (1958), Merton (1968). On the subject, cf. Mises (1966), Popper (1960b), Hayek (1979).
46 Hayek (1979: 159).
47 Op. cit.: 160.
48 Ibid.: 154; cf. also Hayek (1960: 60–2).
49 Comte (1974a: 145).
50 Popper (1960a: 3–4; 1966a II: 94–5). Here it must be made clear that all of this happens because Comte, like Plato, asked the question 'Who should rule?' And the reply is: the 'scientific class'. Marx was to say the revolutionary-philosopher. Others, asking the same question, were to say the 'race'. This is always the conse-quence of the idea that there is one person or class who has the monopoly of Truth; this leads to the monopoly of political legitimation, namely to the totali-tarian universe. Popper was right (1966 I: 121) – as we have already recalled – when he asserted that, if we want an 'open society', the previous question should be replaced by a different one: *'How can we organize political institutions that bad or incompetent rulers can be prevented from doing too much damage?'* Cf. Mises (1985: 42–6). Popper's position comes from the understanding that nobody is omni-scient: 'our knowledge can be only finite, while our ignorance must necessarily be infinite' (Popper 1960a: 28). Cf. Bartley III (1984).
51 Hegel (1955 I: 29). I use the original German version of Hegel's work, because the English translation does not contain the passages quoted here.
52 On the ontological, methodological and political aspects of collectivism, cf. also Antiseri (1992: 17–23).
53 Hayek (1979: 162).
54 Dilthey (1959: 97–9). Gabriel Tarde's judgement is similar (1899: 158–9).
55 Marx (1975a: 604).
56 Marx (1976 I: 179).
57 Marx (1936: 30).
58 Marx (1977a: 61).
59 Ibid.: 62.
60 Marx (1977b: 73).
61 Ibid.
62 The two expressions are taken from Marx (1976 I: 171–2); see also Engels (1959: 393).
63 Hegel (1942: 197–8).
64 Popper (1948: 336). Mill's psychologistic method and methodological collec-tivism fall thus into 'historicism', because both see in institutions the projection of individual plans. Cf. Popper (1966 II: 91–2).
65 Popper (1960b: 156).
66 Marx (1976 I: 102).
67 Comte (1970: 220).
68 It is perhaps useful to recall that the formula by which Marx calculated the rate of profit is given by the relation between the surplus value of labour and total

capital. The introduction of new machinery and the extended use of the old have an inevitable consequence. The organic composition, that is the relation between constant capital and total capital (c + v) invested in the production, increases. This means that in the productive combination, the weight of materials, tools and machines increases in relation to that of human labour. This leads to a fall in the rate of profit; in fact the numerator of the fraction decreases while the denominator increases. Marx obtained this result because he put the surplus value, rather than the profit, as numerator, and because he did not consider the increase in productivity consequent upon the introduction of new machines. On this point, see Mises (1966: 145), Schneider (1971), Boudon (1981: 83), Elster (1982: 453–82; 1985; 1986: 60–76), Infantino (1985: 41–2).

69 Here I use an expression of Boudon's (1989: 27–50).

70 Marx (1977b: 73).

71 Sorokin (1942: 14–15).

72 War makes intermediate positions weaken and splits society into two hostile camps. This is why, in Marx's programme, the disappearance of the middle classes is also foreseen.

73 It is worth adding that, in order to unify individual interests, Marx used, beside the threat of survival generated for the time being by the economic mechanism, the promise of a magnificent future reward constituted by the establishment of the Realm of Freedom. In this way, another optical illusion is created: individuals show that they wish to 'release' themselves from their closest interests; but in reality such 'releasement' is made possible by the expectation of a definitive 'gain', precisely that of the Realm of Freedom, in which the 'integral' fulfilment of man goes as far as remoulding the human condition.

74 Marx (1977c: 389). The conclusion reached here coincides with that of Popper (1966 II: 89–99).

75 Hence, José Ortega y Gasset's formula, 'I am myself and my circumstance', is valid (cf. Infantino 1990). It emphasises Simmel's dialogue between the self and the world, of which more will be said later.

76 Engels (1934: 58).

77 Marx (1975b: 318).

78 Here I use an expression of Merton's (1968: 475–90).

79 The idea of unintentional consequences which he made use of in his schema must therefore have 'immunized' Marx against the illusion of being able to 'order' the future society by means of a 'single plan'. But his desire prevailed over his critical reasoning.

80 To complete the argument, it must be added that the 'predictions' of Marx's theory, based on a false premise, have obviously been repudiated by events. Rather than correct the theory, the Marxists have tried to save it by means of ad hoc hypotheses, thus preventing scientific comprehension of the social dynamic. They have proceeded like the doctor who, in order to save his own mistaken diagnoses, refuses to understand the patient's ailments and hence renders his recovery impossible. On this point, cf. Antiseri (1986: 34–5).

4   DURKHEIM AND THE APPLICATION OF THE COLLECTIVISTIC METHOD

1 Parsons (1968: 310).

2 Durkheim (1964: 42).

3 Op. cit.: 415, my italics.

4 Durkheim (1992: 11), my italics.

5 Op. cit.: 24.
6 Op. cit.: 56.
7 Ibid.: 29.
8 Ibid.: 15, 73.
9 Op. cit.: 91.
10 Op. cit.: 92.
11 Op. cit.: 93.
12 Ibid.: 93–4.
13 Op. cit.: 16, my italics.
14 Ibid.: 94.
15 Ibid.
16 Ibid.: 105.
17 Rousseau (1997b: 60).
18 Op. cit.: 71.
19 Durkheim (1992: 105).
20 Ibid.: 105–6, my italics.
21 Durkheim (1964: 28).
22 Ibid.: 329–30. Cf. Durkheim (1992: 14).
23 Durkheim (1964:28).
24 Ibid.
25 Ibid.: 27.
26 Durkheim (1992: 36).
27 Op. cit.: 72.
28 Op. cit.: 74.
29 Ibid.
30 Ibid.: 49.
31 Ibid.: 30, my italics. Cf. Durkheim (1962: 72–3).
32 Durkheim (1992: 49–50).
33 Op. cit.: 57.
34 Durkheim (1975a: 400). This statement is from 1902. Some years later, in 1907, Durkheim wrote, in a controversy with Simon Deploige: 'all of these German works of which M. Deploige speaks have been made known in France by me; it is I who have shown that, although they are not works of sociology, they can still serve the progress of sociology. And I *have certainly exaggerated rather than lessened the importance of their contribution*' (1975a: 402, my italics). But here Durkheim seems to have been more interested in defending himself than in speaking the truth.
35 Hegel (1942: 154).
36 Ibid.: 155.
37 Hegel (1955 I: 111). It is worth comparing the positive opinion of Hegel and Durkheim with the negative opinion of Adam Smith (1976b I: 146):

> The pretence that corporations are necessary for the better government of the trade, is without any foundation. The real and effectual discipline which is exercised over a workman, is not that of a corporation, but that of his customers. It is the fear of losing their employment which restrains his fraud and corrects his negligence. An exclusive corporation necessarily weakens the force of this discipline. A particular set of workmen must then be employed, let them behave well or ill. It is upon this account that in many large incorporated towns no

tolerable workmen are to be found, even in some of the most necessary trades.

38 Durkheim (1961: 117).
39 Cited by Mises (1983: 40). Lewis A. Coser has rightly commented (1977: 145): 'Durkheim's stay in Germany was mainly devoted to the study of methods of instruction and research . . . In his subsequent reports on his German experiences, Durkheim . . . stressed that France *should emulate Germany in making philosophical instruction serve social as well as national goals*' (my italics). However, we shall have to give some attention to this point later on.
40 Parsons (1968: 301). Nor is Guy Aimard's modest work (1962) able to invalidate Parsons' opinion. In a letter to Célestin Bouglé, Durkheim wrote (1975b: 392):

> I wish to tell you that reading the economists may be of more use to you that it has been to me. I, too, when I began fifteen years ago, believed that I would find in them the answer to the questions that preoccupied me. Thus, I spent many years without having anything in return except what one can obtain from a negative influence.

Durkheim's statement seems exaggerated and yet it does not modify the fact of his meagre knowledge of economics. We can add, to the indications in this text, the fact that, in a work on the German economists, Durkheim (1975c: 271) unconcernedly associated Carl Menger, the founder of Austrian marginalism and a vigorous opponent of Gustav Schmoller, with Schmoller himself and with Adolf Wagner, *Kathedersozialisten*.

41 Durkheim (1964: 39).
42 Op. cit.: 416.
43 Op. cit.: 418.
44 Op. cit.: 279.
45 Op. cit.: 280.
46 Op. cit.: 227.
47 Op. cit.: 203.
48 Ibid.
49 Op. cit.
50 Op. cit.: 203–4.
51 Op. cit.: 203.
52 Smith (1976a: 223).
53 Durkheim (1970: 86). In his controversy with Simon Deploige, Durkheim (1975a: 405) declared that he owed to his own neo-Kantian master, C. Renouvier, the 'axiom' that 'a whole is not equal to the sum of the parts'. Commenting on this, Steven Lukes (1973: 57) wrote that 'Renouvier himself did not use the axiom in this way [as Durkheim]; indeed, he criticized the social realism of Saint-Simon and of Comte'. In order to understand Durkheim's statement, it is probably necessary to realise that, in the face of attacks made against his own theories, he was trying to play down his less 'confessable' intellectual debts. Without going any further, the idea that the 'whole is not identical with the sum of its parts' can be found, as will shortly be seen, in Rousseau; it can be found also in Wilhelm Wundt (1912: 33–8). According to Ortega y Gasset (1962: 30–2), the generation of Sigwart, Teichmüller, Wundt, Dilthey and Brentano was drawn together by, among other things, the fact of their being

'rabidly anti-Kantian' and maintaining that the 'whole' was in fact superior to the parts.

54 Here I use an expression of Coser's (1977: 145).
55 Durkheim (1965b: 66).
56 Rousseau (1997a: 134).
57 Op. cit.: 125.
58 Op. cit.: 151.
59 Op. cit.: 138.
60 Op. cit.: 165–6.
61 Op. cit.: 170.
62 Op. cit.: 186–7.
63 Smith (1976c: 249–50).
64 Ibid.: 250.
65 Cf. Colletti (1975: 268).
66 Rousseau (1997a: 145).
67 Ibid.: 147.
68 Ibid.: 172–3.
69 Op. cit.: 173.
70 Op. cit.: 173–4.
71 Rousseau (1997b: 48).
72 Op. cit.: 49–50.
73 Ibid.: 53.
74 Rousseau (1997c: 153).
75 Op. cit.: 154.
76 Ibid., my italics.
77 Op. cit.: 155, my italics.
78 Ibid., my italics.
79 Rousseau (1974: 49), my italics.
80 Durkheim (1965b: 93–4).
81 Rousseau (1997a: 175). Here Rousseau, not unlike Descartes, sings the praises of Sparta, which seems to be the point of reference common to many 'constructivists'.
82 Ibid.: 159.
83 Ibid.: 125.
84 Parsons (1968: 354–5).
85 Cf. note 77 of this chapter.
86 Cf. note 13 of this chapter.
87 Rousseau (1997b: 68–9). In Rousseau's idea of an intelligence, 'who saw all of man's passions and experienced none of them', there is an anticipation of Rawls's (1973) 'veil of ignorance'.
88 Op. cit.: 87.
89 Op. cit.: 60.
90 Durkheim (1974: 26).
91 Op. cit.: 67. Cf. (1982: 82–3), where Durkheim compares personal preferences to 'shifting sand'.
92 Piaget (1928: 205).
93 Durkheim (1964: 64).
94 Durkheim (1982: 59, note 3).
95 Durkheim (1964: 68).
96 Durkheim (1982: 45). Dahrendorf (1973) also dwelt on the social understood as an exclusive external 'constraint'.
97 Simmel (1896–7: 74).

98 Op. cit.: 75.
99 Simmel (1978: 509).
100 Simmel (1992) p.101.
101 Simmel (op. cit.: 103) gives the well-known example of the 'Society of the Broken Dish', an association – to express it in more general terms – in which the entry of new members or the replacement of the deceased is not possible. In this way, the group dies out, it does not outlive the individual members, it does not place itself 'above' them. Simmel (op. cit.: 565), about the 'open' group, adds: 'the departure of the old elements and the entry of new ones takes place so gradually and without a break that it [the group] appears to be a unitary subject, in the same way as an organic body which changes its atoms'. Following Simmel, Berger and Luckman (1967: 225, note 59) write: 'the theoretical key to the question is the distinction between objectivation and reification'.
102 Durkheim (1965a: 237, 240).
103 Parsons (1968: 442).
104 Op. cit.: 441–2.
105 Durkheim (1975c: 296).
106 Op. cit.: 300).
107 Ibid.
108 Op cit.: 297.
109 Durkheim (1961: 116).
110 Ibid.
111 Ibid.: 117.
112 Ibid.: 116.
113 Op. cit.: 115, my italics.
114 Op. cit.: 114, my italics.
115 Hegel (1977: 296).
116 Hegel (1942: 10).
117 Hegel (1977: 265).
118 The expression 'collective consciousness' which Durkheim probably took from Schäffle and from Wundt, coincides with the *volksgeist* or with the *volksseele* of the idealistic tradition.
119 Durkheim (1982: 85–6).
120 When Talcott Parsons (1971 I: 1) said, on the subject of one of his own works, that the matrix which has been most influential is that established by 'German idealism, as it passed from Hegel through Marx to Weber', he was making Durkheim's idealistic position his own. By doing this, he fell into two serious errors. First, he renounced the voluntaristic-creative element of social action which is what he had previously (1968: 444–50) reproved Durkheim's idealism for. Second, he placed Weber close to Hegel, not taking account of the separation between Destiny and science, on which Weber so much insisted. Cf. Sanderson (1990: 124–6).
121 It should be added that Durkheim spoke of 'certainty' with reference to science. But science does not recognise 'certainties'; to use Popper's expression, it proceeds by way of 'conjectures and refutations'; and it is partial and fallible.
122 It is not out of place here to recall that Max Scheler (1954: 94) placed Comte's positivism within the 'romantic movement', as it tended in particular towards restoring a 'vision of the organological world' and towards 'unipathy'. José Ortega y Gasset in his turn (1964: 31) observed that the 'profound error' of positivism 'is the opposite of what is generally supposed; it does not consist in treating ideas as if they were corporeal realities, but rather in treating realities – bodies or not – as if they were ideas, concepts, that is, identities'. Ortega also

declared that the works of Hegel and Comte are 'without doubt' 'works of genius', but that, if we consider them 'from the point of view that interests us most, that of intellectual responsibility and as a token of the moral climate, we quickly realize that, *coeteris paribus*, they would not have been possible in any other epoch of philosophical thought, in any other time of moderation and of passionate respect for the mission of the intellect' (op. cit.: 26).

123 Cited from Lukes (1973: 52).
124 Op cit.: 506, note 44.
125 Simmel (1996: 80). Cf. note 75 of Chapter 3.
126 Op. cit.: 56–7.
127 Thus, the 'social' is not explained as the 'social', but as the co-operative life of men. It is well known that Durkheim (1975a: 403) declared that he owed the distinction between sociology and psychology first of all to his neo-Kantian master Émile Boutroux, who 'often repeated that each science should be explained . . . through its own principles: psychology through psychological principles, biology through biological principles'. If this means that sociology ought to have its own principles, one could not but agree. Nevertheless, this was not what Durkheim thought. He wrote (1974: 29): 'We must, then, explain phenomena that are the product of the whole by the characteristic properties of the whole, the complex by the complex, social facts by society'. This is like saying that the social should be explained tautologically by the social. This idea should be rejected. We shall see in the following chapter how Durkheim can be read 'individualistically'. This, obviously, makes the 'circle' mentioned above disappear.

5 IS AN 'INDIVIDUALISTIC' READING OF DURKHEIM POSSIBLE?

1 Alpert (1939: 155).
2 Durkheim (1975c: 300).
3 Durkheim (1982: 128), my italics.
4 Durkheim (1974: 25–6).
5 Durkheim (1965a: 240).
6 Durkheim (1974: 44–5), my italics.
7 Durkheim (1975d: 335).
8 Durkheim (1975a: 404–6).
9 Robertson Smith (1907: 254–5).
10 Ibid.: 257.
11 Ibid.: 265.
12 Durkheim (1982: 125).
13 Op. cit.: 129.
14 Op. cit.: 134.
15 Ibid.
16 Durkheim (1964: 234).
17 Op. cit.: 245.
18 Op. cit.: 270.
19 However, the explanation given by Mandeville and Smith differs from that of Durkheim in its antecedents. According to Mandeville and Smith, the increase of competition depends on the slackening of the 'grip' of the administrative–bureaucratic apparati of the state and of the corporations on civil society, and on the consequent increase of individual autonomy. Putting it in different terms, Durkheim (1964: 256–7) said:

The growth of the division of labor is . . . brought about by the social segments losing their individuality, the divisions becoming more permeable. In short, a coalescence takes place which makes new combinations possible in the social substance . . . Consequently, there is an exchange of movements between parts of the social mass which, until then, had no effect upon one another. The greater the development of the cellular system, the more are our relations enclosed within the limits of the cell to which we belong. There are, as it were, moral gaps between the various segments. On the contrary, these gaps are filled in as the system is leveled out. Social life, instead of being concentrated in a moltitude of little centres, distinctive and alike, is generalized. Social relations, – more exactly, intra-social – consequently become more numerous, since they extend, on all sides, beyond their original limits. The division of labor develops, therefore, as there are more individuals sufficiently in contact to be able to act and react upon one another. If we agree to call this relation and the active commerce resulting from it dynamic or moral density, we can say that the progress of the division of labor is in direct ratio to the moral or dynamic density of social.

In other words, it is autonomy that allows greater social exchanges and that produces, unintentionally with respect to individual projects, the increase of the division of labour.

20 Durkheim (1964: 275).
21 Ibid.
22 Durkheim (1952: 48).
23 Ibid.
24 Op. cit.: 51–2.
25 Halbwachs (1930).
26 Durkheim (1952: 368). In repudiation of Durkheim's theory, data relating to the beginning of the new century actually registered a reduction in suicides.
27 Boudon and Bourricaud (1986: 589).
28 Durkheim (1964: 133).
29 Ibid.: 130.
30 Ibid.: 131.
31 Op. cit.: 329.
32 Boudon and Bourricaud (1986: 591). For a more complete criticism of Durkheim's sociologistic theory of suicide, the reader is referred to Douglas (1967) and Baechler (1975). However, it is worth pointing out that Halbwachs (1930: 264) had already perceived, although very cautiously, the 'circularity' of Durkheim's schema.
33 Durkheim (1965a: 425–6).
34 Op. cit.: 426.
35 Op. cit.: 426–7.
36 Op. cit.: 426.
37 Op. cit.: 427.
38 Durkheim (1964: 415).
39 Op. cit.: 55–6, my italics.
40 Op. cit.: 56.
41 Montesquieu (1949: 25).
42 Quoted from Hayek (1982 II: 185, note 7).
43 Wolff (1958: 593).

44 Spencer (1885–96 III: 601). However, on Durkheim's debts to Spencer, despite his polemic, see Andreski (1971: 22).
45 Durkheim (1964: 203).
46 Spencer (1860: 90–1), my italics.
47 Op. cit.: 95.
48 Durkheim (1964: 243).
49 Spencer (1907: 120).
50 Durkheim (1982: 133; 1964: 233–55).
51 Spencer (1860: 91–2), my italics.
52 Op. cit.: 91.
53 Op. cit.: 92.
54 Spencer (1873: 6).
55 Op. cit.: 15.
56 Op. cit.: 21
57 Spencer (1885–96 I: 449–50), my italics. Lewis Coser (1977: 99), has written: 'This is not the place to judge whether Spencer really managed to reconcile his individualism and his organicism – I rather think that he did not – but only to note that Spencer thought he had done so by stressing that no social body possessed a collective sensorium.' Here Coser does not take account of the fact that Spencer himself knew that the organicistic is an analogy, to be used only to the extent that it can be useful to sociology.
58 Spencer (1873: 21–2).
59 Op. cit.: 329.
60 Spencer (1885–96 III: 325).
61 Spencer (1873: 329).
62 Op. cit.: 346.
63 Nozick (1974: 314). Here it is worthwhile recalling that for Spencer (1857: 485), 'the sincere man of science ... becomes by each new inquiry more propoundly convinced that the Universe is an insoluble problem ... In all directions, his investigations eventually bring him face to face with the unknowable; and he ever more clearly perceives it to be unknowable.'
64 Simmel (1896–97: 74–5).
65 Durkheim (1960: 363).
66 Ibid.
67 Simmel (1996: 80).
68 Simmel (1978: 75).
69 Op. cit.: 156.
70 Op. cit.: 128–9.
71 Op. cit.: 292.
72 Op. cit.: 99, my italics.
73 Op. cit.: 291, my italics.
74 Ibid.
75 Ibid.
76 Ibid.
77 Simmel (1977: 55).
78 Jameson (1991).
79 Simmel (1971: 387).

6 ECONOMISTS AND SOCIOLOGISTS COMPARED

1 Menger (1985: 36).
2 Ibid.

3 Op. cit.: 38.
4 Ibid. As is well known, the idea of co-operation between the theoretical moment and the historical and statistical moment was taken up by Joseph Schumpeter (1954). Moreover, Menger (1985: 38) singled out a third group of sciences, 'the so-called *practical* sciences, or *technologies*', whose 'problem is . . . to determine the basic principles by which, according to the diversity of conditions, effort of a definite kind can be most suitable pursued. . . . Technologies of this kind in the field of economy are *economic policy* and the science of finance'.
5 Op. cit.: 59.
6 Op. cit.: 61, my italics.
7 Op. cit.: 57.
8 Op. cit.: 62.
9 The term 'compositive' comes from a manuscript note of Carl Menger's. Cf. Hayek (1979: 67, note 4. The expression 'methodological individualism', on the other hand, comes from Schumpeter (1908: 90).
10 Menger (1985: 58).
11 Op. cit.: 56–7.
12 Menger (1994: 154).
13 Op. cit.: 108.
14 Op. cit.: 120–1.
15 Op. cit.: 74–5.
16 Ibid.
17 Op. cit.: 52, note 4, my italics.
18 Op. cit.: 191.
19 Ibid.
20 Op. cit.: 116, note 3.
21 Op. cit.: 191.
22 Op. cit.: 192.
23 Op. cit.: 192–3.
24 Op. cit.: 192.
25 Ibid.
26 Op. cit.: 147.
27 Ibid.
28 Ortega y Gasset (1946c: 481–2).
29 Menger (1985: 177).
30 Op. cit.: 158–9, my italics.
31 Op. cit.: 151–9.
32 Op. cit.: 174–77. Since Menger relied to a great extent on Savigny and on the historical school of law, while he argued with the historical school of economics, it is useful to recall their methodological difference. In a comment on the position of Roscher, who declared that he was remaking the historical school of law, Max Weber wrote (1975a: 60–1): 'In fact – and in its essentials this point has already been made by Menger – his methodological model is a peculiar *novel interpretation* of this method'. Further, it is significant that Gustav Schmoller (1883: 250), head of the 'young' historical school of economics, did not hesitate to accuse Menger of being an exponent of the school of Burke and Savigny. Cf. Hayek (1979: 112, note 1).
33 Menger (1985: 146).
34 Hayek (1979: 145–6).
35 Menger (1985: 177).
36 On the connections between Smith and Burke, cf. Fay (1960: 1–20).
37 Hayek (1979: 146).

38 Hayek (1949: 4, note 3).
39 Laidler and Rowe (1980: 97).
40 Menger (1901: 160–1).
41 Laidler and Rowe (1980: 100).
42 This assessment of Machlup is mentioned by Laidler and Rowe (1980: 10–1, note 5).
43 Small (1907: 4).
44 Small (1924: 172).
45 Menger (1985: 25).
46 In Gassen and Landmann (1958: 101).
47 Cited by Weber (1975a: 71).
48 This is valid for all the exponents of the German historical school of economics, from Roscher, by way of Schmoller, to Sombart. Referring to the last-named, Ludwig von Mises (1983: 33) wrote:

> The straight line that leads from the work of the historical School to Nazism cannot be shown in sketching the evolution of one of the founders of the School. For the protagonists of the *Methodenstreit* era had finished the course of their lives before the defeat of 1918 and the rise of Hitler. But the life of the outstanding man among the School's second generation illustrates all the phases of German university economics in the period from Bismarck to Hitler.

Mises added (op. cit.: 34), 'Such was the progress of German academic economics from Schmoller's glorification of the Electors and Kings of Hohenzollern to Sombart's canonization of Adolf Hitler'.
49 Menger (1985: 55–6).
50 Op. cit.: 60.
51 Op. cit.: 87.
52 Op. cit.: 92.
53 Ibid.: 92–3.
54 Op. cit.: 93.
55 Op. cit.: 194, note 129. Max Weber, who had benefited from the methodological results obtained by Menger, wrote (1975a: 1): 'This concept of "volksgeist" does not function as a provisional heuristic device for the preliminary description of a large number of concrete perceptual phenomena the logical status of which remains unclarified. On the contrary, it is treated as a real, uniform entity which has a metaphysical status.' And straight afterwards he added (ibid.): 'it is not the *result* of countless cultural influences. Just to the contrary, it is viewed as the *actual ground* of all the individual cultural manifestations of a volk, the source from which they all *emanate*'; translated into a language more familiar to us, this means that with individualistic methodology one proceeds from the data of a problem towards the 'solution', while with the collectivistic method one goes from the 'solution', from the 'intuitive totality' towards the data, which therefore have to be adapted to the solution that is already known.
56 Menger (1985: 194, note 29).
57 It should be recalled here that the methodological dispute with the German historical school of economics was started by Menger with the publication in 1883 of his *Untersuchungen über die Methode der Sozialwissenschaften*. The reply came from Gustav Schmoller (1883), with a polemical review, *Zur Methodologie der Staats – und Sozialwissenschaften*, the second part of which contains positive

evaluations of Dilthey's contemporary *Einleitung in die Geistwissenschaften*. As Ludwig von Mises (1983: 29) pointed out, Schmoller 'did not grasp the fact that the tenor of Dilthey's doctrine was the annihilation of the fundamental thesis of his own epistemology, viz. that some laws of social development could be distilled from historical experience'. The 'benevolent' attitude shown towards Dilthey's position was repeated by Schmoller (1901) over Simmel's *Philosophie des Geldes*, another work methodologically opposed to the position of the historical school of economics and, not by chance, criticised by the 'universalist' Othmar Spann (1925). On the connections between Schmoller and Simmel, cf. Frisby (1978: 8–9; 1981: vii, 18, 110, 117), Köhnke (1990: 101).

Returning to our main theme, it should be added that Menger promptly counter-attacked Schmoller's thesis with his *Die Irrtümer des Historismus*. For full bibliographical references to this dispute, I would mention the recent Italian translation of the *Die Irrtümer des Historismus*, the editor of which, Dario Antiseri (1991), has provided it with a full bibliography. On this subject, cf. the well-documented work by Cubeddu (1992b: 72–98).

58 Simmel (1977: vii–viii).
59 Op. cit.: viii–ix.
60 Ranke (1973: 44, my italics).
61 Ortega y Gasset (1966c: 526, note 1).
62 Simmel (1996: 36).
63 Op. cit.: 57.
64 Simmel (1917: 32).
65 Simmel (1977: 76–7).
66 Op. cit.: 78.
67 Menger (1985: 36).
68 Simmel (1894: 277). (The English translation of Simmel's work does not contain this passage.) It is not out of place here to point out that Durkheim (1960: 357) directed this clumsy exclamation against Simmel's 'formal' sociology: 'what a strange idea it would be to imagine the group as a sort of empty form of trivial cast that can indifferently receive any kind of material whatever!'
69 Menger (1994: 64), my italics.
70 Simmel (1978: 96).
71 Op. cit.: 75, my italics.
72 Ibid.
73 Op. cit.: 66.
74 Op. cit.: 67.
75 Op. cit.: 63.
76 Op. cit.: 78. Simmel declared again (ibid.):

> It has been said that the divine principle, after having created the elements of the world, withdrew and left them to the free play of their own powers, so that we can now speak of an objective cosmos, subject to its own relations and laws . . . In the same way, we invest economic objects with a quantity of value as if it were an inherent quality and then hand them over to the process of exchange, to a mechanism determined by those quantities, to an impersonal confrontation between values, from which they return multiplied and more

intensely enjoyable to their final purpose, which was also their point of origin: subjective experience.

77 Op. cit.: 156.
78 Op. cit.: 162.
79 Op. cit.: 212. It is appropriate to recall the attention paid by Simmel (1917: 71–103) to the unintentional origins of 'courtesy'.
80 Simmel (1978: 212).
81 Mandeville (1924 II: 350).
82 Simmel (1978: 285).
83 Hayek (1982 II: 109–10). Here it is useful to recall what Simmel (1992: 64) wrote about the link between the 'great society' and the division of labour:

> A very large number of men can make up a unit only in the presence of a clearly marked division of labour: not only for immediately comprehensible motives of economic technique, but also because only this generates the framework and the reciprocal dependence that connects each person with others, and without which a very extensive group would disintegrate at every opportunity.

84 Lachmann (1978: 57–9).
85 Menger (1985: 87).
86 Schmoller (1883: 244).
87 Op. cit.: 243.
88 Mises (1981b: 24). It follows that 'in life, everything is continually in flux', even if 'for thought we must construct an imaginary state of rest' (op. cit.: 108). Mises (1981a: 142) said also: 'The stationary condition is that point of equilibrium to which we conceive all forms of economic activity to be tending, and which would actually be attained if new factors did not, in meantime, create a new point of equilibrium'; and he added (op. cit.: 173): 'The idea of a stationary state is an aid to theoretical speculation. In the world of reality there is no stationary state, for the conditions under which economic activity takes place are subject to perpetual alterations which it is beyond human capacities to limit.' In other words, for Mises, individual life is never in a state of equilibrium, and nor is collective life.
89 Mises (1981b: 79).
90 Ibid.
91 Op. cit.: 80.
92 Ibid, my italics. Menger could have upheld the same thesis as Mises. It was not by chance that he declared in his *Grundsätze* (1994: 97): 'human economy and property have a joint economic origin, since both have, as the ultimate reason of their existence, the fact that goods exist whose available quantities are smaller then the requirement of men.' Hume (1923 II: 190–205) had already emphasised this, dwelling on the 'scarcity' of goods in comparison with needs.
93 Mises (1981b: 80).
94 Op. cit.: 157–8.
95 Mises (1981a: 95).
96 Op. cit.: 97.
97 Mises (1981b: 81).
98 Op. cit.: 34.
99 Ibid.

100 Op. cit.: 94, my italics
101 Op. cit.: 179.
102 Ibid.
103 Op. cit.: 118.
104 Op. cit.: 34.
105 Locke (1967: 302). In tune with Locke, Hayek (1982 I: 56) wrote: 'The freedom to pursue his own aims is, however, at least as important for the complete altruist as for the most selfish. Altruism . . . certainly does not presuppose that one has another person's will. But it is true that much pretended altruism manifests itself in a desire to make others serve the ends which the "altruist" regards as important'.
106 Scheler (1973: 105–6).
107 Mises (1981b: 81).
108 Boudon (1994: 260), also agreed on this.
109 Weber (1949b: 106).
110 Op. cit.: 95.
111 Weber (1949a: 3).
112 Op. cit.: 46.
113 Op. cit.: 7.
114 Hayek (1979: 52, note 7) where Hayek himself added: 'I believe that most peculiarities of his (Mises's) views which at first strike many readers as strange and unacceptable trace to the fact that in the consistent development of the subjectivist approach he has for a long time moved ahead of his contemporaries.'
115 Cf. Mises (1978: 104). As a clearer illustration of Mises's position, it is helpful to recall that he believed in the primacy of the theoretical moment in the construction of science; thus Mises (1981b: 28) wrote that 'a theory is already contained in the very linguistic terms involved in every act of thought'. Moreover, he upheld the partiality of knowledge: 'Reason and science deal only with isolated fragments detached from the living whole and thereby killed' (op. cit.: 44). And he considered that no theory can be 'regarded as conclusively established' (op. cit.: 30). It is helpful also to add that Mises, when he published *Soziologie und Geschichte* in 1929, criticised Weber's ideal type, because it was developed by means of the 'unilateral emphasis on *one* or a *few* points of view', and because it was different from Menger's 'types', which represent the phenomena in their 'absolute purity'. In 1932, however, *Der sinnhafte Aufbau der sozialen Welt*, by Alfred Schutz, appeared in Vienna; and Mises, who in 1933 published a collection of his own epistemological essays, left unchanged his statement of 1929, but added (1981b: 125–6, note 27) that Weber's ideal type could be accepted in the reinterpretation of Schutz (his pupil).
    Schutz (1972: 243) considered that there are two versions of the ideal type in Weber. The first, linked to the requirements of historical knowledge, in which in fact the 'ideal type' is derived directly from an 'empirical wealth' or, to repeat Weber's words, from 'those one-sidedly emphasized viewpoints'; the second, much more oriented towards sociological knowledge, in which man is taken 'in his everyday social life not as a living individual person with a unique consciousness, but only as a personal ideal type without duration or spontaneity'. This second meaning of the ideal type is the one approved of by Mises, and one can understand why; not because Weber did not recognise (1949b: 84–94) 'the meaninglessness of the idea' of those who believe 'that the "true" content and the essence of historical reality is portrayed in such theoretical constructs'. But it is because Mises, favouring the economic theory, worked with instruments which have – to explain it with what Simmel (1978: 216) said on the subject of money

– 'the very positive property that is designated by the negative concept of lack of character'.

116 Weber (1968 I: 19).
117 Mises (1981a: 259).
118 Weber (1922a: 361).
119 Op. cit.: 372, note 1.
120 Op. cit.: 372.
121 Mises (1981b: 152).
122 Op cit.: 153–4.
123 Op. cit.: 3, my italics.
124 Op. cit.: 57.
125 Weber (1949b: 63–4). Here it is worth while recalling some remarks by Ortega y Gasset (1970a: 341–2, my italics): 'for man, life, from the very first instant and before anything else, affords the effort to act in such a way that there is what does not yet exist; this means that he himself, who benefits from what there is, is definitely production. By this I mean that life is not fundamentally contemplation, thought, theory, as was believed for many centuries. No. Life is production, building, and, only because these things demand it, but after and not before, it is thought, theory, science. *To live . . . or indeed to find the means to carry out the project that we are*. Moreover, Ortega (op. cit.: 351) explained that even sport, which appears to be a 'vital luxury . . . is at the same time a force', seeing that 'it presupposes a previous domination of the lower layers of existence'; it presupposes a previous accumulation or saving up of 'means'. This is like saying that not even sport can be removed from the 'economic' dimension; to use an expression of Weber's, it needs some form of 'intramondane asceticism'.
126 Mises (1981b: 42).
127 Ibid.
128 Mises (1981b: 42). Mises wrote again (op. cit.: 110):

> The increase in productivity brought about by division of labor is what gives impetus to the formation of society and to progressive intensification of social cooperations. We owe the origin and development of human society and, consequently, of culture and civilization, to the fact that work performed under the division of labor is more productive than when performed in isolation. The history of sociology as a science began with the realization of the importance for the formation of society of the increase in productivity achieved under the division of labor.

129 Weber (1949a: 16). Weber (op. cit.: 15) declared also that 'the assertion that "formal" propositions, for example, those in Kantian ethics, contain no material directives, represents a grave but widespread misunderstanding'.
130 Op. cit.: 163.
131 Mises (1981a: 388).
132 Op. cit.: 363, my italics.
133 Op. cit.: 358.
134 Op. cit.: 357.
135 Op. cit.: 390.
136 Op. cit.: 357.
137 Weber (1922b: 418).
138 Ibid.: 415.

139 Ibid.
140 Weber (1968 I: 13).
141 Op. cit.: 18.
142 Mises (1981b: 43).
143 Op. cit.: 44.
144 Op. cit.: 58.
145 Ibid.
146 Weber (1968 I: 78).
147 vol. xlvii, April 1920: 86–121. The English translation was edited by Hayek (1935).
148 Weber (1968 I: 107).
149 Op. cit.: 108.
150 Taking his own view to its logical conclusion, Mises not only made planification coincide with the impossibility of economic calculation, but also held that it was impossible to articulate a complex society on the basis of a single plan of production and distribution; that is, he foresaw the collapse of the socialist systems. Cf., at greater length, Infantino (1992) and Huerta de Soto (1992).
151 Mises (1981b: 81–2).
152 Ibid.
153 Ibid.
154 Weber (1968 I: 24–5).
155 Op. cit.: 4.
156 Mises (1981b: 83).
157 Op. cit.: 93.
158 Weber (1922a: 379).
159 Mises (1981b: 94).
160 Op. cit.: 92–3.
161 Op. cit.: 85.
162 Ibid.
163 Op. cit.: 84–5.
164 Op. cit.: 88.
165 Weber (1968 I: 25).
166 Mises (1981b: 84). Schutz (1962b: 67–96) adopted a similar attitude to that of Mises.
167 Weber (1975b: 193).
168 Weber (1968 I: 26).
169 Ibid.
170 Weber (1968 I: 25).
171 Weber (1991a: 120), said:

> we must be clear about the fact that all ethically oriented conduct may be guided by one of two fundamentally differing and irreconcilable opposed maxims: conduct can be oriented to an 'ethic of ultimate ends' or to an 'ethic of responsibility'. This is not to say that an ethic of ultimate ends is identical with irresponsibility or that an ethic of responsibility is identical with unprincipled opportunism. Naturally nobody says that. However, there is an abysmal contrast between conduct that follows the maxim of an ethic of ultimate ends – that is, in religious terms, 'The Christian does rightly and leaves the results with the Lord' – and conduct that follows the maxim of an ethic of

responsibility, in which case one has to give an account of the foreseeable result of one's action.

172 Schutz (1962b: 93). On this question, cf. Lachmann (1970: 42–8), who, not
unlike Schutz, emphasised the continual reformation of 'personal plans' made
necessary by the *information* that the subject acquires by acting, and that he transforms into new action. Schütz and Lachmann show obvious effects of Hayek's
influence.

7 THE EARLY PARSONS: BETWEEN SOCIOLOGY AND ECONOMICS

1 Schumpeter (1908: 90).
2 Levine (1971: xlviii).
3 Knight (1940: 460).
4 Parsons (1968: 3).
5 Op. cit.: 4.
6 Op. cit.: 4. It is, however, well known that Parsons (1961) wrote, much later, an
eulogistic introduction to a new edition of Spencer's *Study of Sociology*. This
makes early Parsons' condemnation of Spencer even more unjust.
7 Spencer (1885–96 III: 325).
8 Cf. Chapter 5, note 64).
9 Parsons (1968: 686–94).
10 Parsons (1979: 41–2).
11 Op. cit.: 42.
12 Ibid.
13 Op. cit.: 43.
14 Parsons (1993: 52).
15 Simmel (1978: 99).
16 Op. cit.: 99–100.
17 Parsons (1993: 52–3).
18 Op. cit.: 53, note 23.
19 Simmel (1978: 175) wrote:

> If all interaction ceases there is no longer any society. In the same way, a
> living organism can continue to exist if one or the other of its functions
> ceases . . . because 'life' is nothing but the sum of interacting forces
> among the atoms of organism. It is, therefore, almost a tautology to say
> that exchange brings about socialization: for exchange is a form of
> socialization. It is one of those relations through which a number of
> individuals become a social group, and 'society' is identical with the
> sum total of these relations.

20 Parsons (1979: 43).
21 Ibid.
22 Weber (1922a: 379).
23 Mises (1977: 103). Mises also reported the evidence of Marianne Weber (1926:
213), who mentioned that her husband, when he was teaching economics at
Freiburg, spoke ironically of his 'great' lectures.

24 It is helpful to add here that, in the pages dedicated to Mises in the previous chapter, we deliberately used only writings earlier than *The Structure of Social Action*.

25 Parsons (1934a).

26 Robbins (1935: xv–xvi). As is well known, Robbins, who taught at the London School of Economics and Political Science, not only invited Hayek to teach at that university, but also had Mises's *Theorie des Geldes und der Umlaufsmittel* (1934) and *Gemeinwirtschaft* (1936) translated into English. Because of this, the LSE was regarded as a 'suburb of Vienna' (cf. Ebeling 1993: 59). However, as Kirzner says (1992: 126), it should be made clear that Robbins, by treating ends as 'given', suppressed 'the future from the very notion of human purpose'. In other words, 'Despite all his virtues and all its Austrian credentials, the subjectivism which Robbins brought from Vienna was only the "static" aspect of that theory' (ibid). 'In a market economy, neither the ranking of ends nor the availability of means can be considered as given, to any agent apart from the decision . . . of other individuals,' (ibid.: 127). As we have pointed out in Chapter 2, when speaking of the 'invisible hand', each operator is simultaneously *price taker* and *price maker*.

27 Robbins (1935: 95).

28 Op. cit.: 96, note 1.

29 Smith (1976b I: 116).

30 Parsons (1968: 96, note 2).

31 Jeremy Bentham said: 'I was the spiritual father of Mill, and Mill was the spiritual father of Ricardo: so that Ricardo was my spiritual grandson'; quoted by Halévy (1928: 266). It should be added that Parsons made use not only of Halévy's book, but also of Leslie Stephen's work, *The English Utilitarians* (1900). Stephen obviously did not place Smith within 'philosophical radicalism'; he emphasised the excessive 'abstractness' of Ricardo's theories; he recalled that Smith's was primarily a 'theory of the market', and that Ricardo's, on the other hand, was a theory of 'distribution' (op. cit. II: 191–3). This is why the labour theory of value, though present in Smith, does not harm his work, while in Ricardo 'labour', according to Leslie Stephen (op. cit. II: 217–8) becomes an 'independent variable'.

32 On this point, Parsons was misled by Ralph W. Souter: from his review (Souter 1933: 387 ff.) of Robbins' book, Parsons borrowed the idea (1934a: 515) of the staticity of the neo-Austrian theory and of the suppression of the time variable. This is totally indefensible. Carl Menger (1994: 68) had earlier written:

> the time period lying between command of goods of higher order and possession of the corresponding goods of lower order can never be completely eliminated. Goods of higher order acquire and maintain their goods-character, therefore, not with respect to needs of the immediate present, but as a result of human foresight, only with respect to needs that will be experienced when the process of production has been completed.

He emphasised the 'uncertainty' that affects production (op. cit.: 69–70). Eugen von Böhm-Bawerk (1959: 439), Ludwig von Mises's master, had declared that 'the explanation of interest would derive from the influence of *time* on the value placed by men on goods'; Parsons should have known Böhm-Bawerk's theory, at least through the work of Irving Fisher (1930) or through his own 'masters' at

Harvard, Taussig and Schumpter. Ludwig von Mises had, *inter alia*, criticised the theory of general equilibrium, precisely because the time variable continually modifies the 'data' of the problem (Chapter 6, note 88).

33 Parsons (1968: 50).
34 Op. cit.: 65–66, (my italics).
35 Descartes (1960: 50).
36 Ortega y Gasset (1964: 16, my italics).
37 Parsons (1968: 90).
38 Parsons (1935b: 290).
39 Op. cit.: 291.
40 Ibid.
41 Ibid. Referring to economics, Parsons could thus maintain that the utilitarian schema hypostatises the 'intrinsic' means–end relationship, but that it is extraneous to the 'symbolic' relationship, which aims at ends not scientifically controllable and relevant, in a Weberian way, only for the subject who acts. The recovery of the subjective dimension of action and the criticism of philosophical radicalism obviously enabled Parsons to criticise the behaviourism present in American culture; cf. Camic (1989: 63–77).
42 Hayek (1978: 14).
43 Parsons (1934a: 515–6).
44 Ricossa (1988: 11–12).
45 Kirzner (1992: 128).
46 Parsons (1935a: 655).
47 Smith (1976b I: 117).
48 Op. cit.: 118.
49 Here I use an expression of Mises (1981a: 388).
50 Scheler (1973: 6).
51 Marshall (1969: 394).
52 Op. cit.: 73.
53 Op. cit.: 72.
54 Op. cit.: 76.
55 Parsons (1935a: 443). Parsons (1968: 143) also declared: 'Any sense of the sordidness of economic acquisition as such is totally absent. Indeed, it can be said that on the whole Marshall saw the field of business enterprise as the principal opportunity for the exercise of what he considered the noblest traits of human character.'
56 Parsons (1968: 143).
57 Smith (1976b I: 27).
58 Op. cit.: 127.
59 Parsons (1935a: 443, my italics).
60 Marshall (1969: 676).
61 Parsons (1968: 167).
62 Marshall (1969: 306–7).
63 Op. cit.: 185–6, my italics.
64 Mises (1981a: 181–2). In more recent years, Mises (1966: 252) also wrote: 'the outcome of action is always uncertain. Action is always speculation . . . In any real and living economy, every actor is always an entrepreneur'. All of this fits in perfectly with the idea expressed by Ortega y Gasset (1966b: 400), that the uncertainty of life makes each of us a highly 'programmatic character', a being who continually runs the risk of not being.

It should also be added that Mises's position harmonises perfectly with Hayek's theory (1978: 178–90), of 'competition as a discovery procedure', and with the 'Austrian' theory of Israel Kirzner (1973: 69–75), who sees the entrepreneur as the one who seeks to respond, with his offer, to situations of disequilibrium).

65 Parsons (1968: 185–96).
66 Pareto (1935: 77, para. 150).
67 Parsons (1968: 185–228).
68 Pareto (1935: 1476, para. 2143).
69 Op. cit.: 1460, para. 2112.
70 Op. cit.: 1476, para. 2143.
71 Parsons (1935b: 306, note 20) maintained that it is possible to establish a 'direct parallel' between at least some 'residues' and the 'common system of ultimate ends' which we shall discuss in the next section. But this obscures the real intention of Pareto's work, which was to separate the 'determinants' of actions from their rationalisations or 'derivations.'
72 Schumpeter (1952: 141).
73 Parsons (1935a: 647–8).
74 Parsons (1968: 160).
75 Op. cit.: 64.
76 Op. cit.: 63.
77 Op. cit.: 64.
78 Op. cit.: 60.
79 Op. cit.: 64–5.
80 Parsons (1934a: 517–8).
81 Op. cit.: 518.
82 Cf. Parsons (1968: 96–7).
83 Halévy (1928: 15–6).
84 Op. cit.: 16.
85 Parsons (1968: 96–7).
86 Halévy (1928: 17).
87 Op. cit.: 506.
88 Op. cit.: 17, 499.
89 Hayek (1978: 260).
90 See note 80 above.
91 Spencer (1851: 1 ff).
92 Halévy (1928: 514).
93 Guyau (1885: 5).
94 Cf. Descartes (1960: 45).
95 Hayek (1982 II: 20). It is not out of place at this point to add that Bentham's 'artificialism' came about through the force of numbers. In fact, he (1838–43 V: 211) did not hesitate to write that 'in case of collision or contest, happiness of each party being equal, prefer the happiness of the greater to that of the lesser number'. The illiberality of this position was recognised also by John Stuart Mill (1950: 85–9), inspired by Alexis de Tocqueville. However, this did not prevent Mill (1965 II: 754) from theorising about the 'stationary state' as 'the best state for human nature', 'that in which, while no one is poor, no one desires to become richer, nor has any reason to fear being thrust back, by the efforts of other to push themselves forward'. In other words: the 'optimum' that Mill went in search of is given by a situation in which there is no disequilibrium and no competition; and, we could add, no life.

A further note is needed. With its ambition to 'maximise' rationality, philosophical radicalism dwells within the idea of intentional order and gives rise, from the economic point of view, to the need for planning, or at the least, as in the case of welfare economics, to the intention of constructing (and maximising) a function of social welfare. This is why one can say, with Friedrich von Hayek (1949: 1–32), that the individualism of philosophical radicalism is a 'false individualism'; in effect, it is a psychologism with the illusion that it can reach social harmony. Not by chance, from the normative point of view, it gives rise to juridical positivism, that is, the claim that rules originate from the 'deliberate choice of means for known ends' (Hayek 1982 II: 23). Therefore, utilitarianism *à la* Bentham is the culture of the Lawgiver and of the Planner).

96 Parsons (1968: 101).
97 Op. cit.: 102.
98 Parsons (1934a: 524).
99 Parsons (1935b: 299).
100 Op. cit.: 295.
101 Ibid.
102 Op. cit.: 299.
103 Parsons (1934a: 523; cf. also p. 531).
104 Durkheim (1964: 79), Parsons (1968: 309).
105 Parsons (1968: 337, my italics).
106 Op. cit.: 312. Parsons did not realise that by putting the 'conditions of action' as *given*, he fell into the same errors as those for which he reproved economic theory. This is why his 'structural functionalism' is no different from Walras's schema of general economic equilibrium; on this subject, cf. Camic (1987: 431), impulsively criticised by Mark Gould (1989: 637–54; 1991: 85–107).
107 Parsons (1935b: 306).
108 Op. cit.: 295.
109 Parsons (1968: 251).
110 Ortega y Gasset (1962: 40).
111 Dussort (1963: 30).
112 It is not by chance that Cohen (1914 I, III: 21) declared: 'We begin with thought. Thought cannot have any origin outside itself, otherwise its purity would necessarily finish up limited and obscured.' Cohen (op. cit. I, VIII: 35) proclaimed, that is, 'the autonomy and originality' of pure thought.
113 Ortega y Gasset (1962: 44).
114 Commenting on Hermann Cohen's position, Mises (1981a: 389), emphasised that the idea of the division of labour is not present in Kant and the neo-Kantians; in fact, by showing that each person is at the same time means and end, this idea does not make the survival of the categorical imperative possible. Parsons should have known about this criticism. Following Parsons, not even Münch (1987) takes into account such a criticism.
115 This becomes even clearer, if one gives up the schema of action and moves on, as in Parsons' second phase, to a macrosocial approach.
116 Parsons (1968: 354–55). An analogous passage can be found in Parsons (op. cit: 367).
117 Mises (1989a: 357).
118 This shows, *inter alia*, that action carried out to completion on consensual bases can never be defined as 'egoistic' in the sense of being the bearer of advantages for Ego alone.
119 Parsons (1968: 644).
120 Hayek (1982), Oakeshott (1975).
121 Parsons (1968: 248).
122 Pareto (1904: 194).
123 Pareto (1935: 1466–7, para. 2129).

124 Op. cit.: 1471, para. 2133.
125 Amartya Sen (1970) has discussed the incompatibility of point *P* with the prin-
    ciples of a free society. The incompatibility between the maxim *of* the society and
    a liberal order, the question that interests us here, is analysed further on in the
    text.
126 Pareto (1935: 1473, para. 2137).
127 Op. cit.: 1471–2, para. 2134. Pareto (1904: 198), had also clearly written:

> The opposition between sections of individuals who make up a whole is
> often described as opposition between individuals and *society*. Thus, the
> people who want to bring about the moral, intellectual and religious
> *unity* of society, modestly depict themselves as representatives of this
> society and declare that those who oppose them are merely 'disturbing
> individuals'. But among the latter are those who act in this way because
> they also want to bring about unity in society by imposing their ideas
> on other 'disturbing individuals', who do not accept them willingly.

128 Parsons (1968: 248).
129 Weber's letter is quoted by Boudon and Bourricaud (1986: 1).
130 Parsons (1968: 621). In support of his own accusation, Parsons (op. cit.: 670,
    note 1) recalled the opinion expressed by Othmar Spann, one of the most rigid
    exponents of methodological collectivism.
131 Op. cit.: 607.
132 Op. cit.: 670.
133 Ibid.
134 Weber (1916: 124).
135 Weber (1991a: 125).
136 In this way, Parsons misrepresented the meaning of the 'drama' lived by Weber,
    who had explicitly stated (1949b: 94):

> Nothing, however, is more dangerous than *confusion* of theory and
> history stemming from naturalistic prejudices. This confusion
> expresses itself . . . in the use of these constructs as a procrustean bed
> into which history is to be forced or . . . in the hypostatization of such
> 'ideas' as real 'forces' and as a 'true' reality which operates behind the
> passage of events and which works itself out in history.

Therefore, it is not by chance that Franco Ferrarotti (1974: 59) places Parsons
among those who most contributed to the 'embalming' of Weber's work.
137 Simmel (1978: 175). This is a good opportunity to point out that in his well-
    known essay on Parsons, François Bourricaud (1981, pp. 38–9) did not realise
    the impossibility of linking an 'individualistic' position with 'the sociologistic
    theorem'.
138 Parsons (1968: 95).
139 Hayek (1982 II: 15–7).
140 Parsons (1935b: 299). Cf. also Parsons (1934b: 326).
141 Coleman (1990: 338).
142 Ibid.
143 Ibid.
144 Ibid. As we have already pointed out in note 106 of this chapter, the insistence
    on equilibrium brings Parsons' sociological schema near to the economic schema

of Walras. Equilibrium and the lack of action go along side by side; hence, the criticisms that Dahrendorf (1959) and Gouldner (1971) levelled at Parsons' work.

145 Alexander (1990: 342).
146 Simmel (1992: 53).
147 Ibid.
148 Cf. Parsons (1934b).
149 Hayek (1978: 265).
150 Parsons (1968: 67).
151 Op. cit.: 112–3. Here Parsons showed a confusion between evolutionism and 'progressism'. Cf. also op. cit.: 120–2.
152 Pareto (1935: 1475, para. 2142).
153 Parsons (1968: 113).
154 Pareto (1935: 1230, para. 1770).
155 Parsons (1968: 228).
156 In harmony with this, it is not out of place to recall what Giuseppe Montalenti (1967: 13), wrote:

> [evolutionism denies] finalism as a pre-established design such as is well declared in the 'conclusion admitted up to the present day' of Lamarck, and it seeks to interpret finality and, in particular, adaptation to the environment, in a scientific way, as an acquisition of the organism, as an active process permanently becoming, fruit of a continual dialectic between organism and environment.

157 It is useful to recall what Mises (1981a: 281) wrote on this subject:

> When the formulas of Darwinism, which had sprung from ideas taken over by Biology from social science, reverted to social science, people forgot what the ideas had originally meant. Thus arose that monstrosity, sociological Darwinism, which, ending in a romantic glorification of war and murder, was peculiarly responsible for the over-shadowing of liberal ideas and for creating the mental atmophere which led to the World War and the social struggles of today . . . Even Darwin, when he speaks of the struggle for existence, does not always mean the destructive combat of living creatures . . . He often uses the expression figuratively to show the dependence of living beings on each other and on their surroundings. It is a misunderstanding to take the phrase quite literally, for it is a metaphor. The confusion is worse confounded when people equate the struggle for existence with the war of extermination between human beings, and proceed to construct a social theory based on the necessity of struggle.

Mises (op. cit.: 286) added:

> Fighting in the actual original sense of the word is anti-social. It renders co-operation, which is the basic element of social collaboration, impossible among the fighters and, where the co-operation already exists, destroys it. Competition is an element of social collaboration,

the ruling principle within the social body. Viewed sociologically, fighting and competition are extreme contrasts.

158 If the problem of the *beginning* of society is not asked, and methodological individualism does not do it, the question of the 'randomness' of ends does not arise. The individual is a social being, he benefits from what we have called 'social in the broad sense',which is then established by tradition; on this point, cf. Mises (1981a: 108–9), Popper (1949: 120–35), Hayek (1960: 60–3). The 'second' Parsons (1991: 121) recognised, *inter alia*, that there is a 'relational limitation', which 'rests upon the fact that it is inherent in the nature of social interaction that the gratification of ego's need-dispositions is contingent on alter's action and vice versa', since 'the action system of each actor is a finite system of limited possibilities'.

159 Parsons (1934b: 326;1935b: 299).

160 Parsons (1968: 160).

161 Here I use an expression of Hayek's (1982 III: 190, note 7).

162 Cipolla (1970: 10).

163 Parsons (1935a: 648).

164 Parsons (1934b: 319). On this subject, Parsons obviously disregarded even Max Weber, one of 'his' authors. Leaving on one side the foundation of the thesis on the relation between religion and capitalism, one should recall that Weber (1968 II: 586), had declared: 'By a peculiar paradox, asceticism actually resulted in the contradictory situation . . . that it was precisely its rationally ascetic character that led to the accumulation of wealth'.

165 It could be added that, in an essay of 1949, which is a sort of appendix to the 'early' Parsons, the American sociologist (1949: 49) went as far as to recognise, while confirming many of his previous misunderstandings towards political economy, that its starting point was provided with a 'basis' endowed with 'a very fundamental insight'; that is, the understanding of the 'mutual advantages of exchange'. Parsons also admitted that political economy had 'successfully analysed' human activity 'as a dynamic system of interrelated variable elements'.

166 Here I make use of expressions originally used by O'Driscoll and Rizzo (1985: 5) to criticise the idea of economic equilibrium and to explain the *process* generated by the market.

167 In his *Prolegomena to a Theory of Social Institutions*, Parsons (1934b: 327) declared that: 'the moment in which we conceive a plurality of individuals acting in the same environment, it becomes evident that their actions will give rise to, and be in various ways involved in a set of relations to each other'. But voluntarism, which prevented him from passing *unintentionally* from individual action to social order, forced him to take the path in which there are predefined order and individual adaptation. This is even clearer in the 'second' Parsons (1991: 15), when he went as far as accepting also the principle of 'maximisation'. 'Reduced to the simplest possible terms . . . a social system consists in a plurality of individual actors interacting with each other in a situation which has at least a physical or environmental aspect, actors who motivated in term of a tendency to the *optimization of gratification*'.

168 Ricossa (1991: 170–1); cf. Pizzorno (1968: 20–1).

169 Pareto (1904: 194).

170 Hayek (1982) II: 112).

171 Parsons (1968: 440).

172 Op. cit.: 367.

173 Here it is useful to recall that Mises (1981a: 60–2), discussing the functions of democracy, emphasised that it has the task of allowing the peaceful replacement of rulers (as well as the task of selecting them). Thus, it avoids violent revolution; 'it performs functions which the citizen is not prepared to do without.' Hence, it is an ultimate-value, namely 'condition' considered to be unrenounceable.

174 Durkheim (1982: 59).

8 CONCLUSIONS

1 Popper (1966 II: 91).
2 Popper (1960b: 157–8).
3 Schumpeter (1908: 554).
4 Mises (1981b: 3).
5 Robbins (1935: 84). We should add to what Robbins said that Böhm-Bawerk (1959: 430, note 81) reinforced his position, drawing support from Max Weber, from the essay in which Weber did indeed separate the Austrian theory of value from psychology (cf. Chapter 6).
6 Cf. Chapter 3.
7 Mandeville (1924 II: 189).
8 Smith (1976a: 110).
9 Mises (1981a: 271–2), my italics.
10 Popper (1966 II: 93).
11 For the revival of methodological individualism on the part of Hayek, Popper and Schutz, cf. Leonardi (1986: 40–71). It is as well at this point to provide, in connection with the debate on methodological individualism and methodological collectivism, some further bibliographical references: Watkins (1952, 1958); Mandelbaum (1955); Brodbeck (1958); Gellner (1959); Goldstein (1956, 1958); Scott (1961); Kirzner (1967); Lukes (1968); Wisdom (1970); Buchanan (1975); Nozick (1977); Rothbard (1979); Boudon (1982); Galeotti (1988); Petroni (1989); Rainone (1990); Laurent (1994).
12 Schütz (1962c: 168).
13 Homans (1967: 60).
14 Op. cit.: 62. Therefore, Joseph Agassi (1975: 145) had some foundation for writing that methodological individualism refutes psychologism and gives autonomy to the social sciences. Consequently, one can say that the individualistic method stands as the third solution with respect to psychologism and methodological collectivism. Unlike what Cesareo (1993) has stated, it is not necessary to go 'beyond the holism–individualism dilemma', because methodological individualism is already 'third'. As Leonardi (1994: 77) has correctly written, 'methodological individualism represents the classic and most thought-out form for a synthesis and for an integration between the dimension of individuality and that of the collectivity'. Leonardi's essay can be found in a monograph issue of *Sociologia e Ricerca Sociale* entirely devoted to methodological individualism, which also includes essays by B. Giesen, M. Schmid, G. Statera, and contributions by S. Agnoli, R. Viale, A. Fasanella, R. Egidi, E. Campelli, P. de Nardis, A. Marradi.
15 Schumpeter (1908: 88). Those who believe, on the other hand, that methodological individualism entails political individualism are: Pizzorno (1989: 140–1); Boniolo (1990: 143); Izzo (1991: 425); Pellicani (1992: 174–5).
16 Engels (1934: 58).
17 Mises (1981a: 97).
18 Toennies (1905: 127).

19 Mises (1966: 42).

20 Ibid.

21 Ibid. On this subject, it is useful to recall what Ferdinand Toennies wrote (1905: 116): 'The visible existence of an assembly means that members are visible as beings assembled, but the assembly as a body can be recognized only by a reflecting spectator who knows what those forms mean, who "realizes" their significance, who *thinks* the assembly.'

22 Following the rekindling of the debate on method, Alessandro Pizzorno (1989: 145), declared:

> The imaginary observer of Methodological Individualism is omniscient, the imaginary subject of action to be studied is perfectly transparent and, to define what sort of action is concerned, the components of the context in which the action is carried out are wholly without influence.

Here Pizzorno probably has in mind philosophical radicalism, to the positions of which he arbitrarily reduced methodological individualism. However, an example of the application of the individualistic method can be found in the analysis carried out by Pizzorno (1986: 3–25), *Sul confronto intertemporale delle utilità*, where he examines, *inter alia*, the action of a subject who attributes the greatest importance to loyalty towards the group to which he belongs. The widespread practice of identifying methodological individualism with philosophical radicalism is what impelled Michele Salvati (1993: 206) to say, referring to the theory of general economic equilibrium, that a 'slacker strategy of research (even if still within methodological individualism) is necessary'; a strategy of 'slack rationality', in which the 'history' of individuals would be made up 'of the habits and repetition, of slow adaptations, made by the individuals whose actions are guided by calculation, but the calculation would in its turn be "encapsulated" by sticky outlines both institutional and cognitive' (op. cit.: 207). Salvati cites Etzioni (1991) Nelson and Winter (1982). But it is clear that what he invokes is the 'double entry account' between the *actor* and the *situation*, which is precisely what characterises methodological individualism. Therefore, one can say that Salvati's aspiration is to make philosophical radicalism 'slack', reforming its constructivism which, on the contrary, the individualistic method does not have.

23 Boudon (1986: 29). However, Boudon also wrote (ibid): 'action sociologies . . . can be seen as a branch growing from the same trunk. Another such branch is economics, of which both the classical and the neoclassical varieties share the principle that any economic phenomenon can only be analysed in terms of the elementary individual actions that go towards its make up'. In other words, Boudon does not separate philosophical radicalism from political economy. For this reason, he is obliged to say that the model of the rational choice of the *homo oeconomicus* must be integrated by 'cognitive rationality' and 'assiological rationality'. This threefold division can be criticised in the same way as Mises (cf. Chapter 6) criticised Weber's fourfold division. Another supporter of different types of rationality is Neil J. Smelser (1982: 8–12).

24 Popper (1976: 101).

25 Op. cit.: 102. Popper maintained that psychology and (even) psychoanalysis are impossible without social categories.

26 Simmel (1978: 388–9).

27 Op. cit.: 493. In the wake of Simmel, Ortega y Gasset (1970b V: 384).

28 Smith (1976b I: 116).

29 Mises (1981b: 92–3). Here it can be added that Pareto insisted on the 'data of the problem' to which 'logico–experimental reasoning was to be applied', cf. Pareto (1935: 1476, para. 2143).

30 This is why Mises (1978: 36) saw a theory of 'non-action' in the theory of equilibrium. Obviously, Smith's work cannot be put beside the idea of equilibrium – as we have already seen in our discussion of him – since in Smith, just as later in Hayek, the market is a permanent 'discovery procedure'. Michele Salvati (1993: 205) has recently written: 'the theorists of general equilibrium have had to lean on that hyper-rational monad that Smith would never have accepted'.

31 Swedborg (1990: 326). Among those who criticise the idea of maximisation there is also Neil J. Smelser (1982: 208–9), who however, in *Economy and Society* (1972: 20), written jointly with Talcott Parsons, did not hesitate to declare that 'maximizing utility or the economic value of the total available means to want satisfaction . . . defines the system goal of an economy'. On the problems of maximisation, cf. Fisichella (1994: 48–55).

32 Burke (1976: 113).

33 Parsons (1991:. 120–1).

34 Op. cit.: 121.

35 Robbins (1935: 24–25).

36 Hayek (1982 II: 113).

37 Here I use Herbert A. Simon's well-known expression (1976: 133). The fact that, action being always economic, the actor pursues only 'good solutions' shows that the positions of Gary S. Becker (1976) and of James S. Coleman (1994) are extremist.

38 Simmel (1978: 99).

39 The conclusion reached here can be linked with the idea of 'economy as instituted process' formulated by Karl Polanyi (1971: 243–70) and also with the position of Mark Granovetter (1985: 481–510).

40 Mises (1966: 234).

41 Ibid.

42 Merton (1936: 894). See Merton (1968) for further discussion of this point.

43 Hayek (1979: 68–9).

44 Op. cit.: 69.

45 Popper (1966 II: 93).

46 Popper (1948: 342). Here it can be added that Merton (1968: 120) wrote: 'In short, it is suggested that the *distinctive* intellectual contributions of the sociologist are found primarily in the study of unintended consequences (among which are latent functions) of social practices'. And Albert O. Hirschman (1991: 35–6), though he has seen in perverse effects a basic characteristic of 'reactionary rhetoric', has recently declared:

> One of the great insights of the science of society – found already in Vico and Mandeville and elaborated magisterially during the Scottish Enlightenment – is the observation that, because of imperfect insight, human actions are apt to have unintended consequences of considerable scope. Reconnaissance and systematic description of such unintended

consequences have ever since been a major assignment, if not the *raison d'être*, of social science.

47 Simmel (1978: 175).
48 Ibid., my italics.
49 'In producing we become producers.'

REFERENCES

Agassi, J. (1975) 'Institutional individualism', *British Journal of Sociology* 26: 144–5.

Aimard, G. (1962) *Durkheim et la science économique*, Paris: Presses Universitaires de France (PUF).

Alexander, J. C. (1990) 'Commentary: structure, value, action', *American Sociological Review* 55: 339–45.

Alpert, H. (1939) *Emile Durkheim and his Sociology*, New York: Columbia University Press.

Andreski, S. (1971) *Herbert Spencer: Structure, Function and Evolution*, London: Joseph.

Antiseri, D. (1981) *Teoria unificata del metodo*, Padova: Liviana.

—— (1986) *Critiche epistemologiche al marxismo*, Roma: Borla.

—— (1989) *Teoria della razionalità e scienze sociali*, Roma: Borla.

—— (1991) *Nota Bio-bibliografica* to Carl Menger, *Gli errori dello storicismo*, Milano: Rusconi.

—— (1992) *L'individualismo metodologico: una difesa*, in D. Antiseri and L. Pellicani *L'individualismo metodologico*, Milano: Angeli.

Baechler, J. (1975) *Les suicides*, Paris: Calmann-Lévy.

Baldini, M. (1994) *Storia delle utopie*, Roma: Armando.

Bartley, W. W., III (1984) *The Retreat to Commitment*, La Salle PA: Open Court Publishing.

Becker, G. S. (1976) *The Economic Approach to Human Behavior*, Chicago: University of Chicago Press.

Bentham, J. (1838–43) *The Works of Jeremy Bentham*, Edinburgh: Tait.

Berger, P. L. and Luckmann, T. (1967) *The Social Construction of Reality*, London: Allen Lane/Penguin.

Böhm-Bawerk, E. (1959) *Capital and Interest. Vol. II: The Positive Theory of Capital*, South Holland: Libertarian Press.

—— (1962) 'Whether legal rights and relationships are economic goods', in *Shorter Classics of Eugen von Böhm-Bawerk*, South Holland: Libertarian Press.

Boniolo, G. (1990) *Questioni di filosofia e di metodologia*, Roma: Borla.

Boudon, R. (1981) *The Logic of Social Action*, London: Routledge and Kegan Paul.

—— (1982) *The Unintended Consequences of Social Action*, London: Macmillan.

—— (1984) 'L'individualisme méthodologique en sociologie', *Commentaire* 7: 268–77.

—— (1986) *Theories of Social Change*, Cambridge: Polity Press.

—— (1989) *Razionalità soggettiva e disposizioni*, in L.Sciolla and L. Ricolfi *Il soggetto dell'azione*, Milano: Angeli.

—— (1994) *The Art of Self-Persuasion*, Cambridge: Polity Press.

Boudon R. and Bourricaud, F. (1986) *Dictionnaire critique de la sociologie*, Paris: Presses Universitaires de France (PUF).

Bourricaud, F. (1981) *The Sociology of Talcott Parsons*, Chicago: University of Chicago Press.

Brentano, L. (1891) *The Relation of Labor to the Law of Today*, New York: Putnam.

Brodbeck, M. (1958) 'Methodological individualism: definition and reduction', *Philosophy and Science* 23: 297–329.

Bryson, G. (1945) *Man and Society: The Scottish Inquiry of the Eighteenth Century*, Princeton NJ: Princeton University Press.

Buchanan, J. (1975) *The Limits of Liberty*, Chicago: University of Chicago Press.

Burke, E. (1976) *On Government, Politics and Society*, New York: International Library.

Burrow, J. W. (1974) *Evolution and Society*, Cambridge: Cambridge University Press.

Camic, C. (1987) 'The making of a method: a historical reinterpretation of the early Parsons', *American Sociological Review*, 52: 421–39.

—— (1989) '"Structure" after 50 years: the anatomy of a charter', *American Journal of Sociology*, 54: 38–107.

Cannan, E. (1904) 'Preface', *Adam Smith: An Inquiry . . .*, London: Methuen.

Cesareo, V. (1993) *Sociologia*, Milano: Vita e Pensiero.

Cipolla, C. M. (1970) 'Introduction', *The Economic Decline of Empires*, London: Methuen.

Coase, R. H. (1960) 'The problem of social cost', *Journal of Law and Economics* 3: 1–44.

—— (1974) 'The lighthouse in economics', *Journal of Law and Economics* 17: 357–76.

Cohen, H. (1914) *Logik der reinen Erkenntnis*, Berlin: Cassirer.

Coleman, J. S. (1990) 'Commentary: social institutions and social theory', *American Sociological Review*, 55: 333–9.

—— (1994) *Foundations of Social Theory*, Cambridge MA: Harvard University Press.

Colletti, L. (1975) *Ideologia e società*, Bari: Laterza.

Comte, A. (1903) *A Discourse on the Positive Spirit*, London: Reeves.

—— (1970) *Cours de philosophie positive*, in *Oeuvres*, vol. IV, Paris: Anthropos.

—— (1974a) 'Plan of the scientific operations necessary for reorganizing society', in *The Crisis of Industrial Civilization: The Early Essays of August Comte*, London: Heinemann.

—— (1974b) 'Considerations on the spiritual power', in *The Crisis of Industrial Civilization: The Early Essays of August Comte*, London: Heinemann.

—— (1974c) *The Crisis of Industrial Civilization: The Early Essays of August Comte*, London: Heinemann.

Coser, L. A. (1977) *Masters of Sociological Thought*, New York: Harcourt Brace Jovanovich.

Cubeddu, R. (1992a) 'Friedrich A. von Hayek e Bruno Leoni', *Il Politico* 57: 393–420.

—— (1992b) *Il liberalismo della Scuola austriaca: Menger, Mises, Hayek*, Napoli: Morano.

Dahrendorf, R. (1959) *Class and Class Conflict in Industrial Society*, London: Routledge and Kegan Paul.

—— (1973) *Homo sociologicus*, London: Routledge and Kegan Paul.

Descartes, R. (1960) *Discourse on Method*, Harmondsworth: Penguin.

Dilthey, W. (1959) *Einleitung in die Geisteswissenschaft*, Stuttgart: Teubner.

Douglas, J. (1967) *The Social Meanings of Suicide*, Princeton NJ: Princeton University Press.

Downie, R. S. (1976) 'Comments', in T. Wilson and A. S. Skinner (eds), *Essays in Honour of Adam Smith*, Oxford: Clarendon Press.

Durkheim, E. (1952) *Suicide*, London: Routledge and Kegan Paul.

—— (1960) 'Sociology and its scientific field', in K. H. Wolff (ed.) *Emile Durkheim, 1858–1917: A Collection of Essays*, Columbus OH: Ohio State University Press.

—— (1961) *Moral Education*, New York: Free Press.

—— (1962) *Socialism*, London: Collier-Macmillan.

—— (1964) *The Division of Labor in Society*, New York: Free Press.

—— (1965a) *The Elementary Forms of Religious Life*, New York: Free Press.

—— (1965b) *Montesquieu and Rousseau: Forerunners of Sociology*, Ann Arbor MI: University of Michigan Press.

—— (1970) *La science sociale et l'action*, Paris: Presses Universitaires de France (PUF).

—— (1974) *Sociology and Philosophy*, New York: Free Press.

—— (1975a) *Sur l'influence allemande*, in *Textes*, vol. I, Paris: Minuit.

—— (1975b) *Lettres a Célestin Bouglé*, in *Textes*, vol. II, Paris: Minuit.

—— (1975c) *La science positive de la morale en Allemagne*, in *Textes*, vol. I, Paris: Minuit.

—— (1975d) *Textes*, Paris: Minuit.

—— (1982) *The Rules of Sociological Method*, London: Macmillan.

—— (1992) *Professional Ethics and Civic Morals*, London: Routledge.

Dussort, H. (1963) *L'école de Marbourg*, Paris: Presses Universitaires de France (PUF).

Ebeling, R. M. (1993) 'Economic calculation under socialism: Ludwig von Mises and his predecessors', in J. M. Herbener (ed.) *The Meaning of Ludwig von Mises*, Norwell: Kluwer.

Elster, J. (1982) 'Marxism, functionalism and game theory: the case of methodological individualism, *Theory and Society*, 11: 453–82.

—— (1985) *Making Sense of Marx*, Cambridge: Cambridge University Press.

—— (1986) *Marxisme et individualisme méthodologique*, in P. Birnbaum and J. Leca (eds) *Sur l'individualisme*, Paris: Presse de la fondation nationale des sciences politiques.

Engels, F. (1934) *Ludwig Feuerbach and the Outcome of Classical German Philosophy*, London: Laurence.

—— (1959) *Anti-Dühring,* Moscow: Foreign Languages Publishing House.

Etzioni, A. (1991) 'Encapsulated competition', *Journal of Post-Keynesian Economics*, 7: 287–302.

Fay, C. K. (1960) *The World of Adam Smith*, Cambridge: Heffer.

Ferguson, A. (1966) *An Essay on the History of Civil Society*, Edinburgh: Edinburgh University Press.

Ferrarotti, F. (1974) *Max Weber e il destino della ragione*, Bari: Laterza.

Fisher, I. (1930) *The Theory of Interest*, New York: Macmillan.

Fisichella, D. (1994) *Epistemologia e scienza politica*, Roma: Nuova Italia Scientifica.

Forbes, D. (1954) '"Scientific" Whiggism: Adam Smith and John Millar', in *Cambridge Journal* 7: 643–70.

—— (1966) 'Introduction', in A. Ferguson *An Essay on the History of Civil Society*, Edinburgh: Edinburgh University Press.

REFERENCES

Freud, S. (1949) *An Outline of Psycho-Analysis*, London: Hogarth Press.

Frisby, D. (1978) 'Introduction', in Georg Simmel *The Philosophy of Money*, London: Routledge and Kegan Paul.

—— (1981) *Sociological Impressionism*, London: Heinemann.

Galeotti. A. E. (1988) *Individuale e collettivo: L'individualismo metodologico nella teoria politica*, Milano: Angeli.

Gassen, K. and Landmann, M. (eds) (1958) *Buch des Dankes an Georg Simmel*, Berlin: Duncker and Humblot.

Gellner, E. (1959) 'Holism versus individualism in history and sociology', in P. Gardiner (ed.) *Theories of History*, Glencoe: Free Press.

Goldstein, L. G. (1956) 'The inadequacy of the principle of methodological individualism', *Journal of Philosophy* 53: 801–13.

—— (1958) 'The two theses of methodological individualism', *British Journal for the Philosophy of Science* 9: 1–11.

Gould, M. (1989) 'Voluntarism versus utilitarianism', *Theory, Culture and Society* 6: 637–54.

—— (1991) 'The structure of social action: at least sixty years ahead of its time', in R. Robertson and B. S. Turner (eds) *Talcott Parsons: Theorist of Modernity*, London: Sage.

Gouldner, A. W. (1971) *The Coming Crisis of Western Sociology,* London: Heinemann.

Granovetter, M. (1985) 'Economic action and social structure: the problem of embeddedness', *American Journal of Sociology* 91: 481–510.

Guyau, J. M. (1885) *La morale anglaise contemporaine*, Paris: Alcan.

Haakonsen, K. (1981) *A Science of Legislation*, Cambridge: Cambridge University Press.

Halbwachs, M. (1930) *Les causes du suicide*, Paris: Alcan.

Halévy, E. (1928) *The Growth of Philosophical Radicalism*, London: Faber.

Hayek, F. A. von (ed.) (1935) *Collectivist Economic Planning*, London: Routledge.

—— (1937) 'Economics and knowledge', *Economica* 13: 33–54

—— (1945) 'The use of knowledge in society', *American Economic Review* 35: 519–30.

—— (1949) *Individualism and Economic Order*, London: Routledge and Kegan Paul.

—— (1960) *The Constitution of Liberty*, London: Routledge.

—— (1978) *New Studies in Philosophy, Politics, Economics and the History of Ideas*, Chicago: University of Chicago Press.

—— (1979) *The Counter-Revolution of Science. Studies in the Abuse of Reason*, Indianapolis: Liberty Press.

—— (1982) *Law, Legislation and Liberty*, London: Routledge.

—— (1988) *The Fatal Conceit: The Errors of Socialism*, London: Routledge.

Hegel, G. W. F. (1942) *Philosophy of Right*, Oxford: Clarendon Press.

—— (1955) *Vorlesungen über die Philosophie der Geschichte*, Hamburg: Meiner.

—— (1977) *Phenomenology of Spirit*, Oxford: Oxford University Press.

Hirschmann, A. O. (1977) *The Passions and the Interests*, Princeton NJ: Princeton University Press.

—— (1991) *The Rhetoric of Reaction*, Cambridge MA: Belknap Press, Harvard University.

Hollander, S. (1973) *The Economics of Adam Smith*, Toronto: Toronto University Press.

Homans, G. L. (1967) *The Nature of Social Science*, New York: Harcourt-Brace.

Huerta de Soto, J. (1992) *Socialismo, cálculo económico y función empresarial*, Madrid: Unión Editorial.

Hume, D. (1923) *A Treatise of Human Nature*, London: Dent.

—— (1963) *Essays Moral, Political and Literary*, Oxford: Oxford University Press.

Huxley, T. M. (1893) 'Evolution and Ethics', in G. J. Romanes (ed.) *Romanes Lectures: Decennial Issue (1892–1900)*, Oxford: Clarendon Press.

Infantino, L. (1985) *Dall'utopia al totalitarismo*, Roma: Borla.

—— (1990) *Ortega y Gasset: Una introduzione*, Roma: Armando.

—— (1992) *Ludwig von Mises e la società aperta*, Roma: Luiss.

Izzo, A. (1991) *Storia del pensiero sociologico*, Bologna: Il Mulino.

Jameson, F. (1991) *Postmodernism or the Cultural Logic of Late Capitalism*, London: Verso.

Jhering, R. von (1924) *Law as a Means to an End*, New York: Macmillan.

Jones, E. D. (1975) 'Faith, sincerity and morality: Mandeville and Bayle', in I. Primer (ed.) *Mandeville Studies*, Hague: Nijhof.

Kettler, D. (1965) *The Social and Political Thought of Adam Ferguson*, London/Columbus OH: Ohio State University Press.

Kirzner, I. M. (1967) 'Methodological individualism, market equilibrium and market', *Il Politico*, 32: 787–99.

—— (1973) *Competition and Entrepreneurship*, Chicago: University of Chicago Press.

—— (1992) *The Meaning of Market Process*, London: Routledge.

—— (1994) 'The limits of markets: the real and imagined', in *Marktwirtschaft und Rechtsordnung*, Baden-Baden: Nomos Verl.

Knight, F. H. (1940) 'Professor Parsons on economic motivation', *Canadian Journal of Economics* 6: 460–5.

Köhnke, K. C. (1990) 'Four concepts of social science at Berlin University: Dilthey, Lazarus, Schmoller and Simmel', in M. Kaern, B. S. Phillips and R. S. Cohen (eds) *Georg Simmel and Contemporary Sociology*, Dordrecht: Kluwer.

Kuhn, T. S. (1962) *The Structure of Scientific Revolutions*, Chicago: University of Chicago Press.

Lacan, J. (1949) 'Le stade du miroir comme formateur de la fonction du Je', in *Ecrits*, Paris: Editions du Seuil.

Lachmann, L. M. (1970) *The Legacy of Max Weber*, London: Heinemann.

—— (1978) 'Carl Menger and the incomplete revolution of subjectivism', *Atlantic Economic Journal* 11: 57–9.

Laidler, D. and Rowe, N. (1980) 'Georg Simmel's *Philosophy of Money*: a review article for economists', *Journal of Economic Literature* 18: 97–105.

Laurent, A. (1994) *L'individualisme méthodologique*, Paris: Presses Universitaires de France (PUF).

Lecaldano, E. (1976) 'Dal "senso pubblico" in Hutcheson alla "simpatia" in Hume', in A. Santucci (ed.) *Scienza e filosofia scozzese nell'età di Hume*, Bologna: Il Mulino.

Lehmann, W. C. (1930) *Adam Ferguson and the Beginnings of Modern Sociology*, New York: Columbia University Press.

—— (1960) *John Millar of Glasgow, 1735–1801: His Life and Thought and his Contributions to Sociological Analysis*, Cambridge: Cambridge University Press.

Leonardi, F. (1986) *Di che parla il sociologo?*, Milano: Angeli.

—— (1994) 'In ultima istanza. Ovvero: il destino dell'individualismo metodologico', *Sociologia e Ricerca Sociale* 15: 77.

Leoni, B. (1961) *Freedom and the Law*, Princeton NJ: Van Nostrand.

—— (1980) *Scritti di scienza politica e teoria del diritto*, Milano: Giuffrè.

Levine, D. N. (1971) 'Introduction', Georg Simmel, *On Individuality and Social Forms*, Chicago: University of Chicago Press.

Locke. J. (1967) *Two Treatises of Government*, Cambridge: Cambridge University Press.

Lukes, S. (1968) 'Methodological individualism reconsidered', *British Journal of Sociology*, 19: 119–29.

—— (1973) *Emile Durkheim: His Life and Work*, London: Allen Lane.

Magri, T. (1987) 'Introduzione', B. de Mandeville, *La favola delle api*, vol. I, Bari: Laterza.

Mandelbaum, T. M. (1955) 'Societal Facts', in P. Gardiner (ed.) *Theories of History*, Glencoe: Free Press.

Mandeville, B. de (1924) *The Fable of the Bees; or Private Vices, Public Benefits*, Oxford: Clarendon Press.

Mannheim, K. (1954) *Ideology and Utopia*, London: Routledge.

Marshall, A. (1969) *Principles of Economics*, London: Macmillan.

Martino, A. (1994) *Economia di mercato fondamento delle libertà politiche*, Roma: Borla.

Marx, K. (1936) *The Poverty of Philosophy*, London: Laurence.

—— (1973) *Economic and Philosophic Manuscripts of 1844*, London: Laurence and Wishart.

—— (1975a) 'Peuchet: on suicide', in K. Marks and F. Engels *Collected Works*, London: Laurence and Wishart..

—— (1975b) 'Letter to F. Domela Nieuwenhnis of 22 February 1881', in *Marx–Engels: Selected Correspondence*, Moscow: Progress Publishers.

—— (1976) *Capital*, London: Penguin.

—— (1977a) 'On the Jewish question', in D. McLellan (ed.) *Selected Writings*, Oxford: Oxford University Press.

—— (1977b) 'Towards a critique of Hegel's *Philosophy of Right*', in D. McLellan (ed.) *Selected Writings*, Oxford: Oxford University Press.

—— (1977c) 'A critique of political economy', in D. McLellan (ed.) *Selected Writings*, Oxford: Oxford University Press.

—— (1977d) *Selected Writings*, D. McLellan (ed.), Oxford: Oxford University Press.

Marx, K. and Engels, F. (1969) 'Address of the Central Committee of the Communist League', in K. Marx and F. Engels *Selected Works*, Moscow: Progress Publishers.

—— (1975) *Collected Works*, London: Laurence and Wishart.

Mead. G. H. (1934) *Mind, Self and Society*, Chicago: University of Chicago Press.

Meek, R. L. (1954) 'The Scottish contribution to Marxist ideology', in J. Saville (ed.) *Democracy and the Labour Movement*, London: Laurence and Wishart.

Menger, C. (1884) *Die Irrtumer des Historismus in der Deutschen Nationalökonomie*, Vienna: Holder.

—— (1901) 'Philosophie des Geldes', *Literarisches Centralblatt*, 4: 160–1.

—— (1985) *Problems of Economics and Sociology*, New York: New York University Press.

—— (1994) *Principles of Economics*, Grove City: Libertarian Press.

Merton, R. K. (1936) 'The unanticipated consequences of purposive social action', *American Sociological Review* 1: 894–904.

—— (1968) *Social Theory and Social Structure*, New York: Free Press.

Mill, J. S. (1892) *A System of Logic Ratiocinative and Inductive*, London: Routledge.

—— (1950) *On Bentham and Coleridge*, London: Chatto and Windus.

—— (1965) *Principles of Political Economy*, Toronto: University of Toronto Press.

—— (1967) 'Essays on some unsettled questions of political economy', in *Essays in Economics and Society*, Toronto: University of Toronto Press.

Mises, L. von (1935) 'Economic calculation in the socialist commonwealth', in F. A. von Hayek (ed.) (1935) *Collectivist Economic Planning*, London: Routledge.

—— (1957) *Theory and History*, New Haven CT: Yale University Press.

—— (1966) *Human Action*, Chicago: Contemporary Books.

—— (1969) *Omnipotent Government*, New Roschelle: Arlington House.

—— (1977) *A Critique of Interventionism*, New Roschelle: Arlington House.

—— (1978) *Notes and Recollections*, South Holland: Libertarian Press.

—— (1985) *Liberalism*, San Francisco: Cobden Press.

—— (1981a) *Socialism*, Indianapolis: Liberty Fund.

—— (1981b) *Epistemological Problems of Economics*, New York: New York University Press.

—— (1983) *The Historical Setting of the Austrian School of Economics*, Auburn: Ludwig von Mises Institute.

Mongardini, C. (1970) *L'epoca della società*, Roma: Bulzoni.

Montalenti, G. (1967) 'Introduzione', *C. Darwin: L'origine delle specie*, Torino: Boringhieri.

Montesquieu, C. de (1949) *The Spirits of the Laws*, New York: Hafner Press.

Morra, G. (1987) *M. Scheler: Una introduzione*, Roma: Armando.

Morrow, G. R. (1923a) *The Ethical and Economic Theories of Adam Smith*, New York: Longmans Green.

—— (1923b) 'The significance of the doctrine of sympathy in Hume and Adam Smith', *Philosophical Review* 32.

Münch, R. (1987) *Theory of Action*, London: Routledge and Kegan Paul.

Nelson, R. and Winter, S. (1982) *An Evolutionary Theory of Economic Performance*, Cambridge: Cambridge University Press.

Nisbet, R. A. (1967) *The Sociological Tradition*, London: Heinemann.

—— (1975) *The Sociology of Emile Durkheim*, London: Heinemann.

Nozick, R. (1974) *Anarchy, State and Utopia*, Oxford: Blackwell.

—— (1977) 'On Austrian Methodology', *Synthese* 36: 353–92.

Oakeshott, M. (1975) *On Human Conduct*, Oxford: Clarendon Press.

O'Driscoll, G. P. and Rizzo, M. J. (1985) *The Economics of Time and Ignorance*, Oxford: Blackwell.

Oncken, A. (1897) 'The consistency of Adam Smith', *Economic Journal* 7: 443–50.

Ortega y Gasset, J. (1946a) 'Meditaciónes del Quijote', in J. Ortega y Gasset *Obras completas*, vol. I, Madrid: Revista de Occidente.

—— (1946b) 'Verdad y perspectiva', in J. Ortega y Gasset *Obras completas*, vol. I, Madrid: Revista de Occidente.

—— (1946c) 'Adán en el Paraíso', in J. Ortega y Gasset *Obras completas*, vol. I, Madrid: Revista de Occidente.

—— (1946–83) *Obras completas*, Madrid: Revista de Occidente.

—— (1962) 'Prólogo para Alemanes', in J. Ortega y Gasset *Obras completas*, vol. VIII, Madrid: Revista de Occidente.

—— (1964) 'Historia como sistema', in J. Ortega y Gasset *Obras completas*, vol. VI, Madrid: Revista de Occidente.

—— (1966a) 'Reforma de la inteligencia', in J. Ortega y Gasset *Obras completas*, vol. IV, Madrid: Revista de Occidente.

—— (1966b) 'Pidiendo un Goethe desde dentro', in J. Ortega y Gasset *Obras completas*, vol. IV, Madrid: Revista de Occidente.

—— (1966c) 'La "Filosofia de la historia" de Hegel y la historiologia', in J. Ortega y Gasset *Obras completas*, vol. IV, Madrid: Revista de Occidente.

—— (1969) 'El hombre y la gente', in J. Ortega y Gasset *Obras completas*, vol. VII, Madrid: Revista de Occidente.

—— (1970a) 'Meditación de la tecnica', in J. Ortega y Gasset *Obras completas*, vol. V, Madrid: Revista de Occidente.

—— (1970b) 'Ideas y creencias', in J. Ortega y Gasset *Obras completas*, vol. V, Madrid: Revista de Occidente.

Pareto, V. (1935) *The Mind and Society: A Treatise of General Sociology*, New York: Dover Publications.

—— (1973) [1904] 'L'individuale e il sociale', in C. Mongardini (ed.) *Vilfredo Pareto: Dall'economia alla sociologia*, Roma: Bulzoni.

Parsons, T. (1934a) 'Some reflections on "The Nature and Significance of Economics"', *Quarterly Journal of Economics* 48: 511–45.

—— (1934b) 'Prolegomena to a theory of social institutions', *American Sociological Review* (1990) 55: 319–33.

—— (1935a) 'Sociological elements in economic thought', *Quarterly Journal of Economics* 49: 645–67.

—— (1935b) 'The place of ultimate values in sociological theory', *International Journal of Ethics* 45: 282–316.

—— (1949) 'The rise and decline of economic man', *Journal of General Education* 4: 47–53.

—— (1968) *The Structure of Social Action*, New York: Free Press.

—— (1971) *The System of Modern Societies,* Englewood Cliffs: Prentice Hall.

—— (1979) 'Letter to J. C. Alexander, 19 January 1979', in *Teoria sociologica (1993) 1: 41–4, The Social System*, London: Routledge.

—— (1993) 'Georg Simmel and Ferdinand Toennies: social relationships and elements of action', in *Teoria sociologica (1993)* 1: 45–71, *The Social System*, London: Routledge.

Parsons, T. and Smelser, N. J. (1972) *Economy and Society*, London: Routledge and Kegan Paul.

Pellicani, L. (1992) *L'individualismo metodologico: una critica*, in D. Antiseri and L. Pellicani *L'individualismo metodologico*, Milano: Angeli.

Petroni, A. M. (1989) 'L'individualismo metodologico', in A. Panebianco (ed.) *L'analisi della politica*, Bologna: Il Mulino.

Piaget, J. (1928) 'Logique génetique et sociologie', *Revue Philosophique*, vol. CV.

Pizzorno, A. (1986) 'Sul confronto intertemporale delle utilità', *Stato e mercato* 6: 3–25.

—— (1989) *Individualismo metodologico: prediche e ragionamenti*, in L. Sciolla and L. Ricolfi (eds) *Il soggetto dell'azione*, Milano: Angeli.

217

Polanyi, K. (1971) 'The economy as instituted process', in K. Polanyi, C. M. Arens-
berg and H. W. Pearson (eds) *Trade and Market in the Early Empires*, Chicago:
Gateway Edition.

Popper, K. R. (1948) 'Prediction and prophecy in the social sciences', in *Conjectures
and Refutations*, London: Routledge.

—— (1949) 'Towards a rational theory of tradition', in *Conjectures and Refutations*,
London: Routledge.

—— (1960a) 'On the sources of knowledge and of ignorance', in *Conjectures and Refutations*, London: Routledge.

—— (1960b) *The Poverty of Historicism*, London: Routledge and Kegan Paul.

—— (1965) *Conjectures and Refutations*, London: Routledge.

—— (1966) *The Open Society and its Enemies*, London: Routledge and Kegan Paul.

—— (1976) 'The logic of the social sciences', in *Positivist Dispute in German Sociology*,
London: Heinemann.

—— (1977) 'The self and its brain', in K. Popper and J. C. Eccles *The Self and its
Brain*, Berlin/New York: Springer International.

—— (1979) *Objective Knowledge*, Oxford: Clarendon Press.

—— (1990) *La scienza e la storia sul filo dei ricordi: an interview*, G. Ferrari (ed.),
Bellinzona: Jaka Book-Edizioni Casagrande.

Preti, G. (1957) *Alle origini dell'etica contemporanea: A. Smith*, Bari: Laterza.

Rainone, A. (1990) *Filosofia analitica e scienze storico-sociali*, Pisa: ETS.

Ranke, L. von (1973) *The Theory and Practice of History*, Indianapolis: Bobbs-Merrill.

Rawls, J. (1973) *A Theory of Justice*, Oxford: Oxford University Press.

Ricossa, S. (1982) *Dizionario di economia*, Torino: Utet.

—— (1988) 'Sugli abusi del razionalismo nell'economia politica', *Politica economica*,
78: 7–14.

—— (1991) *Aspetti attuali della teoria economica neoclassica*, Torino: Utet.

Robbins, L. (1935) *An Essay on the Nature and Significance of Economic Science*, London:
Macmillan.

Robertson Smith, W. (1907) *Lectures on the Religion of the Semites*, London: Black.

Rothbard, M. N. (1970) *Man, Economy and the State*, Los Angeles: Nash Publishing.

—— (1979) *Individualism and the Philosophy of Social Sciences*, San Francisco: Cato Institute.

Rousseau, J.-J. (1974) *Emile*, London: Dent.

—— (1997a) 'Discourse on the origin and foundation of inequality among men', in
The Discourses and Other Early Political Writings, Cambridge: Cambridge University
Press.

—— (1997b) 'Of the social contract', in *The Social Contract and Other Later Political
Writings*, Cambridge: Cambridge University Press.

—— (1997c) 'Geneva manuscript', in *The Social Contract and Other Later Political Writings*, Cambridge: Cambridge University Press.

—— (1997d) *The Social Contract and Other Later Political Writings*, Cambridge:
Cambridge University Press.

Saint-Simon, C.-H. de (1877–8) *Oeuvres de Saint-Simon et d'Enfantin*, Paris: Leroux.

Salomon, A. (1945) 'Adam Smith as sociologist', *Social Research* 12: 28–9.

Salvati, M. (1993) 'Economia e sociologia: un rapporto difficile', *Stato e mercato* 13:
197–240.

Salvemini, G. (1964) *La rivoluzione francese: 1788–1798*, Milano: Feltrinelli.

Sanderson, S. K. (1990) *Social Evolutionism: A Critical History*, Oxford: Blackwell.

Sartori, G. (1979) *La politica: Logica e metodo in scienze sociali*, Milano: Sugarco.

Scheler, M. (1954) *The Nature of Sympathy*, London: Routledge and Kegan Paul.

—— (1973) *Formalism in Ethics and Non-Formal Ethics of Values*, Evanston IL: Northwestern University Press.

—— (1980) *Problems of Sociology of Knowledge*, London: Routledge and Kegan Paul.

Schmoller, G. (1883) 'Zur Metodologie der Staats-und Sozialwissenschaften', *Jahrbuch für Gesetzgebung Verwaltung und Volkswirtschaft* 7: 239–51.

—— (1901) 'Simmels Philosophie des Geldes', *Jahrbuch für Gesetzgebung Verwaltung und Volkswirtschaft* 25: 799.

Schneider, L. (1971) 'Dialectic in sociology', *American Sociological Review* 36: 667–78.

Schumpeter, J. A. (1908) *Das Wesen und der Hauptinhalt der theoretischen Nationalökonomie*, München/Leipzig: Duncker und Humblot.

—— (1914) 'Epochen der Dogmen-und Methodengeschichte', in *Grundriss der Sozialökonomik*, I, Tübingen: Mohr.

—— (1952) *Ten Great Economists*, London: Allen and Unwin.

—— (1954) *History of Economic Analysis*, Oxford: Oxford University Press.

Schutz, A. (1962a) 'Common sense and scientific interpretation of human action', in *Collected Papers*, vol. I, Hague: Nijhoff.

—— (1962b) 'Choosing among projects of action', in *Collected Papers*, vol. I, Hague: Nijhoff.

—— (1962c) 'Scheler's theory of intersubjectivity and the general thesis of the alter ego', in *Collected Papers*, vol. I, Hague: Nijhoff.

—— (1962d) 'On multiple realities', in *Collected Papers*, vol. I, Hague: Nijhoff.

—— (1962e) *Collected Papers*, vol. I, Hague: Nijhoff.

—— (1972) *The Phenomenology of the Social World*, London: Heinemann.

Scott, K. J. (1961) 'Methodological and epistemological individualism', *British Journal for the Philosophy of Science* 11: 331–6.

Scott, W. R. (1937) *Adam Smith as Student and Professor*, Glasgow: Jackson.

Scribano, M. E. (1980) *Natura umana e società competitiva: Studio su Mandeville*, Milano: Feltrinelli.

Sen, A. (1970) 'The impossibility of a Paretian Liberal', *Journal of Political Economy* 78: 152–7.

—— (1987) *On Ethics and Economics*, Oxford: Blackwell.

Simmel, G. (1894) 'Das Probleme der Soziologie', *Jahrbuch für Gesetzgebung Verwaltung und Volkswirtschaft in Deutschen Reich* 18: 271–7.

—— (1896–97) 'Comment les formes sociales se maintiennent', *L'année sociologique* 1: 71–109.

—— (1917) *Grundfragen der Sociologie (Individuum und Gesellschaft)*, Berlin: Goschen'sche.

—— (1971) 'The conflict in modern culture', in G. Simmel *On Individuality and Social Forms*, Chicago: University of Chicago Press.

—— (1977) *The Problems of the Philosophy of History*, New York: Free Press.

—— (1978) *The Philosophy of Money*, London: Routledge and Kegan Paul.

—— (1992) *Soziologie*, Frankfürt a Main: Suhrkamp.

—— (1996) *Hauptprobleme der Philosophie*, Frankfürt a Main: Suhrkamp.

Simon, H. A. (1976) 'From substantive to procedural rationality', in S. Latsis (ed.) *Method and Appraisal in Economics*, Cambridge: Cambridge University Press.

Small. A. W. (1907) *Adam Smith and Modern Sociology*, Chicago: University of Chicago Press.

—— (1924) *Origins of Sociology*, Chicago: University of Chicago Press.

Smelser, N. J. (1982) 'On the relevance of economic sociology', in T. Huppes (ed.) *Economics and Sociology: Toward an Integration*, Boston: Kluwer.

Smith, A. (1976a) 'The theory of moral sentiments', in *Works and Correspondence*, Oxford: Clarendon Press.

—— (1976b) 'An inquiry into the nature and causes of the wealth of nations', in *Works and Correspondence*, Oxford: Clarendon Press.

—— (1976c) 'Essays on philosophical subjects', in *Works and Correspondence*, Oxford: Clarendon Press.

—— (1976d) 'Lectures on rhetoric and belles lettres', in *Works and Correspondence*, Oxford: Clarendon Press.

—— (1976e) 'Lectures on jurisprudence', in *Works and Correspondence*, Oxford: Clarendon Press.

—— (1976f) 'Correspondence of Adam Smith', in *Works and Correspondence*, Oxford: Clarendon Press.

—— (1976g) *Works and Correspondence*, Oxford: Clarendon Press.

Sombart, W. (1923) 'Die Anfänge der Soziologie', in *Hautprobleme der Soziologie: Erinnerungsgabe für Max Weber*, München/Leipzig: Duncker und Humbolt.

Sorokin, P. (1942) *Man and Society in Calamity*, New York: Dutton.

Souter, R. W. (1933) 'The nature and significance of economic science in recent discussions', *Quarterly Journal of Economics* 47: 377–413.

Spann, O. (1925) *Tote und lebendige Wissenschaften*, Jena: Fischer.

Spencer, H. (1851) *Social Statistics*, London: Williams and Norgate.

—— (1857) 'Progress: its law and cause', *Westminster Review* 11: 431–85.

—— (1860) 'The social organism', *Westminster Review* 17: 90–132.

—— (1873) *The Study of Sociology*, London: King.

—— (1885–96) *Principles of Sociology*, London: Williams and Norgate.

—— (1907) *The Data of Ethics*, London: Williams and Norgate.

Stark, W. (1958) *The sociology of Knowledge*, London: Routledge and Kegan Paul.

Stephen, L. (1900) *The English Utilitarians*, London: Duckworth.

—— (1902) *History of English Thought in the Eighteenth Century*, London: Murray.

Swedberg, R. (1990) *Economics and Sociology*, Princeton: Princeton University Press.

Tarde, G. (1899) *Social Laws. An Outline of Sociology*, London: Macmillan.

Taylor, O. H. (1967) *Economics and Liberalism*, Cambridge MA: Harvard University Press.

Tocqueville, A. de (1967) *L'ancien régime et la révolution*, Paris: Gallimard.

Toennies, F. (1905) 'The present concept of social structure', *American Journal of Sociology* 10: 116–127; now in F. Toennies, *On Sociology: Pure, Applied and Empirical*, Chicago: University of Chicago Press.

Viner, J. (1927) 'Adam Smith and laissez faire', *Journal of Political Economy* 35: 198–232.

—— (1937) *Studies in the Theory of International Trade*, London: Allen and Unwin.

Watkins, J. W. N. (1952) 'Ideal types and historical explanation', *British Journal for the Philosophy of Science* 3: 22–43.

—— (1958) 'The alleged inadequacy of methodological individualism', *Journal of Philosophy* 56: 390–5.

Weber, Marianne (1926) *Max Weber: Ein Lebensbild*, Tübingen: Mohr.

Weber, Max (1916) 'Zwischen zwei Gesetzen', *Die Frau* Februar

—— (1922a) 'Die Grenznutzlehre und das "psychophysiche Grundgesets"', in *Gesammelte Aufsatze zur Wissenschaftslehre*, Tübingen: Mohr.

—— (1922b) 'Ueber einige Kategorien der verstenden Soziologie', in *Gesammelte Aufsatze zur Wissenschaftslehre*, Tübingen: Mohr.

—— (1922c) *Gesammelte Aufsatze zur Wissenschaftslehre*, Tübingen: Mohr.

—— (1949a) 'The meaning of "ethical neutrality" in sociology and economics', in *The Methodology of the Social Sciences*, Glencoe: Free Press.

—— (1949b) '"Objectivity" in social science and social policy', in *The Methodology of the Social Sciences*, Glencoe: Free Press.

—— (1949c) *The Methodology of the Social Sciences*, Glencoe: Free Press.

—— (1968) *Economy and Society*, New York: Bedminster Press.

—— (1975a) 'Roscher's Historical Method', in *Roscher and Knies: The Logical Problems of Historical Economics*, New York: Free Press.

—— (1975b) 'Knies and the problem of irrationality', in *Roscher and Knies: The Logical Problems of Historical Economics*, New York: Free Press.

—— (1975c) *Roscher and Knies: The Logical Problems of Historical Economics*, New York: Free Press.

—— (1991a) 'Politics as a vocation', in H. H. Gerth and C. Wright Mills (eds) *Essays in Sociology*, London: Routledge.

—— (1991b) 'Science as a vocation', in H. H. Gerth and C. Wright Mills (eds) *Essays in Sociology*, London: Routledge.

—— (1991c) *Essays in Sociology*, H. H. Gerth and C. Wright Mills (eds) London: Routledge.

West, E. G. (1990) *Adam Smith and Modern Economics*, Aldershot: Elgar.

Wildelband, W. (1893) *A History of Philosophy*, New York: Macmillan.

Winch, D. (1978) *Adam Smith Politics*, Cambridge: Cambridge University Press.

Wisdom, J. O. (1970) 'Situational individualism and the emergent group-properties', in R. Borger and F. Cioffi (eds) *Explanation in the Behavioural Sciences*, Cambridge: Cambridge University Press.

Wolff, K. H. (1958) 'The challenge of Durkheim and Simmel', *American Journal of Sociology* 63: 590–6.

Wundt, W. (1912) *Ethik*, Stuttgart: Enke.

INDEX